The Emergence of
Literature

The Emergence of Literature

An Archaeology of Modern Literary Theory

Jacob Bittner

BLOOMSBURY ACADEMIC

NEW YORK · LONDON · OXFORD · NEW DELHI · SYDNEY

BLOOMSBURY ACADEMIC
Bloomsbury Publishing Inc
1385 Broadway, New York, NY 10018, USA
50 Bedford Square, London, WC1B 3DP, UK

BLOOMSBURY, BLOOMSBURY ACADEMIC and the Diana logo are trademarks of
Bloomsbury Publishing Plc

First published in the United States of America 2020

For legal purposes the Acknowledgments on p. vii constitute an extension
of this copyright page.

Cover design by Eleanor Rose | Cover photographs © Getty Images

Bloomsbury Publishing Inc does not have any control over, or responsibility for, any
third-party websites referred to or in this book. All internet addresses given in this
book were correct at the time of going to press. The author and publisher regret any
inconvenience caused if addresses have changed or sites have ceased to exist but can
accept no responsibility for any such changes.

Library of Congress Cataloging-in-Publication Data
Names: Bittner, Jacob, author.
Title: The emergence of literature : an archaeology of modern literary
theory / Jacob Bittner.
Other titles: Archaeology of modern literary theory
Description: New York : Bloomsbury Academic, 2020. |
Includes bibliographical references and index. |
Summary: "Examines the philosophic-historical conditions of literary
theory"– Provided by publisher.
Identifiers: LCCN 2019028811 (print) | LCCN 2019028812 (ebook) |
ISBN 9781501354243 (hardback) | ISBN 9781501354250 (epub) |
ISBN 9781501354267 (pdf)
Subjects: LCSH: Literature–History and criticism–Theory, etc. |
Critical theory–History. | Criticism–History. | Authorship–History. |
Literature–Philosophy.
Classification: LCC PN441 .B58 2020 (print) | LCC PN441 (ebook) |
DDC 801/.95—dc23
LC record available at https://lccn.loc.gov/2019028811
LC ebook record available at https://lccn.loc.gov/2019028812

ISBN: HB: 978-1-5013-5424-3
ePDF: 978-1-5013-5426-7
eBook: 978-1-5013-5425-0

Typeset by Newgen KnowledgeWorks Pvt. Ltd., Chennai, India

To find out more about our authors and books visit www.bloomsbury.com
and sign up for our newsletters.

CONTENTS

Acknowledgments vii
Note on Text viii
List of Abbreviations ix

Introduction: Writerly Necessity 1

Part 1 The Emergence of Literature as Absolute 17

1 Literature as Pure Writing 19

2 The Literary Absolute 27

3 The Born Poet 51
   Threshold 60

Part 2 The Paradigm of Writerly Necessity 65

4 Between the Subject and Language 67

5 The Paradigm of Writerly Necessity 79

6 The Writer Who Cannot Not-Desire to Write 87
   Threshold 100

Part 3 Literary Criticism 103

7   The Author (Sincerity) 105

8   The Death of the Author (Intransitivity) 111

9   The Politics of a priori Poetry 119
    Threshold 124

Part 4 Aesthetics 127

10 Literature in the Age of Criticism 129

11 The Critic 135

12 To Write as an Intransitive Verb 143
    Threshold 153

Afterthought on Literary Inoperativity 155

Conclusion 159

Notes 161
Bibliography 211
Index 229

ACKNOWLEDGMENTS

I am grateful to Prof. Patrick ffrench for his guidance during my time at King's College London. His support, benevolence, and critique have been decisive for my research. I cannot thank him enough. I would also like to say a very special thanks to Dr. Jo Malt for her feedback, support, and encouragement during my research at King's. I am very grateful for her advice and help. Furthermore, I would like to thank Dr. Hector Kollias and Dr. Sanja Perovic for reading parts of my work at different stages during my research and providing me with valuable perspectives and suggestions. I would like to thank Prof. Howard Caygill, Dr. Ian James, and the anonymous reviewers for their questions, comments, and advice. And I would like to thank my editor at Bloomsbury, Haaris Naqvi.

NOTE ON TEXT

Earlier versions of parts of this work have been published as the following:

Bittner, Jacob, "Hölderlin and the Romantics: The Paradigm of Writerly Necessity in Philippe Lacoue-Labarthe and Jean-Luc Nancy's The Literary Absolute," *MLN* (German Issue), vol. 131, no. 3 (2016), 770–90.

Bittner, Jacob, "Roland Barthes and the Literary Absolute: The Conditions of the Necessity to Write Intransitively," *Barthes Studies*, vol. 3 (2017), 2–24.

ABBREVIATIONS

I have used the following abbreviations in the text for frequently cited works. When I cite a text both in translation (English) and in its original, the first page number refers to the English translation and the second to the original version.

A   Hegel, G. W. F., *Hegel's Aesthetics: Lectures on Fine Art, Volume I*, translated by T. M. Knox (Oxford: Clarendon Press, 1975). [*Vorlesungen über die Ästhetik I–II*, Werke 13–14, edited by Eva Moldenhauer and Karl Markus Michel (Frankfurt am Main: Suhrkamp, 1986)].

AM   Foucault, Michel, *Aesthetics, Method, and Epistemology. Essential Works of Foucault, 1954–1984. Vol. 2*, edited by James D. Faubion (London: Penguin, 2000). [*Dits et écrits I. 1954–1975*, edited by Daniel Defert, François Ewald, and Jacques Lagrange (Paris: Gallimard, 2001); *Dits et écrits II. 1976–1988*, edited by Daniel Defert, François Ewald, and Jacques Lagrange (Paris: Gallimard, 2001)].

CJ   Kant, Immanuel, *Critique of the Power of Judgment*, translated by Paul Guyer and Eric Matthews (Cambridge: Cambridge University Press, 2000). [*Kritik der Urteilskraft*, edited by Wilhelm Weischedel (Frankfurt am Main: Suhrkamp, 1974)].

CR   Kant, Immanuel, *Critique of Pure Reason*, translated by Paul Guyer and Allen W. Wood (Cambridge: Cambridge University Press, 1998). [*Kritik der reinen Vernunft*, 1–2, edited by Wilhelm Weischedel (Frankfurt am Main: Suhrkamp, 1974)].

"CS"   Lacoue-Labarthe, Philippe, "The Caesura of the Speculative," in *Typography: Mimesis, Philosophy, Politics*, edited by Christopher Fynsk (Stanford, CA: Stanford University Press, 1989), 208–35. ["La Césure du spéculatif," in *L'Imitation des modernes (Typographies 2)* (Paris: Galilée, 1986), 39–69].

DS   Nancy, Jean-Luc, *The Discourse of the Syncope: Logodaedalus*, translated by Saul Anton (Stanford, CA: Stanford University Press,

2008). [*Le Discours de la syncope: I. Logodaedalus* (Paris: Aubier-Flammarion, 1976)].

E   Lacan, Jacques, *Écrits: The First Complete Edition in English*, translated by Bruce Fink (London: W. W. Norton, 2006). [*Écrits*, 1–2 (Paris: Seuil, 1999)].

EL   Hölderlin, Friedrich, *Essays and Letters*, edited by Jeremy Adler and Charlie Louth (London: Penguin, 2009). [*Sämtliche Werke (Grosse Stuttgarter Ausgabe)*, edited by Friedrich Beissner (Stuttgart: W. Kohlhammer Verlag, 1943)].

EP   Heidegger, Martin, *The End of Philosophy*, translated by Joan Stambaugh (Chicago, IL: University of Chicago Press, 2003). [*Nietzsche II* (Pfullingen: Neske, 1961)].

ET   Hölderlin, Friedrich, *Essays and Letters on Theory*, edited by Thomas Pfau (Albany: State University of New York Press, 1988). [*Sämtliche Werke (Grosse Stuttgarter Ausgabe)*, edited by Friedrich Beissner (Stuttgart: W. Kohlhammer Verlag, 1943)].

FA   Hölderlin, Friedrich, *Sämtliche Werke: Historisch-Kritische Ausgabe (Frankfurter Ausgabe)*, edited by D. E. Sattler (Frankfurt am Main: Stroemfeld/Roter Stern, 1975).

HP   Heidegger, Martin, *Hegel's Phenomenology of Spirit*, translated by Parvis Emad and Kenneth Maly (Bloomington: Indiana University Press, 1994). [*Hegels Phänomenologie des Geistes*, Gesamtausgabe, Band 32 (Frankfurt am Main: Vittorio Klostermann, 1980)].

IC   Blanchot, Maurice, *The Infinite Conversation*, translated by Susan Hanson (Minneapolis: University of Minnesota Press, 1993). [*L'Entretien infini* (Paris: Gallimard, 1969)].

KP   Heidegger, Martin, *Kant and the Problem of Metaphysics*, translated by Richard Taft, 5th ed., Enlarged (Bloomington: Indiana University Press, 1997). [*Kant und das Problem der Metaphysik*, Fünfte, vermehrte Ausgabe (Frankfurt am Main: Vitorrio Klostermann, 1991)].

LA   Lacoue-Labarthe, Philippe, and Jean-Luc Nancy, *The Literary Absolute: The Theory of Literature in German Romanticism*, translated by Philip Barnard and Cheryl Lester (Albany: State University of New York Press, 1988). [*L'Absolu littéraire: théorie de la littérature du romantisme allemand* (Paris: Seuil, 1978)].

LD   Agamben, Giorgio, *Language and Death: The Place of Negativity*, translated by Karen E. Pinkus and Michael Hardt

(Minneapolis: University of Minnesota Press, 1991). [*Il linguaggio e la morte: un seminario sul luogo della negatività* (Torino: Giulio Einaudi, 1982)].

MC   Agamben, Giorgio, *The Man without Content*, translated by Georgia Albert (Stanford, CA: Stanford University Press, 1999). [*L'uomo senza contenuto* (Macerata: Quodlibet, 1994)].

OT   Foucault, Michel, *The Order of Things: An Archaeology of the Human Sciences* (London: Routledge, 2002). [*Les Mots et les choses: une archéologie des sciences humaines* (Paris: Gallimard, 1966)].

PN   Barthes, Roland, *The Preparation of the Novel: Lecture Courses and Seminars at the Collège de France, 1978–1979 and 1979–1980*, edited by Nathalie Léger, translated by Kate Briggs (New York: Columbia University Press, 2011). [*La Préparation du roman: cours au Collège de France 1978–1979 et 1979–1980*, edited by Nathalie Léger (Paris: Seuil, 2015)].

PS   Hegel, G. W. F., *Phenomenology of Spirit*, edited by J. N. Findlay, translated by A. V. Miller (Oxford: Oxford University Press, 1977). [*Phänomenologie des Geistes*, Werke 3, edited by Eva Moldenhauer and Karl Markus Michel (Frankfurt am Main: Suhrkamp, 1986)].

SA   Hölderlin, Friedrich, *Sämtliche Werke (Grosse Stuttgarter Ausgabe)*, edited by Friedrich Beissner (Stuttgart: W. Kohlhammer Verlag, 1943).

SL   Blanchot, Maurice, *The Space of Literature*, translated by Ann Smock (Lincoln: University of Nebraska Press, 1982). [*L'Espace littéraire* (Paris: Gallimard, 1955)].

SP   Lacoue-Labarthe, Philippe, *The Subject of Philosophy*, edited by Thomas Trezise (Minneapolis: University of Minnesota Press, 1993). [*Le Sujet de la philosophie: typographies I* (Paris: Aubier-Flammarion, 1979)].

SR   Nancy, Jean-Luc, *The Speculative Remark (One of Hegel's Bons Mots)*, translated by Céline Surprenant (Stanford, CA: Stanford University Press, 2001). [*La Remarque spéculative (un bon mot de Hegel)* (Auvers-sur-Oise: Éditions Galilée, 1973)].

ST   Heidegger, Martin, *Schelling's Treatise on the Essence of Human Freedom*, translated by Joan Stambaugh (Athens: Ohio University Press, 1985). [*Schellings Abhandlung über das Wesen der menschlichen Freiheit (1809)*, edited by Hildegard Feick (Tübingen: Max Niemeyer Verlag, 1995)].

SW   Benjamin, Walter, *Selected Writings. Vol. 1, 1913–1926*, edited
        by Michael W. Jennings and Marcus Paul Bullock (Cambridge,
        MA: Belknap Press of Harvard University Press, 2004).
        [*Gesammelte Schriften*, edited by Rolf Tiedemann and Hermann
        Schweppenhäuser (Frankfurt am Main: Suhrkamp, 1991), vol.
        I–VII].

WF   Blanchot, Maurice, *The Work of Fire*, translated by Charlotte
        Mandell (Stanford, CA: Stanford University Press, 1995). [*La Part
        du feu* (Paris: Gallimard, 1949)].

Sie sehen nach außen, und das vor allem dürften Sie jetzt nicht tun. Niemand kann Ihnen raten und helfen, niemand. Es gibt nur ein einziges Mittel. Gehen Sie in sich. Erforschen Sie den Grund, der Sie schreiben heißt; prüfen Sie, ob er in der tiefsten Stelle Ihres Herzens seine Wurzeln ausstreckt, gestehen Sie sich ein, ob Sie sterben müßten, wenn es Ihnen versagt würde zu schreiben. Dieses vor allem: fragen Sie sich in der stillsten Stunde Ihrer Nacht: muß ich schreiben? Graben Sie in sich nach einer tiefen Antwort. Und wenn diese zustimmend lauten sollte, wenn Sie mit einem starken und einfachen "ich muß" dieser ernsten Frage begegnen dürfen, dann bauen Sie Ihr Leben nach dieser Notwendigkeit; Ihr Leben bis hinein in seine gleichgültigste und geringste Stunde muß ein Zeichen und Zeugnis werden diesem Drange.

—RAINER MARIA RILKE, *BRIEFE AN EINEN JUNGEN DICHTER*, PARIS, FEBRUARY 17, 1903

Introduction: Writerly Necessity

Rainer Maria Rilke's first letter to the young poet, Franz Xaver Kappus, addresses a *necessity to write* (Paris, February 17, 1903). For Rilke, the poet is by definition somebody who writes because he *must* write. He cannot live without writing. Nobody can help him. The poet must write because his life is at stake in writing. Rilke thus says that the poet is someone who would die if he could not write: "Admit to yourself whether you would die if it should be denied you to write."[1] Moreover, the necessity to write is an imperative of life: "And if it should be affirmative, if it is given to you to respond to this serious question with a loud and simple '*I must*' ['ich muß'], then construct your life according to this necessity."[2] For Rilke, the verbs *to be* and *to write* coincide since the poet must not only live in order to be able to write but must also write so as to live.

But this question of life does not only concern the poet: "Most unsayable of all are works of art, mysterious existences whose life endures alongside ours, which passes away."[3] Poetry is life, Rilke says; a work of art is "a piece, and a voice, of your life. A work of art is good if it has arisen out of necessity. The verdict on it lies in this nature of its origin: there is no other."[4] The condition of the poet's being as well as the criterion of poetry consists in this necessity to write. For Rilke, therefore, every subject who *can* not-write is in advance excluded from the possibility of becoming a poet:[5] "But perhaps even after this descent into yourself and into your solitariness you will have to give up the idea of becoming a poet (the feeling that one could live without writing is enough, as I said, to make it something one should never do)."[6] The condition for being a poet is the feeling that one cannot not-write. What are we to think of this proposition that a "necessity to write" constitutes the poet's very being as well as the criterion of poetry? We might agree or disagree with Rilke's proposition; however, how are we to judge whether this "feeling" is true or false? What are the conditions for this criterion of poetry?

Let us consider some other criteria of poetry. During the 1920s, a lecturer at Cambridge undertook an experiment to issue "printed sheets of poems … to audiences who were requested to comment freely in writing upon them."[7] The majority of the audience "were undergraduates reading English with a view to an Honours Degree."[8] The lecturer is I. A. Richards who published the documentation of this experiment in the seminal *Practical Criticism* (1929). An anonymous participant writes about a particular poem, "This poem is a good one because it is a sincere expression of the writer's feeling."[9] Richard notes, "'Sincere' is a great favourite in its primitive unanalysed condition—we have the poem up before us and apply the test."[10] We should note that the criterion of sincerity also was a great favorite in the literary-critical writing during the entire nineteenth century.

In opposition to such a criterion of poetry, Paul de Man writes in *Allegories of Reading* (1979) that "Rilke's most advanced poetic achievement" is the poetry that is "by necessity brief and enigmatic, often consisting of one single sentence."[11] The criterion of poetry is its tendency to enigmatic disappearance. In *The Space of Literature* (*L'Espace littéraire*, 1955), with reference to Rilke, Maurice Blanchot writes that the "experience of art" is to "read the word death *without* negation" (*SL*, 242). The criterion of literature emerges as the withdrawal of any criterion insofar as literature is the interruption of "the power to negate" (*SL*, 242) and thus of any dialectical positing. A year earlier, Wiliam K. Wimsatt had written in *The Verbal Icon* (1954) that the criterion of poetry is its "unity and wholeness"[12] since a poem is "a fullness of actually presented meaning."[13]

Is there any relation between these apparently contradictory claims? Let us consider yet another criterion, which is not simply a criterion of poetry but a criterion of criticism itself. In 1797, Friedrich Schlegel writes in *Critical Fragment* 117 (*Kritische Fragmente* 117), "Poetry can only be criticized by way of poetry."[14] A critical judgment of poetry must itself be poetry; however, as Schlegel indicates in the review "On Goethe's Meister" ("Über Goethes Meister," 1798), the criterion of poetry is also that poetry itself must be "poetic criticism [*poetische Kritik*]."[15] For Schlegel, it is not possible to distinguish between poetry and the criticism of poetry. But how can we understand poetry to emerge as criticism? What are the conditions for these criteria of poetry? The modern sense of the *word* literature comes into existence at the end of the eighteenth century.[16] This is also the time when the concept of the literary absolute emerges.

In my archaeology of literary theory, I investigate how *the necessity to write literature* emerges as a paradigm that conditions these criteria of poetry. In *The Literary Absolute* (*L'Absolu littéraire*, 1978), Jean-Luc Nancy and Philippe Lacoue-Labarthe examine the inauguration of the concept of literature as absolute. My main claim is that the literary absolute emerges not simply as a concept but also as a *paradigm of writerly necessity* that constitutes subjects as writers who cannot not-write literature, and that this paradigm instantiates different subject positions that function as conditions of the apparently contradictory criteria of literature from Schlegel to Blanchot.

The Literary Absolute constitutes the point of departure of my archaeology of literary theory. I am here concerned with "literary theory" both in a "metaphysical" sense in which literature is understood to produce itself *as* theory and "literary theory" in a "pragmatic" sense in which one can say that there are different "schools" of literary theory. With respect to the pragmatic sense, I focus on the conditions of an extensive but not exhaustive list of schools that includes biographism, New Criticism, structuralism, poststructuralism, deconstruction, and phenomenology.

There are several reasons why my starting point is Nancy and Lacoue-Labarthe's *The Literary Absolute*. First, my concern coincides with Nancy and Lacoue-Labarthe's object of study, since my concern is not romanticism as such but a paradigm that emerges in a constellation between Kant, Hegel, and the Romantics, among others. Nancy and Lacoue-Labarthe explicitly state that their "object of study is exclusively the *question of literature*" and not "the philosophy of the romantics" (*LA*, 13). In my book, I analyze in detail what this means. But, generally, the question is thus the emergence of the literary absolute. Second, Nancy and Lacoue-Labarthe present the concept of the literary absolute in relation to the question of writing (influenced by their reading of Blanchot, Barthes, and Derrida). In my archaeology, I elaborate on the question of writing and situate this question within a philosophic-historical context. Third, I view it as a distinct strength of Nancy and Lacoue-Labarthe's study that it shows how the concept of the literary absolute relates to the "metaphysics of will," which has been analyzed by Martin Heidegger and in recent years Giorgio Agamben. By relating the paradigm of writerly necessity to the metaphysics of will, my archaeology provides a link between literature and other fields of knowledge. It will thus be possible for future investigations to elaborate and further analyze how the paradigm of writerly necessity, which I explore here, relates to fields such as law, theology, and politics.[17]

My archaeology is thus an investigation into the philosophic-historical conditions that made "Rilke" possible. It is an examination of how subjects constitute themselves as writers who cannot not-write literature. Following Michel Foucault, I construe the concept of *subject* as "a particular, vacant place that may in fact be filled by different individuals."[18] The subject is a certain position that an individual can come to occupy and which constitutes this living being's mode of writing, insofar as this being is produced by this subject position. I focus on this subject who cannot not-write literature.[19] The inability to not-write, which I call *writerly necessity*,[20] is a discursive site that produces certain possibilities and limitations for an individual who occupies this subject position.

But my archaeology is not a bare study of certain writers who apparently must write; rather, it concerns the modern condition of literature in the "age of criticism" (*CR*, Axi), which means that literary writing itself emerges as an operation of criticism. I examine the philosophic-historical conditions of the positing of literature as an object for a subject who writes literature and for the subjects who think critically about the concept of literature. This archaeology should be understood as a critical history of literary thought. In a text written under the pseudonym Maurice Florence, Foucault addresses the aims of such a "critical history":

> If what is meant by thought is the act that posits a subject and an object, along with their various possible relations, a critical history of thought would be an analysis of the conditions under which certain relations of subject to object are formed or modified, insofar as those relations constitute a possible knowledge [*savoir*]. (*AM*, 459/II: 1450–1)

My investigation is a history of the emergence of the literary subject and the object of literature. On the one hand, it is an investigation of what discursive positions since the end of the eighteenth century a subject needed to occupy in order to write literature. On the other hand, it is an investigation of how literature has been posited as an object of knowledge for subjects who write literature or are occupied with literary theory and criticism. This question of how literature is posited as an object of knowledge concerns the emergence of forms of acceptability by which discourses can be said to be true or false: "In sum, the critical history of thought is neither a history of acquisitions nor a history of concealments of truth; it is the history of 'veridictions,' understood as the forms according to which discourses capable of being declared true or false are articulated concerning a domain of things" (*AM*, 460). My archaeology concerns the history of how the paradigm of writerly necessity conditions the possibility of "saying the truth" about literature.[21] In literary history, it is especially "sincerity" and "intransitivity" that emerge as criteria of the predication of literary truth. In the nineteenth century, sincerity is a necessary characteristic of (true) literature, whereas in the twentieth century intransitivity (self-reference *or* unworking) functions as the truth of literature. My archaeology considers the historical conditions of these criteria themselves. What are the conditions that make these criteria function *as* true? What are the conditions for the emergence of "sincerity" and "intransitivity" as criteria of true predication in literary studies? In order to answer this question, I read several critical texts that are or have been generally accepted to be saying something true about literature, and I then show how the paradigm of writerly necessity makes possible the criteria for truth-saying that are explicitly proposed in these texts.

Method: The Question of Literature

I claim that writerly necessity functions as a *paradigm* within literary-critical thought. I here understand the concept of paradigm as a reconceptualization of the "historical *a priori*," which Foucault introduces as a central methodological concept of (philosophical) archaeology of history. I understand the relation of "a certain type of object to certain modalities of the subject" to be the instantiation of "the historical a priori of a possible experience for a period of time, an area and for given individuals" (*AM*, 460). The paradigm of writerly necessity is thus a historical a priori that constitutes a certain literary experience. This paradigm itself subsists as a subject–object relation of literature, which has arisen *in* history. In order to understand how this paradigm instantiates itself as a subject–object relation, we should understand the temporality of the historical a priori.

The Latin a priori designates "from what is before." Formally, the a priori is that which is always already "earlier" in relation to historical facts. For Kant, knowledge is a priori when it is not based on experience, which means that knowing a priori excludes any form of historical experience a posteriori (see *CR*, B2–3). The historical a priori is however not a (Kantian) formal a priori but a condition of possibility of experience that itself emerges *in* history *as* the condition of this history. As Agamben writes, the historical a priori "realizes the paradox of an a priori condition that is inscribed within a history and that can only constitute itself a posteriori with respect to this history in which inquiry—in Foucault's case, archaeology—must discover it."[22] The methodological concept of the paradigm retains this concept of an a priori condition that is itself inscribed within a history, which this condition itself makes possible.

I understand the paradigm of writerly necessity to *be* a singular literary subject–object relation as well as that which *constitutes* the domain of literary objects and as that which *manifests* the intelligibility of the literary domain. The paradigm is neither simply a universal condition nor a particular entity but the exposition of how an a priori condition instantiates itself as a historical subject–object relation.[23] My investigation of the paradigm of writerly necessity shows how every singular literary subject–object relation exposes the a priori conditions that this relation itself instantiates. In my archaeology, I thus read a series of texts and examine how writerly necessity emerges each time as at once a singular historical relation and as the condition of this relation.

But the methodological question is then how we should understand the temporality of the paradigm (the historical a priori): What does it mean that the a priori condition is inscribed within history? As a reconceptualization of the historical a priori, the paradigm of writerly necessity subsists on the level of discourse. But the paradigm is at the same time irreducible to this discourse since it can only be understood from the perspective of the future historical discourse to which it gives rise. The paradigm only becomes a paradigm by transcending its own discursive actualization in that it reconfigures the possibilities and limitations for the subjects and objects that this paradigm itself makes possible. The paradigm thus itself opens the horizon from which it can be understood.[24]

With respect to the paradigm, each singular literary experience is not simply conditioned by the a priori condition; rather, these experiences *instantiate* their condition *in* history, which means that the condition first emerges *as* a condition of these experiences *retroactively*. This entails a temporality of the paradigm in which each instantiation exposes the historical contingency of the paradigm and therefore its limits as an a priori condition. A paradigm is thus *proactive* in the sense that it is going to arise *as* a paradigm in the present only to the extent that understanding is *retroactive* and produces this paradigm as *its* condition. A paradigm is contingent precisely because it transcends its actualization as a fact: It only arises *as* a condition of possibility *if* it is instantiated *as* a fact retroactively by later understanding.[25]

The historical a priori is thus not attributed to a transcendental Subject (I here capitalize the word *Subject* when I refer to a subject position that understands itself to function as an ahistorical foundation independent of historical contingency). Rather, archaeology shows how an a priori emerges as a specific historical relation between subjects and objects, which conditions these subjects' experience of objects only insofar as the condition is instantiated as this relation. The historical instantiation of the paradigm is the retro condition of the a priori condition inscribed within history.

We should here recognize that the concept of the paradigm entails an aporia since it is not possible to distinguish between the constituting and the constituted: The paradigm can be understood as a reconceptualization of the concept of the historical a priori that must appear within experience in order to take place. However, experience itself presupposes the a priori condition, which means that it is never possible to ascribe priority to the a priori. But this aporia is not a defect of the method of archaeology; rather, this aporia is the very concern of my archaeology insofar as the aporia of the paradigm of writerly necessity exposes the contingency of every positing of a writerly subject in relation to a literary "object" in the history of literature.[26] The understanding of literature as absolute means that literature emerges as an unconditioned condition of all historical understanding; however, the concern of my archaeology of writerly necessity is precisely to expose the historical conditions of this "unconditioned" and thus manifest the contingency of the literary absolute. An unconditioned positing must be a positing without presupposition, but this positing must thus presuppose itself in the very act of positing, which produces an aporia of positing. My archaeology concerns this aporia in which the paradigm of writerly necessity exposes a non-posited space in the withdrawal of its constitutive deferment.[27] The temporality of the paradigm of writerly necessity entails a constitutive delay of positing, a suspension, an interruption of the paradigm, which displays the contingency of the paradigm. Insofar as my archaeology concerns this contingency of the historical positing of a literary subject–object relation, the archaeology of writerly necessity is the exposition of the aporia of positing in which the historicity of the literary absolute manifests itself.

It will in this regard become visible that "intransitivity" occupies a significant position within my study of the literary domain since intransitivity manifests the literary absolute as "the question of literature." Since literature emerged as this "question of literature" in the twentieth century, it has however been an ambiguous "object" of knowledge. In 1948, in "Literature and the Right to Death" ("La Littérature et le droit à la mort"), Blanchot writes, "Let us suppose that literature begins at the moment when literature becomes a question" (WF, 300).[28] Thirty years later, in *The Literary Absolute* (1978), Nancy and Lacoue-Labarthe write that their study concerns "exclusively the *question of literature*" (LA, 13). The "question of literature" entails that literature exposes itself as the suspension of the positing of a subject in relation to an object. It is thus not certain that literature is in fact an "object" of knowledge since the very question posed within the literary domain is whether literature exists as an object given to a subject.

It is a concern of my archaeology to show how the central question within the literary domain is whether literature is the production of the dialectical Subject, of an absolute positing (Hegel), or the very interruption of the dialectical production, the suspension of absolute positing (Blanchot). My archaeology of writerly necessity concerns the conditions for this question of literature. But it is not my aim to answer this question regarding whether literature confirms the Subject or interrupts the Subject. Rather, on the one hand, my aim is to examine how this question of literature emerges as the question of how to understand an act of writing intransitively and, on the other hand, how this act of writing intransitively is linked to the necessity to write literature.

In the paper "To Write: Intransitive Verb?" ("Écrire, verbe intransitif?"), delivered at the seminal conference at Johns Hopkins University in 1966, Roland Barthes identifies the apparent transformation of the verb *to write* from its transitive to its intransitive sense as "the sign of an important change in mentality."[29] In Modernity, the verb *to write* would not be a transitive verb (to write *something*) but an intransitive verb (to write, *tout court*). But the question remains whether *to write* is an intransitive verb (without object) or whether intransitivity conceals that the "subject" who writes becomes the "object" of writing. Does intransitivity in literary writing indicate the self-reference of the Subject or the disappearance of the Subject? My aim is not to undertake a linguistic analysis of the intransitive verb but to situate this question of intransitivity in its philosophical context. My concern is not to answer this question but to show how this question of intransitivity emerges as the question of literature. As I will argue, there is a link between a necessity to write and the act of intransitive writing, which means that literature not only emerges as the *question* of how to understand what is indicated by the act of intransitive writing but also entails that any definite answer remains suspended. My aim is to render inoperative this suspended question in which, I will argue, the thinking of the Subject incessantly reconstitutes itself. My archaeology thus concerns the possibility of interrupting the Subject.

The Question of Literature: Between Hegel and Blanchot

Various contemporary thinkers have looked into the conditions of literature. In this section, I situate my own archaeology in relation to the investigations undertaken by Roland Barthes, Jean-Paul Sartre, Jacques Rancière, and Pierre Bourdieu.

In *What Is Literature?* (*Qu'est-ce que la littérature?*, 1948), Sartre conceives of literature as a (Hegelian) "dialectic of literature,"[30] which sublates itself from the "concrete" alienation of the Middle Ages (content without form) via the "abstract negativity" of the eighteenth century to the modern "absolute negation" of the nineteenth century (form without content).[31] For Sartre, the essence of literature is the self-conscious and transparent dialectical Subject in which "form and content, public and subject, are identical."[32] This (utopian) essence of literature could only emerge in a society in which the writer's self-consciousness would coincide with the consciousness of every man (reader): "The writer, in speaking about them [the readers], would be speaking about himself, and in speaking about himself would be speaking about them."[33]

In sociopolitical terms, Sartre describes this dialectic of literature as the writer's relation to the bourgeoisie: "The political triumph of the bourgeoisie which writers had so eagerly desired convulsed their condition from top to bottom and put the very essence of literature in question."[34] According to Sartre, the French Revolution changes the very conditions of literature, which is intrinsically linked to democracy. During the revolution itself, "literature was naturally revolutionary because the first discovery which it made of itself revealed to it its connections with political democracy."[35] Sartre therefore writes, "Hence, by demanding *for himself* and *as a writer* freedom of thinking and of expressing his thought, the author necessarily served the interests of the bourgeois class."[36] After the revolution, when the bourgeoisie did not struggle against "the privileges of nobility,"[37] the literary writer comes to occupy an ambiguous place in relation to the bourgeoisie. Literature symbolically rejects the bourgeois "ideology" that nevertheless sustains the position of literature, which itself emerges as an ideology of autonomy:

> Thus, it [literature] set itself up as being, in principle, independent of any sort of ideology. As a result, it retained its abstract aspect of pure negativity. It had not yet understood that it *was itself* ideology; it wore itself out asserting its autonomy, which no one contested. This amounted to saying that it claimed it had no privileged subject and could treat any matter whatever.[38]

According to Sartre, the French Revolution produces literature as a form of intransitive writing, but this intransitivity can for Sartre only emerge as a form without content. From Sartre's Hegelian perspective, literature emerges in Modernity as an abstract subjectivity: There is no essential content of literature.

Roland Barthes's *Writing Degree Zero* (*Le Degré zero de l'écriture*, 1953) can be read as a response to Sartre's investigation insofar as Barthes undertakes a history of the a priori conditions of writing. Due to the French horizon of Barthes's investigation, he conceptualizes the 1850s as the modern moment when literature emerges as an object of knowledge.[39] But this modern literary object indicates only the very disappearance of the literary object since "it is the existence of Literature itself which is called into question."[40] Barthes writes, "Modernism begins with the search for a Literature which is no longer possible."[41] The Year of Revolution (1848) is the date for an event at which the classical age of *Belles Lettres* disappears and (modern) literature emerges. This disappearance signifies the fragmentation of "the ideological unity of the bourgeoisie [which] gave rise to a single mode of writing" since "literary form could not be divided because consciousness was not."[42] The disappearance thus manifests the historicity of the (Hegelian) concept of a true classical consciousness in which form and content coincide. This would be an atemporal universal (bourgeois) consciousness that would function as the transparent condition of society. Barthes rejects this consciousness as ideology, but he confirms the (Hegelian) thesis that literature is "tragic" because the writer's "consciousness no longer accounts for the whole of his condition."[43] Since there is no universal norm in (modern) literature, there is a multiplication in the modes of writing, which are however all attempts to find a solution to the (alienated) condition of the writers as "writers without [universal] Literature."[44] Barthes's diagnosis is that the condition of literature means that it is unable to overcome itself: "Literary writing carries at the same time the alienation of History and the dream of History; as a Necessity, it testifies to the division of languages which is inseparable from the division of classes; as Freedom, it is the consciousness of this division and the very effort which seeks to surmount it."[45] Literature embodies a division of the modes of writing, which all aim to overcome their division; however, since literature is also the consciousness of the historicity of the ideological character of the universal (bourgeoisie), it occupies a position of alienation in which its only "utopian" possibility is its own disappearance: "For Literature is like phosphorous: it shines with its maximum brilliance at the moment when it attempts to die."[46] In his later *Roland Barthes by Roland Barthes* (*Roland Barthes par Roland Barthes*, 1975), Barthes comments on a dream that "began with *Writing Degree Zero*."[47] This is the dream "of a world which would be *exempt from meaning* (as one is from military service)."[48] This dream is a political dream in which literature as a form of intransitive writing indicates the very interruption of the dialectical Subject. With this dream, Barthes is concerned with literature as the interruption of absolute positing.

This is a conception of literature that Rancière and Bourdieu neglect in their different examinations of the historical conditions of literature. In my archaeology of writerly necessity, I will argue that literature emerges as the *question* whether it constitutes the dialectic or the interruption of the dialectic. Like Sartre before them, Rancière and Bourdieu presuppose in their investigations that literature constitutes an abstract dialectic, but they thus neglect to consider how it is possible for thinkers of literature such as Barthes, Blanchot, Nancy, and Lacoue-Labarthe to consider literature to be the interruption of the dialectic.

In his work on aesthetics and literature, Rancière undertakes a reworking of Foucault's archaeology of literature. In *The Politics of Aesthetics* (*Le Partage du sensible*, 2000), Rancière addresses the "aesthetic regime," which "can be understood in a Kantian sense—re-examined perhaps by Foucault—as the system of *a priori* forms determining what presents itself to sense experience."[49] In *Mute Speech* (*La Parole muette*, 1998), he uses the term "literature" to signify a specific "historical mode of visibility of the works of the art of writing."[50] Insofar as Rancière's investigation is to be an investigation of the *conditions* of literature, I will argue that there is a problem with the presupposition of his historical analysis of literature as a mode of visibility. Rather than considering literature as the visibility of the *question* whether it is a dialectical reconciliation of form and content or the very interruption of any dialectical identity, Rancière presupposes that literature is always an alienated thought that aims at a form of resolution. Rancière criticizes the formalism of an intransitive writing understood as the self-reference of the Subject but never considers the possibility that intransitivity could indicate the withdrawal of the Subject.

Since Rancière remains within a Hegelian mode of thought, he does not examine the conditions for how intransitivity can become visible as the disappearance of visibility. Accordingly, for Rancière, the poetics of the Early German Romantics appears as a form of classicism in the Hegelian sense: "The work that is a language, the beautiful coincidence of form and signification, of the fabricated work and the living form, or of creative individuality and collective poeticity—everything that Novalis and the Schlegel brothers had assigned to the poetry of the future as its task—all this is a thing of the past."[51] Rancière continues, "As a principle of art, Romantic poetics has already been fulfilled, and it was fulfilled as classicism. … Poetry attempts in vain to surpass itself and become its own theory. It can leave the domain of art but not thereby enter that of philosophy."[52] For Rancière, the journal of the Early German Romantics, the *Athenaeum* (1798–1800), is nothing but the form without content, since "the heart of the problem" with respect to literature is "the antigeneric principle of the equality of all represented subjects."[53] Since Rancière never leaves the horizon of (dialectical) representation, literature can never arise as the question whether intransitivity is this form in which all subject matters are equal or the very disappearance of the form–content relation.

Like Rancière, Bourdieu also does not consider the conditions of literature as the *question* whether intransitivity indicates the dialectic of the Subject or the withdrawal of the Subject. In *The Rules of Art* (*Le Règles de l'art*, 1992), Bourdieu shows convincingly how a "literary and artistic field is constituted as such in and by opposition to a 'bourgeois' world."[54] He poses the question why "so many critics … take such satisfaction in professing that the experience of a work of art … escapes by definition all rational understanding."[55] Focusing on how a *historical transcendental*[56] produces a literary field, he concludes that "it is historical analysis which allows us to understand the conditions of the 'understanding', the symbolic appropriation, real or fictive, of a symbolic object [i.e. literature] which may be accompanied by that particular form of enjoyment which we call aesthetic."[57] But Bourdieu does not undertake a sustained reflection on the reason why literature is said to elude "rational understanding." He assumes that the likely reason why the field of literature poses an obstacle to "scientific objectification" is "the veneration of all those who were raised, often from their earliest youth, to perform sacramental rites of cultural devotion."[58] He thus does not consider whether it is "reason" as such, the knowing Subject itself, which is in question in literature. As we shall see, for writers such as Blanchot and Derrida, literature manifests itself as the question of its own existence, thereby exposing the possibility of interrupting thetic Being,[59] of suspending positing as such, and literature thus also puts in question the very possibility of understanding.

"Literature" is a paradoxical object of a (philosophical) archaeology because, even if this object is without a doubt constituted in history, it is precisely constituted as the interruption of every constitution of knowledge and thus of every historical understanding. The lack of consideration of this historical truth of literature produces a lacuna in Bourdieu's sociological investigation of the "historical transcendental" of the literary field. We should thus also recognize that "literature" sets a limit to the determination of a *date* for its own "emergence." To the extent that literature is the withdrawal of thetic Being (positing), literature has never "existed" (as a spatiotemporal object that could be localized in a temporal chronology). It is thus not possible to set a date for the emergence of literature. But the concern of my archaeology is also not to determine a given date in a historical chronology in which literature could be said to have emerged. It is not a question of determining the identity of an origin of the Subject. Rather, I argue that the issue is to trace how the paradigm of writerly necessity as the condition of literature emerges as a moment of undecidability between the subject and object. With reference to Agamben, it is a question of exposing literature's moment of arising: "The moment of arising is objective and subjective at the same time and is indeed situated on a threshold of undecidability between object and subject."[60] With respect to the emergence of literature, the question is what the relation is between philosophy and literature and between the subject who writes and the object to be written. My focus is therefore how the paradigm of writerly necessity produces the possibilities and limitations for posing the question of literature that consists in the question of whether literature is a form of dialectic or the interruption of dialectic. My archaeology of writerly necessity concerns the conditions for this question of literature. It is an extension and reworking of Nancy and Lacoue-Labarthe's investigation of the concept of the literary absolute, Heidegger's destruction and Agamben's archaeology of the metaphysics of will, Blanchot's examination of the space of literature, and Foucault's archaeology of literature.

The Archaeology of Writerly Necessity: Chapters and Thresholds

An archaeology of writerly necessity entails a double historicization. On the one hand, it must focus on the emergence of the paradigm of writerly necessity at the end of the eighteenth century, which makes possible the criteria of the predication of literary truth in the nineteenth and twentieth century. It is thus only because of certain events at this moment that the modern concept of literature as absolute can emerge. But, on the other hand, since the paradigm only emerges *as* a paradigm insofar as later literary-critical history instantiates writerly necessity as a historical a priori condition, archaeology must also focus on how the emergence of these very criteria retrospectively makes the paradigm of writerly necessity visible as such. The archaeology must show not only how the paradigm emerges as a paradigm at the end of the eighteenth century but also how literary theory of the nineteenth and the twentieth century provides the horizon of "truth" for the reception of the emergence of the paradigm. It is thus necessary to make visible how the emergence of the paradigm of writerly necessity takes place in the constellation between a past in which the paradigm arises in history so as to form an a priori condition of literary history and a present in which this paradigm instantiates itself within a certain horizon of literary truth-saying.

The first part of my archaeology concerns the emergence of the paradigm of writerly necessity. I show how the paradigm of writerly necessity arises within a post-Kantian problematic of how to present philosophy. The modern concept of literature is a "solution" to the post-Kantian question of how to exhibit the absolute. Reading Nancy's analysis and Heidegger's interpretation of Kant and Hegel, I show how literature emerges as the concept of a pure intransitive writing and I examine how Hegel's speculative dialectic produces a philosophical solution to the Kantian problem of philosophical presentation (Chapter 1). I then compare this speculative concept of the absolute with the concept of the literary absolute. I show how the paradigm of writerly necessity makes possible Nancy and Lacoue-Labarthe's identification of the concept of the literary absolute in the journal of the Early German Romantics, the *Athenaeum*. I examine how the concept of the literary absolute emerges as the question of intransitivity, which is the question whether this concept produces an abstract dialectic of the Subject or the very interruption of the dialectical Subject (Chapter 2). I then analyze Friedrich Hölderlin's letters and theoretical texts in order to show how a subject emerges as a writer who cannot not-write literature. Moreover, I explore how the paradigm of writerly necessity makes possible the twentieth-century thought of "unworking" in which literature is understood as the suspension of thetic Being (Chapter 3).

The second part concerns the delimitation of the paradigm of writerly necessity. I read Foucault's archaeology of literature in order to show how the paradigm of writerly necessity emerges between the Subject and language. This leads me to examine Foucault's thoughts on the relations between madness and literature and Blanchot's commentary on Foucault's *History of Madness* (Chapter 4). I then read Blanchot's *The Space of Literature* in order to display how the paradigm of writerly necessity is delimited between the Subject and language. I investigate how the subject who cannot not-write intransitively disperses into different positions of enunciation, and I consider these positions that a subject must occupy in order to write literature (Chapter 5). Hereafter, I examine the psychic form of this subject who cannot not-write literature. With reference to Hölderlin's letters, I analyze the enunciative positions of the subject who cannot not-desire to write literature (Chapter 6).

The third part concerns how the paradigm of writerly necessity constitutes the criteria of literary criticism. I investigate how the concept of sincerity emerges as the primary criterion of the nineteenth century in author criticism and New Criticism (Chapter 7). I then show how the concept of intransitivity emerges as a criterion of twentieth-century literary criticism. With reference to Barthes, Foucault, and Agamben, I examine the question of the death of the author and the emergence of the author as gesture (Chapter 8). This leads me to an investigation of Walter Benjamin's early literary criticism. I examine how the paradigm of writerly necessity emerges in Benjamin's concept of *das Gedichtete*, which Benjamin uses to read Hölderlin's poetry. I argue that *das Gedichtete* is a concept by which Benjamin can think poetry as a political form of writing (Chapter 9).

The fourth part concerns the emergence of literature in the age of criticism in which the question is whether art is a "thing of the past" or a thing of the future. I investigate how the paradigm of writerly necessity emerges in Hegel's lectures on aesthetics. My concern is to see how the modern subject position of writerly necessity differs from the "symbolic" and "classical" subject positions (Chapter 10). I then examine how the position of the critic emerges in the paradigm of writerly necessity. I read Agamben's destruction of aesthetics in order to display how criticism can be understood to produce literature as a thing of the past. I explore how writerly necessity produces the relation between the subject whose life is essentially at stake in art and the critic whose life is essentially indifferent to art (Chapter 11). I then turn to Barthes's late lectures on the preparation of the novel in order to display how a critic can be understood as an amateur writer who cannot be integrated into the paradigm of writerly necessity. I propose the possibility of an *in-transitive* practice of writing as an interrogation of the space of inoperativity (Chapter 12). Finally, I consider the question of literary inoperativity and the possibility of a literary thought beyond the paradigm of writerly necessity ("Afterthought"). Between each part there is a "threshold." The function of these thresholds is both to summarize the main points of the part that came before and to function as the transition to the part which comes after.

My archaeology is not a critique; rather, it is an archaeology that examines how the critique of literary-critical thought became possible as such. It is an investigation into the history of literary theory in which literature emerges as at once its own actual history and the very interruption of any (literary) history. It concerns the historical emergence of literature as absolute. It concerns the contingency of the literary absolute: The question how the absolute literary operation came to function as true for certain subjects. My aim in this archaeology of writerly necessity is thus also not totalizing. I do not pretend that the paradigm of writerly necessity constitutes the criteria of every form of modern criticism that has called itself "literary." Moreover, my archaeology of literary theory is not to be understood as a form of reductionism. Rather, my aim is precisely to delimit this paradigm in order to provide the horizon from which it is possible to think what has been excluded from this literary domain and investigate the possibilities beyond this paradigm. The question is how writerly necessity produces the Subject as the question of its own death. Is this death the negativity of a Hegelian dialectic? Or can we come to understand this death as a Hölderlinian caesura that interrupts the dialectic? The urgency of this question can be measured by the issue that the paradigm of writerly necessity reproduces the *question* of the Subject.

PART ONE

The Emergence of Literature as Absolute

1

Literature as Pure Writing

Literature: A "Solution" to a Kantian Problem

I use the term *writerly necessity* for the subject position of the writer who cannot not-write literature. But what are the necessary conditions for the emergence of this paradigm of writerly necessity? How does a subject who cannot not-write emerge? What constitutes that which this subject is to write (literature)? How is literature absolute? These questions will be the dominant concerns of the first part of my archaeology. In this first part, I focus on Nancy and Lacoue-Labarthe's investigation of literature and examine how Hölderlin emerges as a subject produced by the paradigm of writerly necessity.

In *The Discourse on the Syncope* (*Le Discours de la syncope*, 1976), Nancy claims that the "moment of Kant" (*DS*, 19) "is the moment in which philosophy explicitly designates its own exposition as *literature*" (*DS*, 18).[1] My initial concern is to show how this Kantian moment manifests "literature" as a form of a priori writing, which prepares the later understanding of literature as absolute in the journal of the Romantics, the *Athenaeum*. This Kantian moment will also be a condition for the emergence of the paradigm of writerly necessity, since it will constitute literature as an a priori writing: as an intransitive writing in which the possibility of the objectivity of the literary "object" is always in question.

The notion that the Kantian moment exposes philosophical presentation as "literature" does not mean that Kant *invents* literature; rather, it means that literature arises as a solution to a Kantian problem of how to present philosophy. Kant never recognizes "literature" as a solution as such; however, Nancy traces how the problem of the exposition of philosophy becomes a fundamental problem for Kant. This is the problem of how thinking can exhibit itself: the question of philosophical *Darstellung* or "presentation" (see *DS*, xxii). It is because of this problem that the Kantian moment is the time when it becomes "possible and necessary to expressly distinguish between philosophy and literature" (*DS*, 19).[2]

Nancy's analysis presupposes Heidegger's *Kant and the Problem of Metaphysics* (*Kant und das Problem der Metaphysik*, 1929), which is a reworking of a lecture course first delivered at the University of Marburg in 1927–8.[3] Heidegger understands Kant's first *Critique* as an attempt to find a "secure course of a science" (*CR*, Bxviii), which is to prevent metaphysics from both skepticism and dogmatically overstepping the limits of the sensible in order to grasp the absolute (the supersensible). On the one hand, for Kant the absolute is that which "reason [*Vernunft*] necessarily and with every right demands [*verlangt*] in things in themselves for everything that is conditioned, thereby demanding the series of conditions as something completed [*vollendet*]" (*CR*, Bxx). But, on the other hand, Kant excludes the absolute as a possible object of knowledge: "the unconditioned [*das Unbedingte*] must not be present [*angetroffen*] in things [*Dingen*] insofar as we are acquainted with them (insofar as they are given to us), but rather in things insofar as we are not acquainted with them, as things in themselves" (*CR*, Bxx). For Kant, metaphysics has failed in its attempt to establish itself as a science since it lacks a "procedure" (*CR*, Bxv; see *KP*, 6). The *Critique* is therefore a "treatise" on "method" (*CR*, Bxxii; see *KP*, 11), which is not itself the system of metaphysics but which is to make the system possible. According to Heidegger, method should here not simply be understood as a technique for how to proceed but as the delimitation of the entire structure of ontology (see *KP*, 11). Heidegger thus understands Kant's *Critique* as an attempt to lay the ground for metaphysics: "the fundamental knowledge of beings as such and as a whole" (*KP*, 5).

For Kant, human knowledge is thus not *intuitus originarius*, an infinite divine knowledge or an absolute intuition, which originally produces beings; rather, it is an *intuitus derivativus*, a derived intuition, which cannot make the being come-into-being but must be receptive for the already given being (see *CR*, B72; *KP*, 17). For Heidegger, Kant's aim is to secure an ontological (transcendental) knowledge. In Heidegger's terms, the *Critique* aims to constitute "the Being of the being" (*KP*, 10), which for Kant concerns a knowledge of objects a priori, a cognition, "which is to establish something about objects before they are given to us" (*CR*, Bxvi; see *KP*, 8). Kant's insight is to focus on things insofar as they appear to us since metaphysics might be secured if we distinguish between "objects as appearances" that conform to the human way of representing and "things in themselves" as the things insofar as they are not given to us (*CR*, Bxx; see *KP*, 8).

For Heidegger, the question at the core of the Kantian *Critique* is the question of human finitude since human pure reason is the foundation for establishing metaphysics (see *KP*, 15). Heidegger presents the Kantian problematic of representing in terms of the question of transcendence.

The finite being (the human), in its ecstatic turning "itself toward" and "standing-out-from," lets objects horizontally "stand-against" itself and thereby "holds before itself—a horizon" (*KP*, 84) that first makes possible any experience of objects (objectivity). In Heidegger's admittedly "violent" analysis (see *KP*, 141), which focuses on the *unsaid* of Kant's *Critique*, the main question in the first *Critique* is the question of how to understand the problem of schematism, which Kant describes as "a hidden art in the depths of the human soul" (*CR*, A141/B180-81). For Kant, schematism concerns the synthesis or unification of sensible intuition and pure concepts (categories). The schema is "the sensible concept of an object" (*CR*, A146/B186), the synthesis of intuition and pure concepts, which as a unity makes possible the experience of objects. The "schema" is "the pure synthesis," which is a "transcendental product of the imagination" (*CR*, A142/B181). According to Heidegger, it is thus the transcendental imagination that for Kant "forms the look of the horizon of objectivity as such in advance, before the experience of the being [*Seienden*]" (*KP*, 92/131).

The transcendental imagination is the "root" (*CR*, A15/B29) of the two stems of human knowledge, sensibility and understanding (see *KP*, 25). This is a source that Kant writes "perhaps" exists but in any case is "unknown" to us (*CR*, A15/B29). In Heidegger's analysis, the transcendental imagination becomes the finite "creative" faculty, which is not "ontically 'creative' " (*KP*, 93) since it is not an absolute intuition but which forms the pure image (*Bild*) of time by which objectivity becomes possible. In Heidegger's reading, understanding (conceptual representing) is itself relative to intuition (the pure forms of time and space) since, as Kant writes, the intuition relates "immediately" to the object whereas the understanding "is mediate" (*CR*, A320/B377; see *KP*, 16–17). For Kant, knowing is thus "intuiting thinking" insofar as the faculty for judging is the faculty for thinking: "Judgment is therefore the mediate cognition of an object, hence the representation [concept] of a representation of it [intuition]" (*CR*, A68; *KP*, 20). Moreover, according to Heidegger, there is a division in intuition itself insofar as "time has a preeminence over space" (*KP*, 34). As "the form of inner sense" (*CR*, A33/B49), time manifests itself as successive "states of our mind" (*KP*, 34) without spatial relations. Kant understands time as "the intuition of our self" (*CR*, A33/B49), which is thus nothing but "pure self-affection" (*KP*, 132). In this understanding of time as pure self-affection, Heidegger finds the traces of a more original time that he understands (against Kant) to mean that the subjectivity of the subject itself consists in a time, which forms the possibility of transcendence. In the last instance, transcendental imagination, as the root of the two sources of knowledge (intuition and understanding), is thus itself "rooted in original time" (*KP*, 141) since the pure, finite subject is in itself temporalization. On the one hand, Heidegger can therefore say that, in the Kantian groundlaying of metaphysics, "the grounding of the inner possibility of ontology is brought about as an unveiling

of transcendence, i.e. [an unveiling] of the subjectivity of the human subject"
(*KP*, 144). The fundamental question of the *Critique* is thus the question
of human finitude. But, on the other hand, Kant never firmly established
the transcendental imagination at the core of the subject's transcendental
synthesis. Rather, according to Heidegger, in the second version of the first
Critique, "Kant falls back from the ground which he himself had laid" (*KP*,
150) because this ground (finitude) undermines the very concept of pure
reason (subjectivity) that forms the point of departure for the *Critique*.
From Heidegger's perspective, in order to retain the Subject as a foundation,
Kant neglects to pose the question of the relation between human finitude
and Being (see *KP*, 155). In Nancy and Lacoue-Labarthe's words from *The
Literary Absolute*, this means that "an abyss opens up where a bridge should
have been built" (*LA*, 30; see also *KP*, 151).

According to *The Literary Absolute*, it is this abyss, "this problematic
of the subject unpresentable to itself" (*LA*, 30), which Romanticism
"will receive, not as a bequest but as its 'own' most difficult and perhaps
insoluble question" (*LA*, 30). With Heidegger's analysis in mind, Nancy
and Lacoue-Labarthe will state, regarding the section of the *Critique* on the
transcendental aesthetic ("a science of all principles of *a priori* sensibility";
CR, A21), "What does the transcendental Aesthetic represent? Not the
traditional division of the sensible and the intelligible but rather the division
between *two* forms (*a priori*) within the 'sensible' or intuitive itself. The first
and most fundamental result is that there is no *intuitus originarius*" (*LA*,
30). There is no absolute intuition, no absolute Subject, but only a division
between the two pure forms of intuition, time and space.

In *The Discourse on the Syncope*, Nancy addresses how this Kantian
problem of how to situate the foundation of metaphysics in a common
root (the transcendental imagination) corresponds to the problem of how
to *present* philosophy. This problem of presentation (*Darstellung*) will give
rise to the question of literature, which is also to say that this question
(of literature) is first "posed within philosophy itself" (*DS*, 18). Nancy
addresses the problem of *Darstellung* in relation to Kant's distinction from
"The Transcendental Doctrine of Method" in the first *Critique* between
mathematical cognition and philosophical cognition (see *CR*, A714–15).
According to Kant, mathematics travels "the secure path of a science"
(*CR*, Bx) since it is supposed to establish its objects purely a priori. Nancy
can therefore say that, for Kant, the "only invulnerable presentation is
mathematical presentation" since it is "the only adequate grammar [*régime*]
of a joint presentation of the concept and the intuition that responds to it"
(*DS*, 32/31). Mathematics is the only proper locus in which a presentation of
the unity of understanding and sensibility in the transcendental imagination
could be carried out. But, as Nancy points out, philosophy is restrained by
a linguistic imperative, which means that philosophy *must discourse* (*DS*,
15). Philosophical exposition thus "reveals a particular fragility" (*DS*, 32),

the fragility of its *discursive* status, which for Kant involves the question of the *foundation* of philosophy itself since language can never be a totally adequate form of presentation. Nancy writes that philosophy "must" for this reason "desire elegance" (*DS*, 34) since the exposition of philosophy always already exposes this science to its own insufficiency. The pure system should be presented a priori, but "the grapheme is always inadequate, uncertain, buried, misshapen, or damaged" (*DS*, 104).

The problem of *Darstellung* is thus the problem of the lack of the foundation of the system since it means that the system is always already displaced. The system needs the substitution of elegance since it is exposed to its discursive presentation: "Elegance is the term substituted for the presentation of the mathematical opus, and the desire for it is the desire to write a book. 'Literature' will be the name of the object of desire of the lost opus" (*DS*, 44). At the very core of Kant's *Critique*, the question of writing emerges as the problem of philosophical exposition. Philosophy will never be able to accomplish a "pure writing": An intransitive writing is understood as a writing without anything *actually* written that would thus constitute a *pure* presentation. Literature will be the name of the loss of the desired adequate philosophical presentation: "to write *in not writing*" (*DS*, 126). Literature will be the locus of the pure writing of a "poet-philosopher," an impossible hybrid figure that Nancy proposes: "the mathematician who would write (in prose)" (*DS*, 85). But literature will thus precisely be the impossible *fiction* of a pure writing. The modern category of literature arises within the horizon of the philosophy of finitude (Kant's *Critique*), but literature will at the same time be that which always already transgresses possible experience (see *DS*, 106). From the Kantian perspective, literature is not a philosophical possibility since it is the fiction of an infinite or absolute intuition. The Kantian moment manifests "literature" as the fictional realization of a pure philosophical writing, a form of a priori writing, which would be the writing of pure "reason" itself, independent of all empirical limiting conditions.

The Pure Philosophical Writing: Hegel's Absolute Subject

Literature emerges as a solution to the problem of how to present philosophy: it is the fiction of a pure writing a priori. In his *Dialogue on Poetry* (*Das Gespräch über die Poesie*, 1800) published in the journal *Athenaeum* (1798–1800), Friedrich Schlegel lets the figure Ludovico pose the question of literature: "Do you perhaps consider it impossible to construct future poems *a priori*? [*Halten Sie es etwa für unmöglich, zukünftige Gedichte* a priori *zu konstruieren?*]."[4] The *critical* question of literature is the following: how is poetry a priori possible?[5] Literature arises as the question of how to produce a pure intransitive work. The *Athenaeum* represents the core of the Kantian moment, insofar as this journal inaugurates literature as absolute. But, for later literary theory, this inauguration will be inscribed not only within Kantian transcendental philosophy but also within a pure philosophical writing that manifests itself in Hegel's speculative system.

In the essay "The Unpresentable" ("L'Imprésentable," 1975), Lacoue-Labarthe proclaims that the question of literature is "the echo *after the fact* [*après coup*] of a question never asked or of an 'answer' given to the absence of a question" (*SP*, 117). The *Athenaeum*, the journal of the Romantics, poses the question of literature, but this question *as* a question has been concealed in "the discourse claiming to be the sum and the truth of all [philosophical] discourse in general" (*SP*, 117). The question of literature is concealed within philosophical discourse as the question of writing, but this question has also inscribed itself within Hegel's philosophical *text*:

> The (silent and secret) dissolution or *Auflösung* of literature has left a reminder, a residue—an *abortion*: to begin with—though this is an hypothesis that almost goes without saying today—Hegel's *text*; but also, *before* Hegel's intervention (the logic of the *aftereffect* does not preclude it), "literature itself" to the extent that it has resisted, *in its "own" dissolution*, philosophical dissolution. (*SP*, 118)

Before we address this question of "literature itself" (in the journal *Athenaeum*), we should understand how literature subsists as the question of the philosophical text.

In *The Speculative Remark*, Nancy focuses on Hegel's *text*, on the question of *reading* Hegel and what it means *to write* the philosophical text. This focus is guided by the keyword of speculative Idealism, the word *and* concept of *Aufhebung* (sublation). Nancy's text is moreover itself oriented by Heidegger's interpretation of Hegel in which German Idealism (Hegel) is presented as being first of all "concerned with *overcoming finite knowledge and attaining infinite knowledge* [unendlichen Wissens]" (*HP*, 11/16). In his lecture course *Schelling's Treatise on the Essence of Human Freedom* (*Schellings Abhandlung über das Wesen der menschlichen Freiheit* (1809), 1936/1941–3)—an analysis that Nancy and Lacoue-Labarthe presuppose in *The Literary Absolute* (see *LA*, 134, note 17)—Heidegger says, from the perspective of German Idealism, "Kant did succeed in a critique ... [but the] critique as critique was itself not founded" (*ST*, 41). For German Idealism, the problem of the Kantian Subject's lack of self-presentation means that the system was not secured; the "system [which] alone guarantees the inner unity of knowledge, its scientific character and truth" (*ST*, 41–2). Despite Kant's rejection of the absolute as an object of knowledge, German Idealism will attempt to think the absolute in order to secure a foundation for philosophy. Heidegger shows how Kant's *Critique* manifests a "will to system," a system, which in German Idealism will become "the jointure of Being itself [*Fuge des Seyns selbst*]" (*ST*, 39/47). Since this "totality of Being lacks a relation to other things, is not relative," this system is itself "called the *Ab-solute*" (*ST*, 43).

Kant's philosophy produces the demand of the system, which Kant shows cannot be justified empirically (in time and space). Therefore, against Kant, German Idealism will introduce the possibility of intellectual intuition as the name for a nonsensuous intuition. But, as Kant writes, only if "all of the manifold in the subject were given *self-actively* through that alone, then the inner intuition would be intellectual" (*CR*, B68). Only if the Subject is ontically creative, an absolute Subject, can there be a form of nonfinite intuition. In Fichte's *Foundations of the Entire Science of Knowledge* (*Grundlage der gesammten Wissenschaftslehre*, 1794/95), such an absolute Subject will be the form of the originary *Thathandlung* ("fact/act") by which the ego (*Ich*), as "pure activity [*reine Thätigkeit*],"[6] posits itself as "at once the agent [*das Handelnde*] and the product of action [*das Product der Handlung*]."[7] The idealist work is to be a systematic account *of* the absolute as *self*-activity: the Subject's auto-production that presents this very production as the coming-into-being of givenness (i.e., *intuitus originarius*). In Hegel's *Science of Logic* (*Wissenschaft der Logik*, 1812–16), the absolute is actuality (*Wirklichkeit*) presenting itself. It is a self-manifestation: "the absolute is manifestation not of an inner, nor over against an other, but it *is* only as the absolute manifestation of itself for itself. As such it is *actuality*."[8] This self-active Subject is absolute knowing as knowing *of* the absolute (in both the subjective and objective genitive). In Heidegger's words, the absolute Subject is a knowing unity: "absolute knowing is knowing 'of' the Absolute in the double sense that the Absolute is the knower and the known" (*ST*, 47).

In the lecture course *Hegel's Phenomenology of Sprit* (*Hegels Phänomenologie des Geistes*, 1930–1),[9] Heidegger emphasizes that the knowledge of absolute knowing is not so much a question of a quantitative knowledge, a knowing that would know *everything* there is to know, but of a qualitative knowing that knows itself in its knowing. In order to be absolute knowing, knowing cannot be "*held fast* by what is known" (*HP*, 14) since that would make the knowing dependent on its knowledge. Hegel's absolute Subject cannot be *relative* to what is known; rather, absolute knowing "must not remain bound but must liberate and ab-solve itself from what it knows and yet as so ab-solved [*ab-gelöstes*], as absolute, still be a knowledge [*Wissen*]. To be ab-solved [*Sichloslösen*] from what is known does not mean 'abandoning' it, but 'preserving it by elevating it' ['*erhaltende Aufhebung*']" (*HP*, 15/21).[10]

Absolute knowing is absolvent, detaching, in the sense of *Aufhebung*, Hegel's concept for the negating, elevating, and preserving movement of the absolute. Absolute knowing is thus a knowing that undergoes an experience with itself in the sense that it only becomes itself by becoming other than itself, returning to itself, being only the "absolute unrest of pure self-movement" (*PS*, 101; see *HP*, 23). The absolute unrest is actuality (*Wirklichkeit*) itself. It is actuality that presents itself as the true Concept (see *HP*, 27, 30). But, as Nancy writes in *The Speculative Remark*, "If the exposition, as *plastic* exposition, is the genuine place of truth—speculative presentation—one must therefore understand both the truth of the *aufheben* through the already-past of becoming [*le déjà-passé du devenir*] and the becoming already-past through (or 'as') truth that exposes itself by *aufheben* [by sublating]" (*SR*, 29). Absolute knowing has always already exposed itself but only because it is this very exposition itself, the unrest of coming to itself by becoming other than itself and returning to itself. Nancy understands this plasticity of the exposition in terms of Hegel's explanation of the speculative proposition in the *Phenomenology of Spirit* (*Phänomenologie des Geistes*, 1807). This speculative proposition destroys "the usual subject-predicate relation" (*PS*, 39) since the philosophical proposition is the very movement of the relation itself.[11]

For Hegel, the form of this speculative proposition is the reason why philosophy "has to be read over and over [*wiederholt gelesen werden*] before it can be understood" (*PS*, 39/60; see *SR*, 10–11). Rereading is thus intrinsic to the *thing itself*, that is, not an external requisite but required by the philosophical text as such. Plasticity is the grammar of the speculative proposition. Nancy comments, "To read Hegel's text is thus, if not to rewrite it, at least to repeat its exposition *plastically*" (*SR*, 13). In his reading of Hegel, Nancy thus locates the *unrest* of the speculative absolute in Hegel's *text* itself. Nancy investigates in detail how "*aufheben* never occurs in the same way, is displaced from word to word, slides along from text to text" (*SR*, 87). Nancy's concern is how the determination of the sense of the Concept is always already deferred: "*Hegel's text* is nonetheless doomed never … to finding its meaning (its direction) again" (*SR*, 126).[12]

In Hegel's text, Nancy finds a *philosophical* solution to the Kantian problem of presentation; however, it is a solution that is still exposed to the *writing* of a text. Even if Hegel's pure exposition abandons any romantic program of writing, philosophy must still be written and is thus exposed to its discursive form. But Hegel's speculative system will nevertheless frame the question of literature: insofar as literature emerges as an intransitive writing, the question will be whether this intransitivity is nothing but the negativity of the dialectical system or the very interruption of this system. This question arises at the core of the paradigm of writerly necessity. It will manifest itself as the question of whether the subject who cannot not-write literature *lacks* the objective actuality of the work or *affirms* the absence of work without negation. This will then also be the question of whether literature is a thing of the past or a thing of the future.

2

The Literary Absolute

A Philosophical Study of Literature

How should we read *The Literary Absolute*? Given the reception of Nancy and Lacoue-Labarthe's work since its publication in 1978, this question is anything but arbitrary.[1] But this is not the only reason why we should pose this question, which in fact will take us to the very core of a dominant concern of *The Literary Absolute*. This is the concern for literature as a solution to philosophical presentation. The question of how to read the writing of *The Literary Absolute* will therefore be a constant focus here since the *text* of *The Literary Absolute* demands our attention. So far we have seen *that* literature emerges as the fiction of a pure intransitive writing. Literature arises as the solution to philosophical presentation within the Kantian moment. We have also seen how Hegel produces a pure philosophical writing as the solution to how the philosophical Subject can present itself. It is now time to investigate *how* literature emerges as an intransitive writing in the journal of the Early German Romantics, the *Athenaeum*. How do the Romantics inaugurate literature as absolute between Kant and Hegel? This investigation will lead us to see not only how the subject who cannot not-write becomes possible but also how the paradigm of writerly necessity makes possible Nancy and Lacoue-Labarthe's identification of the literary absolute.

In the preface to *The Literary Absolute*, Nancy and Lacoue-Labarthe quote *Critical Fragment* 115 (*Kritische Fragmente*, 1797), which they rightly say provides the program of the journal of the Early German Romantics:

It [*Critical Fragment* 115] furnishes the entire program of the Athenaeum: "The whole history of modern poetry is a running commentary on the following brief philosophical text: all art should become science, and all science art; poetry and philosophy should be made one." If only for this reason, it seemed to us necessary (in other words *still* urgent) to undertake a properly philosophical study of romanticism. (*LA*, 13)

Nancy and Lacoue-Labarthe will show how Romanticism inaugurates the concept of literature as absolute. Literary writing will emerge as the (apparent) solution to the philosophical problem of how to present philosophy (science). For Nancy and Lacoue-Labarthe, a "properly philosophical" study does not entail a concern for "the 'philosophy of the romantics'" (*LA*, 13); rather, they proclaim, "The object of our study is exclusively the *question of literature*" (*LA*, 13).[2] What does "philosophical" then mean here? What is the sense of this "question of literature"?

In *The Literary Absolute*, the philosophical focus will emerge as a concern for the question of literature, since this question indicates itself in the romantic work but nevertheless remains *unthought* in Romanticism (see *LA*, 57). What makes Nancy and Lacoue-Labarthe's philosophical study *philosophical* is the concern for the *unthought* of Romanticism. With this concern they adopt Heidegger's thoughts on the condition of thinking: "the thinker can never himself say what is most of all his own. It must remain unsaid [*ungesagt*], because what is sayable [*sagbare Wort*] receives its determination from what is not sayable [*Unsagbaren*]" (*EP*, 77–8/484). *The Literary Absolute* concerns the unsaid of the *Athenaeum*, and this unsaid is "the question of literature." We will see soon enough how this question of literature is unthought in Romanticism, and how we should understand literature as a question.

The Method of *The Literary Absolute* I

Nancy and Lacoue-Labarthe identify *fragmentation* as the literary gesture or "the romantic genre *par excellence*" (*LA*, 40). But, in order to approach the romantic fragment, Nancy and Lacoue-Labarthe must first *begin*, and they must think of *how* to begin. They must think about the question of method, since, as they say, "nowhere did any of the romantics propose a definition of the fragment that could, by itself, supply a content for this framework" (*LA*, 42). They therefore choose a way to begin: "From the practice of fragments, then, we must begin, in order to try to grasp the nature of the fragment and the stakes it involves" (*LA*, 42). That we are to understand this focus on *practice* literally as a question of *writing fragments* is manifest from Nancy and Lacoue-Labarthe's exposition of what they call "the romantic 'project' or in other words that brief, intense, and brilliant *moment of writing* (not quite two years and hundreds of pages)" (*LA*, 7). The theme of writing governs the entire analysis in *The Literary Absolute*. The two Schlegel brothers, the initiators of the journal, are identified as writers: "August and Friedrich (the latter no doubt more than the former) have explicit ambitions as *writers*" (*LA*, 7). For Nancy and Lacoue-Labarthe, the Romantics's "literary ambition is always the result of their ambition for an entirely new social function for the writer—that writer who was, for them, a character still to come" (*LA*, 6). Nancy and Lacoue-Labarthe understand the *Athenaeum* to be the locus of a fraternity where "fraternization means collective writing" (*LA*, 9). The two main figures of this fraternity, which also include Novalis (Friedrich von Hardenberg), are the editors: the brothers August Wilhelm Schlegel and Friedrich Schlegel (see *LA*, 8). It is this "experience" of collective writing that leads to the "theoretical breakthrough" (*LA*, 9) of Romanticism, insofar as that which was "new" in the *Athenaeum* "was not 'literature' but criticism" (*LA*, 12). The *Athenaeum* is the inauguration of the concept of literature, of *literary theory*, literature as theory, theory as literature.

For Nancy and Lacoue-Labarthe, it is thus an experience of *writing* that makes the grasping of the romantic fragment possible. But the question then arises: How can they defend this decision to focus on writing? Is this methodological starting point not more or less arbitrary? Why not begin with the concept of "reflection" or the problem of "irony"?[3] For Hegel, the philosophical method is itself "the path by which the Concept of knowledge is reached" (*PS*, 20/38; translation modified). It is the "necessary and complete process of becoming; so that this preparatory path ceases to be casual philosophizing that fastens on to this or that object, relationship, or thought that happens to pop up in the imperfect consciousness" (*PS*, 20). Is *The Literary Absolute* not supposed to be a *philosophical* study, that is, a rigorous exposition that systematically works out the criterion for its method?

It is. Nancy and Lacoue-Labarthe themselves write in a mode informed by Hegel's philosophical text. Following Hegelian logic, writing is the point of departure for a reading of the romantic fragments because writing is also the end point by which the text returns to itself. But in *The Literary Absolute* this very dialectical movement will also displace itself, deconstruct. The anonymous *Athenaeum Fragments* (which share their name with the journal but are not identical to the entire content of the journal) will be the "extreme limit of romantic writing" (*LA*, 14): Reading the writing of the fragments will be the "beginning" (in the Hegelian sense) of *The Literary Absolute*. Nancy and Lacoue-Labarthe are thus explicit about what type of reading and writing the reader of *The Literary Absolute* should expect.[4] They state openly that a dialectical process takes place between the chapters of *The Literary Absolute*:

Thus, having set out from the question of the fragment as a genre (or as "genre"), or in other words, from the moment the question of literature is first raised ("The Fragment: The Fragmentary Exigency"), we took the speculative "step" necessarily raised by the question itself ("The Idea: Religion within the Limits of Art"), before approaching this question for itself and in itself ("The Poem: A Nameless Art"), thereby attaining the properly romantic moment of reflection or of "literature

raised to the second power" ("Criticism: The Formation of Character").
(*LA*, 14–15)

The Literary Absolute will thus itself present "a certain rational progression"
(*LA*, 14) of the two years of writing the *Athenaeum*, which is also to say
that *Aufhebung* takes place (has always already taken place) between and,
as we shall see, within the chapters of Nancy and Lacoue-Labarthe's work
(which also, in the original French edition, includes translations of the main
texts analyzed in the chapters). But, despite this dialectical performance
of the text, or precisely because of it, there will be no pure dialectical
resolution. At least any apparent resolution will always be marked by "the
equivocity of the absence of the work" (*LA*, 126). Instead, there will be
recurrent displacements of words, a fluidity of concepts, which make up the
presentation of *The Literary Absolute*. The reader of *The Literary Absolute*
will therefore have to expect a certain *style*, and it is from this perspective
insufficient when a commentator, not unfamiliar with deconstruction, calls
the prose style of *The Literary Absolute* "irritating"[5] without considering
the methodological presuppositions of this style: the problem of how to
write and present philosophy.

The Method of *The Literary Absolute* II

The question is how Nancy and Lacoue-Labarthe assure that writing is not
an arbitrary methodological point of departure for their investigation. In
order to see how this method is grounded in the "thing itself," the dialectic
occurring from chapter to chapter in *The Literary Absolute* should be made
visible. This will be the movement from the absolute immediate work to
the self-reflection of the work: from the "in itself," which first becomes
itself through its becoming-other and, *as* the "return to itself," becomes
the "romantic moment of reflection," which is thinking exhibiting itself
as literature. In the first chapter, Nancy and Lacoue-Labarthe write, "The
fragment in itself, almost immediately [*immédiatement en quelque sorte*],
also sets forth the truth of the work. Beyond or before the work it proposes
its very operativity [*l'opérativité*]" (*LA*, 47/68). We should note here, at first,
that everything depends on this "almost" or "to some extent" that indicates
the speculative thought of mediation. In *The Speculative Remark*, it is this
"almost" that makes it possible for Nancy to locate the displacements of
the speculative absolute in the restlessness of Hegel's *text* itself. Everything
begins *almost* immediately, almost from the beginning, since the "beginning"
has always already begun and *is* not before its return to itself but is thus
precisely this very production of (its) negativity, of its "not." As Heidegger
says, "The immediate to which we, the mediators, condescend always
already stands under the dominion of mediation and sublation" (*HP*, 48).

The first chapter of *The Literary Absolute* is thus the beginning, but the beginning can only be understood at the end. We will see that Nancy and Lacoue-Labarthe's focus on writing in *The Literary Absolute* is precisely such a beginning that needs a supplement, since it is always already both more and less than itself.

In the second chapter, the "history of fragmentation" (*LA*, 60), as Nancy and Lacoue-Labarthe call the movement of the literary absolute, "passes [*passer*] from the *Fragments* to the *Ideas*" (*LA*, 63/186), but this "passing" is then nothing but the dialectical *Wiederkehr*—the "turn back toward [*faire retour*]" (*LA*, 64/188), the "return to the moral tradition of the fragment" (*LA*, 66).[6] In the third chapter, Nancy and Lacoue-Labarthe will say that the genre of "dialogue represents the fulfilment of what we have called the 'moral genre of the fragment' " (*LA*, 86), but this genre will nevertheless not "fulfil" this role "absolutely" (*LA*, 86). In the final analysis, the reason for this is that the fragmentary epoch is an "epoch that begins with criticism" (*LA*, 110). As Nancy and Lacoue-Labarthe write in the last chapter of *The Literary Absolute* (only superseded by the equivocal "Closure"), the epoch that begins with Kant's *Critique*, the epoch, which opens the very possibility for (the question of) literature, "is an epoch that founds itself, so to speak, on a loss of origin" (*LA*, 110). The epoch of literature is the epoch of the loss of "great poetry" (*LA*, 110) and the loss of an adequate philosophical exposition. The history of fragmentation completes itself in criticism; however, this completion is nothing but the loss of completion, since an epoch that begins with criticism is an epoch that is suspended. It is an epoch that begins with the supplement rather than with the completed literary work:

> Construction (criticism) is art—or more precisely, the *entire* construction is the critical complement or supplement that the work requires in order to be a work (of art). An epoch that begins with criticism is perhaps an epoch that begins (without beginning, for it is in suspense) with the supplement or with the perfection [*parachèvement*] of the work of art rather than with the completed [*achevée*] work of art. Such is undoubtedly the profound duplicity that constitutes the romantic concept of criticism. (*LA*, 110/382)

The romantic concept of criticism produces itself as the supplement of the literary work only to lack the Work itself. In *Of Grammatology* (*De la grammatologie*, 1967), Derrida presents the supplement as that which is neither present nor absent, neither inside nor outside, but a (non)-concept that cannot be thought in any ontology: "Less than nothing and yet, to judge by its effects, much more than nothing. The supplement is neither a presence nor an absence. No ontology can think its operation."[7] The supplement is "less than nothing" since it replaces *nothing* of the absolute presence, which is not supposed to be lacking. It supplements the absolute as "less than nothing," but since it adds itself to that which is supposedly unconditioned, its effects are also "much more than nothing" because it makes the absolute function as origin. Derrida writes, "There is no present before it, it is not preceding by anything but itself, that is to say by another supplement. The supplement is always the supplement of a supplement. One wishes to go back *from the supplement to the source*: one must recognize that there is *a supplement at the source*."[8] The logic of supplementarity is an indefinite process that has "always already *infiltrated* presence"[9] and which makes visible that there was never any absolute presence: "What opens meaning and language is writing as the disappearance of natural presence."[10] In his deconstruction of the history of the metaphysics of presence, Derrida identifies writing as the supplement of the "full" speech of presence.[11]

Nancy and Lacoue-Labarthe follow in the wake of Derrida's deconstruction. Lacoue-Labarthe understands his own investigation of the relation of philosophy and literature to be in debt to Derrida's thought (see *SP*, 1). In March 1973, Nancy presented his work on Hegel at Derrida's seminar at the École Normale Supérieure, a reading of Hegel that Nancy himself understands to be linked to Derrida's *Of Grammatology* in which Derrida considers Hegel to be "the last philosopher of the book and the first thinker of writing."[12] For Derrida, Hegel is the thinker of the book, of absolute knowing, in which writing is effaced, but "Hegel is *also* the thinker of irreducible difference."[13] Hegel is "also" a thinker of writing, which functions as a supplement of the absolute.

When Nancy and Lacoue-Labarthe identify the romantic concept of criticism as the supplement of the literary work, they thus find at the end that which constituted the very beginning of the dialectical movement of *The Literary Absolute*: the methodological presupposition that we should focus on the question of writing when we read the romantic fragments. But insofar as this concept of writing is identified with the supplement, this presupposition also introduces equivocity into the dialectical process of *The Literary Absolute*. The romantic concept of criticism is the supplement of the literary work, but it thus also interrupts the presence of the absolute Work, which this supplement was supposed to supplement. Likewise, writing not only presents itself as the absolute presupposition of the dialectical history of fragmentation in *The Literary Absolute* but also exposes itself *as* presupposition insofar as it is nothing but the supplement of this presupposition. Nancy and Lacoue-Labarthe thus deliberately expose the dialectical logic of *The Literary Absolute* to its written condition, but they do this in order to grasp how an entire dialectical history of fragmentation takes place within the journal of the *Athenaeum*. The fragments constitute the operation of the literary absolute. The question is now how this operation functions and thus how literature emerges as absolute.

Fragmentation: The Operation of *The Literary Absolute*

Nancy and Lacoue-Labarthe show how Romanticism, in relation to speculative thought, "sets the work to work in a different mode" (*LA*, 39). The focus on the fragments as a *gesture of writing* is decisive for their reading of the *Athenaeum* fragments since it means that they will insist on the fact—at least initially (and, I will come back to this)—that the romantic gesture is not simply the "progressive, universal poetry"[14] of *Athenaeum Fragment* 116. Nancy and Lacoue-Labarthe say, "Fragment 116's 'romantic' poetry does not exhaust the romantics' idea or ideal of total, infinite poetry—neither is the fragment simply the work-project of this poetry. It is both more and less [*plus et moins*]" (*LA*, 43/63, translation modified).

In order to try to understand the sense of this "more" and "less" in *The Literary Absolute*, we should pay attention to the textual modifications taking place within the first chapter. It is necessary to note how certain significations are dislocated and deferred in the text. We should thus pay attention to the fact that the text is itself *written*. There is a certain (quasi)-dialectical process taking place *within* the chapter "The Fragment: The Fragmentary Exigency," a dialectic, which evolves around the sense of the "progression" of romantic poetry.

In the first instance, the "more" denotes the fragmentary demand of absolute positing: "It is more in that it posits the exigency of its total closure, basically in opposition to 'progressive' poetry" (*LA*, 43). The "less" indicates the comparison of the fragment to "a *small* work of art" (*LA*, 43). The "more" means that fragmentation takes place as an actual totality in which each fragment is itself plural. The reason for this is that to *write* a fragment is always already to write a plurality of fragments: "The romantics did not publish a unique *Fragment*; to write the fragment is to write fragments" (*LA*, 43–4). The "less" means that the fragment is not "absolutely the Work" but nevertheless must be understood "with respect to its relation to the work" (*LA*, 43).

In the second instance, the totality of the "more" is understood as a "dialectical" absolute insofar as this term marks the form of all metaphysical thinking: "For all of metaphysics, it [the term *dialectical*] covers the thinking of identity through the mediation of nonidentity. For this is precisely what forms the basis of fragmentary totality" (*LA*, 46). Fragmentation constitutes the total closure as the romantic concept of the system, the system of absolute knowledge, which means that the fragment is itself the romantic thinking of the Work: "The absolute fragmentary grasping of the System thus depends on the dialectic concerning the Work taking place within the fragment" (*LA*, 47). The dialectic of the Work takes place within the fragment. How are we to understand this taking place "within"? It indicates that, even if the fragmentary operation aims to grasp itself as absolute, as "more," the fragment is nevertheless comparable only to a *small* work of art, to the "less." The fragment's *quasi*-dialectic of the "more" is always "less" than the speculative dialectic. However, following the logic of the fragment, since the "more" (the grasping of the absolute Work) needs the "less" (the non-Work) in order to grasp itself as "more," the fragment as the *small* work is at once a "sub-work" that is never the Work and a "super-work" that makes the Work function as absolute presence:

> Undoubtedly, the fragment is thus a "small work" in that it is a miniature or microcosm of the Work. But also in that, functioning in some sense as the work of work [*l'œuvre de l'œuvre*], or as putting into-work of the work [*de la mise en œuvre de l'œuvre*], it always operates [*opère*] both as a sub-work [*sous-œuvre*] and as a super-work [*sur-œuvre*]. The fragment figures—but to figure, *bilden* and *gestalten*, is here to work and to present, *darstellen*—the outside-the-work [*le hors-d'œuvre*] that is essential to the work. (*LA*, 48/68–9)

In *Of Grammatology*, Derrida writes that there is no "outside-text" (*hors-texte*) in order to emphasize that there is no "transcendental signified,"[15] which one can refer to as an absolute presence. With the term "outside-the-work" (*hors-d'œuvre*), Nancy and Lacoue-Labarthe understand the fragment to function as precisely such a "transcendental signified," which, inscribed outside the Work as the small non-Work, makes the absolute Work function as absolute. It is crucial to note that at this point in Nancy and Lacoue-Labarthe's argument, the initiating distinction between "more" and "less" is itself sublated (*aufgehoben*) insofar as it is precisely the fragment as "less" (in the sense of the small work of art) that produces the fragment as "more" (as an inscription outside the Work that completes it). Indeed, it is this dialectic *performed* by Nancy and Lacoue-Labarthe's text that means that they will construe *Work in progress* (*LA*, 48), the progression itself, as "the infinite truth of the work" (*LA*, 48). They will do this in obvious contradiction to their initial statement (what I have called the first instance) that "progression" does not exhaust the romantic concept of poetry. But, insofar as the very distinction between "more" and "less" is sublated in progression, *Work in Progress* is now the truth of the romantic work. This is the final moment of the fragmentary dialectic of the first chapter. In this instance, Nancy and Lacoue-Labarthe oppose the Romantics to Hölderlin in order to show why the concept of the literary absolute is inaugurated specifically in the *Athenaeum* (and not in Hölderlin's work). I quote at length:

> The romantic fragment, far from bringing the dispersion or the shattering of the work into play, inscribes its plurality as the exergue

of the total, infinite work. This is no doubt also because the infinite is presented only through its exergue and because, if the *Darstellung* of the infinite after and despite Kant, constitutes the essential preoccupation of idealism, then romanticism, through literature in the fragment, forms the exergue of philosophical idealism. This is where the romantics, along with Hölderlin, occupy the position we have evoked in their name in the "Overture." Purely theoretical completion is impossible (as stated in *Athenaeum* fragment 451 and several others, notably those calling for the unification of philosophy and poetry) because the theoretical infinite remains asymptotic. The actual infinite is the infinity of the work of art. Yet unlike Hölderlin, and much closer to idealism, the romantics simultaneously postulate the motifs of a present, accomplished (*effectué*) infinite in a work that the logic of the fragment stubbornly summarizes within the contours of its ideal, and as a corollary to this, the potential infinite in itself *as* the actuality of the work [*A la différence de Hölderlin, en revanche, et dans une proximité beaucoup plus grande avec l'idéalisme, les Romantiques se proposent simultanément les motifs de l'infini présent, effectué, dans une œuvre que la logique du fragment résume obstinément aux contours de son idéal, et—ce qui est au fond le corrélat de ce qui précède—de l'infini potentiel lui-même en tant qu'actualité de l'œuvre*]. In fact, to return to *Athenaeum* fragment 116, it is in the very "progressivity" and infinity of its movement that "romantic poetry," since Antiquity and for all the future, forms the truth of all poetry. The actuality of romanticism, as is well known, is never *there* (especially during the period of those who do not call themselves romantics, even while writing fragment 116), and likewise, "there is as yet nothing that is fragmentary" (*A* 77). But it is indeed in this not being there, this never yet being there, that romanticism and the fragment *are*, absolutely. *Work in progress* henceforth becomes the infinite truth of the work. (*LA*, 48/69)

It is in the *not being there* that fragmentation *is*, absolutely. How are we to understand this fragmentation? The paragraph simultaneously proposes two motifs. On the one hand, the ideal of the fragment as a present, accomplished infinite. This "ideal" signifies the romantic fragments as the total closure of an actual totality in which each fragment is itself plural, since it is written. On the other hand, the potential infinite is in itself understood as the actuality of the work. This signifies the "Romantic poetry" of *Athenaeum Fragment* 116, which is "a progressive, universal poetry" whose "essence" is that it is forever in a "state of becoming."[16] Nancy and Lacoue-Labarthe thus seem to present us with a paradox since the romantic fragmentation apparently is simultaneously potentiality (*l'infini potentiel*) and effective actuality (*l'infini présent, effectué*) but nevertheless also *Work in Progress*, which means that the fragment *is* in its non-Being.

We might question the sense of such an analysis of the romantic fragment and even more since the analysis in *The Literary Absolute* is not deepened at this point. But then we would miss that the indistinction between potentiality and actuality is a consequence of the "operativity" and "effectiveness" that define ontology in the history of metaphysics. This operativity concerns precisely the "work in progress," the production of the *opus* (work), as effective actuality (*Wirklichkeit*). In his reworking of Heidegger's history of being in *Opus Dei* (2012), Agamben shows how the couple of effect (*Wirkung*) and actuality (*Wirklichkeit*) become indeterminate in the paradigm of operativity. As effectiveness (actuality), "being is inseparable from its effects; [effectiveness] names being insofar as it is effective, produces certain effects, and at the same time is determined by them."[17] When Being is will, operativity, Being is effecting actuality in which potentiality is always already actualized:

> An essential characteristic of effectiveness is operativity. We understand with this term the fact that being does not simply exist but is "brought into work," is effectuated and actualized. Consequently, *energeia* no longer designates being-at-work as a full dwelling of presence [as in Aristotle] but an "operativity" in which the very distinctions between potential and act, operation and work are indeterminated and lose their sense.[18]

The romantic work emerges within the horizon of an understanding of Being in which it is not possible to distinguish between potentiality and actuality since Being is a will that must actualize itself: "If being does not exist, but must actualize itself, then in its very essence it is will and command; and vice versa, if being is will, then it does not simply exist but has to be."[19] The romantic work is that which must always actualize itself, which is never securely actualized, but interrupts its actualization. The literary absolute is different from the speculative absolute: It is not the absolute self-transparent system but a system that interrupts itself. The literary absolute interrupts itself as it produces itself.

Witz: The Question of the Interruption I

For Nancy and Lacoue-Labarthe, the question of the literary truth is the question of the truth of this interruption. From the perspective of Hegel's dialectical Subject, insofar as fragmentation interrupts its actuality, the literary Subject is "abstract" (in the Hegelian sense), one-sided, since the literary absolute does not coincide, in its purity, with actuality itself (see *PS*, 106–7). In Hegelian terms, to produce the absolute systematically thus means to understand the living Subject as the self-manifestation of the absolute and this manifestation as actuality itself. As Nancy and Lacoue-Labarthe remark, "In philosophical [idealist] discourse the systematic power must be given, in actuality, from the outset" (*LA*, 49). Contrary to this speculative living system, the literary absolute interrupts actuality in its production. But is this interruption then only the sign of an abstraction? How are we to understand this interruption of actuality?

It is possible to read *The Literary Absolute* as nothing but a commentary on a short digression in Heidegger's *Schelling*: "Friedrich Schlegel once said (*Athenaeum* fragment 82) that 'a definition that is not *witzig* is worthless.' This is only a romantic transposition of the idealist dialectic" (quoted in *LA*, 135, note 28; *ST*, 82). Nancy and Lacoue-Labarthe cite this comment by Heidegger in a note to *The Literary Absolute* in which they also add, "This affirmation nevertheless raises the question, clearly, of what is in fact at stake in this *transposition*, or of the 'play' that subsists between idealism and romanticism" (*LA*, 135–6, note 28). Insofar as the "advent of writing," according to Derrida, is the advent of "the play of signifying references that constitute language,"[20] the question for Nancy and Lacoue-Labarthe is the play of writing that takes place in the post-Kantian space between Hegel and the *Athenaeum*. In *Athenaeum Fragment* 394 (quoted in *The Literary Absolute*), it is written, "Genuine *Witz* is still conceivable only in written form [*Eigentlichen Witz kann man sich doch nur geschrieben denken*]" (*LA*, 54).[21] Moreover, insofar as (written) *Witz* in *Critical Fragment 9* is understood as "fragmentary genius [*fragmentarische Genialität*],"[22] Nancy and Lacoue-Labarthe can write, "*Witz* ultimately provides the essence of the fragment" (*LA*, 54). But how is *Witz* then the essence of fragmentation? According to Nancy and Lacoue-Labarthe, romantic *Witz* is "constituted in the greatest proximity to what Hegel will call 'Absolute Knowledge'" (*LA*, 53). But, *Witz* at the same time indicates itself as the gap that separates Romanticism and Idealism. In a "Remark" in his *Logic*, Hegel opposes *Aufhebung* to a Ciceronian *Witz* in which the equivocal senses of the Latin *tollere* are deployed.[23] In his entry on the concept of *Aufheben* in the *Dictionary of Untranslatables*, Philippe Büttgen explains this relation between this *Witz* and the concept of *Aufhebung*. Since *tollere* can mean either to "raise" (to the highest office) *or* to "eliminate," Büttgen writes that "the *Witz* proceeds from the fact that Cicero succeeds in making this 'second meaning,' which is threatening, heard in a passage that is apparently favorable to Octavian ('We must praise this young man, adorn him with all the virtues, *tollere* him')."[24] In opposition to the *Witz* in which the sense is *either* to "raise" *or* to "eliminate," *Aufhebung* means to "raise," "preserve," *and* "eliminate," all at once.

In *The Speculative Remark*, Nancy presents this difference of concepts in a similar manner: "*tollere* covers an antinomic duality (to suppress, to push aside *or* to lift up); *aufheben* combines a dialectical or speculative duplicity (to suppress *and* to preserve)" (*SR*, 55–6). The romantic *Witz* thus introduces equivocation into the system where the speculative *Aufhebung* manifests itself as the System presenting itself (see also *SR*, 56). But, when Nancy (re)reads the Hegelian *text* and shows how this text displaces itself, how the sense of the very word and concept of *Aufhebung* is postponed, he also shows how this text produces a remainder. Nancy writes, "The very operation of the *aufheben* entails, in all its rigor and in all its necessity, a remainder, the relief of its own—forever improper—nonsublated *Witz*. ... Hegel's 'painful effort,' the desperate effort of the speculative, might be an effort *not* to master this unrest, *even* while identifying and sublating it" (*SR*, 132). The operation of *Aufhebung*, even if it works within the horizon of the identity of identity and nonidentity, is an operation that includes contingency, even when it apparently sublates contingency into necessity (see *SR*, 147–53). Nancy writes that an "author's pen cannot be deduced. ... It writes in spite of everything—but it is also always in danger of not being able to write in a certain way" (*SR*, 143). *Witz* thus points to the possibility of contingency. It indicates the very interruption of the system, the suspension of the "will to system," since it is not possible *to will Witz*. Nancy writes in the essay "Menstruum Universale" (1978), "One cannot will *Witz*. But what cannot be *willed*, and what *not-to-will* is, philosophy has never been able to think nor literature to practice."[25] But is romantic *Witz* then the interruption of the system? Does the either-or of the antinomy of *Witz* interrupt the both-at-once of dialectical *Aufhebung*?

In *The Literary Absolute*, Nancy and Lacoue-Labarthe dismiss this possibility. They write,

> [Romantic] *Witz* very precisely represents an *a priori* synthesis in the Kantian sense, but one that is removed from Kant's limiting conditions and critical procedures and that involves the synthesis not only of an object but of a subject as well (or at least the synthesis of the power of the producer-subject). In this respect, *Witz*, in short, is the solution of the enigma of transcendental schematism, as discussed in the "Overture." (*LA*, 53)

The concept of *Witz*, as the essence of fragmentation, is the truth of the *Work*, the transcendental synthesis. It is the solution to the system, to transcendental schematism, which also means that it is a solution to the question of presentation since it is an "absolute knowing-seeing [*savoir-voir*]" by which the writer gains "direct access to the productive capacity of works" (*LA*, 53). *Witz* is the creative spark, "the 'sudden idea' (*Einfall*, the idea suddenly 'falls' upon you, so that the find is less found than received)" (*LA*, 52). *Witz* functions as the *other* concept of *Wissen*, of knowing (see *LA*, 53). But insofar as *Witz* is the solution to the system, it is necessary to "retain or contain the 'chaotic', 'telluric' *Witz*" and, yet, to "abandon oneself to its fundamentally involuntary character" (*LA*, 54). In *The Discourse of the Syncope*, Nancy writes that the arbitrary and chaotic *Witz* is also the danger of destroying science. It is the "aesthetic, inadmissible substitute for [mathematical] demonstration" (*DS*, 56). In order to "safeguard science" (*DS*, 57), one cannot give in to "the temptation of play" (*DS*, 57), to the superficial *Witz*, which threatens the purity of science: "The ethics of presentation begins in the mortifying asceticism of the concept" (*DS*, 58). *Witz* is thus also the danger of the lack of method, of the lack of *Critique*, and the risk of returning to or remaining in the dogmatism of a precritical age.

In *The Literary Absolute*, Nancy and Lacoue-Labarthe thus also note that Witz "must be torn from its too-immediately explosive and dangerous existence in the salon. In other words, it must be put to work in the work" (*LA*, 54). Insofar as the absolute Work must be secured, *Witz* can still only be conceived in *written* form. Nancy and Lacoue-Labarthe write, "The writing of the fragment thus constitutes the dialectical *Aufhebung* of the internal antinomy of *Witz*. 'Fragmentary geniality' preserves *Witz* as work and suppresses it as non-work, sub-work, or anti-work" (*LA*, 54). According to Nancy and Lacoue-Labarthe, for the Romantics, *Witz* thus remains within the horizon of the system, which means that the antinomy of Witz always already functions within the dialectic of the Subject.

The Question of the Subject

The literary absolute interrupts itself in its actualization, but the antinomy of *Witz* preserves this very interruption as the absolute Work. The literary absolute thus confirms the thinking of the Subject. My concern is now how this thinking of the Subject manifests itself in the *Athenaeum*. Nancy and Lacoue-Labarthe write, "Our own image comes back to us from the mirror of the literary absolute. And the massive truth flung back at us is that we have not left the era of the Subject" (*LA*, 16). As we have seen, Nancy and Lacoue-Labarthe display how Romanticism (as the *locus* of the literary absolute) arises *within* Idealism between "Hegel (who has not yet appeared) and Fichte, whose ontology of the absolute Self has nonetheless initiated the movement as its most proximate cause" (*LA*, 34), but moreover, since Idealism is itself only possible after Kant, how "crudely translated, this means that Kant opens up the possibility of romanticism" (*LA*, 29). Romanticism is situated between Kant and German Idealism, which in *The Literary Absolute* refers to Fichte, Schelling, and Hegel, but the main focus is nevertheless on Hegel's dialectical thought.

In *Modern French Philosophy* (originally published in French as *Le Même et l'autre*, 1979), Vincent Descombes traces how the figure of Hegel emerges at the center of modern French thought from the 1930s. Besides such readers of Hegel as Jean Hyppolite, Eric Weil, and Jean Wahl, it is especially Alexandre Kojève's course on Hegel given at the Ecole Pratique des Hautes Etudes from 1933 to 1939 that impacted the turn to Hegel in

French thought. Descombes points to the change in connotation of the word *dialectic* as a mark for Hegel's emergence. Before the 1930s, the word *dialectic* "was understood pejoratively; for a neo-Kantian the dialectic was the 'logic of appearances,'" but after the 1930s until the 1960s, with reference to Hegel, "the word [*dialectic*] was almost always used in a eulogistic sense."[26] Nancy and Lacoue-Labarthe's concern with Hegel is thus in line with the traditional focus in recent French thought on German Idealism.

For Nancy and Lacoue-Labarthe, as they say, this focus on Hegel is not meant as a "critique" of "the traditional presentation of the genesis of romanticism, which makes Fichte an obligatory stage" (*LA*, 132, note 7). Nancy and Lacoue-Labarthe in fact rely on Walter Benjamin's dissertation, *The Concept of Criticism in German Romanticism* (*Der Begriff der Kunstkritik in der deutschen Romantik*, 1920), in which Benjamin shows how the romantic concept of reflection emerges as the transposition of Fichte's Absolute (see *LA*, 132, note 7).[27] Here Benjamin argues that romantic reflection does not entail a positing (*Setzung*) (see *SW*, 128) but consists in a "reflection in the medium of art" (*SW*, 134), which is without any ego (*Ich*): "Reflection without the 'I' is a reflection in the absolute of art [*Die Ich-freie Reflexion ist eine Reflexion im Absolutum der Kunst*]" (*SW*, 134/I:1, 40). This reflection is the pure thinking of form, a reflection of reflection, which Benjamin shows produces an ambiguity (*Doppeldeutigkeit*) of reflection when the "reflection of reflection" reflects back on itself:

> The thinking of thinking of thinking can be conceived and performed in two ways. If one starts from the expression "thinking of thinking," then on the third level this is either the object thought of, thinking (of thinking of thinking), or else the thinking subject (thinking of thinking) of thinking. The rigorous original form of second-level reflection is assailed and shaken by the ambiguity [*Doppeldeutigkeit*] in third-level reflection. (*SW*, 129/ I:1, 30–1)

The ambiguity is an antinomy of reflection, which apparently cannot be sublated in a Hegelian dialectic positing. The romantic absolute is apparently not the absolute Subject but the absolute of art. Nancy and Lacoue-Labarthe nevertheless write, "The romantic Fragment conclusively confirms and installs the figure of the artist as Author and Creator" (*LA*, 52). It has been claimed that Nancy and Lacoue-Labarthe forget Benjamin's decisive point about ego-free reflection;[28] however, is this in fact the case?

Nancy and Lacoue-Labarthe understand *The Literary Absolute* to build on Benjamin's dissertation (see *LA*, 135, note 26). They conceive Romanticism as the "experience" of a form of "violence" produced by the "effective philosophical *crisis*" (*LA*, 132, note 7) caused by the abyss of Kant's *Critique*, which consists in the "hiatus introduced at the heart of the subject" (*LA*, 32). The sense of this "hiatus" is the fact that the Kantian

Subject cannot present itself to itself, which means that the foundation of philosophy remains unsecure. Hegel's aim is precisely to make up for this abyss by producing philosophy as the self-presentation of the absolute system. The aim of the *Athenaeum* is also to produce the absolute but in opposition to German Idealism, as Benjamin writes, "For Friedrich Schlegel in the *Athenaeum* period, the absolute was the system in the form of art. Rather than attempting to grasp the absolute systematically, however, he sought conversely to grasp the system absolutely" (*SW*, 138).

Benjamin notes that this is the "essence" of Schlegel's linguistic "mysticism" (*SW*, 138), which emerges in the form of *Witz*: "Mystical terminology played its most general role in early Romanticism in the form of wit [*der Form des Witzes*]" (*SW*, 140/I:1, 48). Benjamin cites Novalis, "In this, Schlegel and Novalis are at one: philosophy 'is a mystical ... penetrating idea that drives us incessantly in every direction.' Novalis' terminology bears the clearest stamp of the mystical tendency of Friedrich Schlegel's philosophizing" (*SW*, 139). For Benjamin, *Witz* constitutes a form of linguistic knowing that presents the antinomy of the medium of reflection since it drives us in every direction. Benjamin writes, "The conceptual medium makes its appearance in the witty observation, as it does in the mystical term, like a bolt of lightning [*blitzartig*]" (*SW*, 140/I:1, 49). The antinomy of *Witz* can thus apparently not be thought in a Hegelian positing. But is romantic *Witz* then for Benjamin the interruption of the Subject?

It is significant that Benjamin understands romantic reflection to be not "an empty infinity [*leere Unendlichkeit*], but [reflection which] is in itself substantial and filled [*in sich selbst substanziell und erfüllt*]" (*SW*, 129/I:1, 31). For Benjamin, even if romantic reflection is not Fichte's absolute positing, *Witz* is not the interruption of the absolute but the very linguistic medium of the absolute. Benjamin thus conceives the romantic project as a form of thinking within the horizon of the absolute, which is the horizon of how to give the system a reasonable foundation. Benjamin writes, "Schlegel reflected vigorously on the essence of a system [*Wesen des System*] and the possibility of its grounding [*die Möglichkeit seiner Begründung*]" (*SW*, 136–7/I:1, 43). For Benjamin, the romantic (literary) absolute thus confirms the system, the Subject, even if reflection is not the positing of an *ego*.[29] Likewise for Nancy and Lacoue-Labarthe, the literary absolute is the thinking of the Subject. In *The Literary Absolute*, they show moreover how the literary absolute manifests itself as a specific understanding of Being as a will that wills itself. This understanding of Being will be my concern in the following section.

The Fragmentary Will

The romantic Subject is not Fichte's self-positing; however, even if the literary absolute is not the ego, it is the operation, the *opus*, the Work.

Nancy and Lacoue-Labarthe write, "To the aims of the Work corresponds the decidedly *operative* status of the subject" (*LA*, 52). When Nancy and Lacoue-Labarthe claim that the literary absolute confirms the thinking of the Subject, they thus mean the Work as Subject and substance. There is here a Heideggerian distinction between subjectivity (*Subjektivität*) and subjectity (*Subiectität* or *Subjektität*), which informs *The Literary Absolute* (see *LA*, 104–5). In order to read the history of metaphysics, Heidegger coins the term *subjectity* (*Subiectität*) which "*should emphasize the fact that Being* [Sein] *is determined in terms of the* subiectum, *but not necessarily by an ego* [Ich]" (*EP*, 46/451). The literary absolute can thus be understood to infinitize the Subject (subjectity) even if reflection is not the production of an *ego* (subjectivity). The subjectity of the literary absolute is the will of the absolute, the will to will, the imperative of Being, which *must* be the Work, but also interrupts its own Being as Work.

The Literary Absolute is thus written within the horizon of Heidegger's history of Being. When Nancy and Lacoue-Labarthe understand Romanticism as a manifestation of "the will to system [*la volonté du système*]" (*LA*, 32/46), this is a reference to Heidegger's identification of the Being of modern metaphysics as self-willing, *exigent*, the "will to be," which means that being has precedence over nothingness: "Ever since the developed beginning of modern metaphysics, Being is will, that is, *exigentia essentiae*" (*EP*, 47).[30] In modern German philosophy, the Being as will becomes "the unification of the unity of totality striving for itself" (*EP*, 48). Kant's transcendental Subject, Hegel's absolute Subject, and the romantic Subject are all specific understandings of Being in which Being is the self-grounding of the effective foundation.[31] Being emerges as the *will to system*, which is the English translation of Nancy and Lacoue-Labarthe's French "volonté du Système,"[32] which itself is a translation of Heidegger's *Wille zum System*.[33] In Heidegger's analysis, this *Wille zum System* is also rendered as *Systemwille*.[34] The German *zu-* (preposition in Dative) in *Wille zum System* corresponds to the English *to* indicating that the system is *to do*; however, the German *Systemwille* furthermore underlines that it is the system itself that wills. Nancy and Lacoue-Labarthe choose no doubt to render this in French as *volonté du Système* in order to underline both senses:[35] the system is to (*de-*) do, but it is the system *itself* that is to produce itself and, in this sense, the preposition *de-* simply brings the two nouns *volonté* and *Système* together as in the German *Systemwille*. The system is thus the system of the will, the Subject's will, the system *as* Subject. Lacoue-Labarthe and Nancy therefore choose to give the name *System-subject* (*LA*, 34) to the absolute system, which must be the *living System* (*LA*, 34). The Subject is thus a certain understanding of Being as the system that is actuality itself: an absolute will that wills its own actuality.

Unworking: The Question of the Interruption II

The romantic Being as the "will to be" also emerges in the concept of the "Fragmentary Exigency" (*LA*, 39), insofar as this fragmentary exigency signifies that the literary absolute inscribes itself within the metaphysics of presence. With this term Nancy and Lacoue-Labarthe allude to Blanchot's essay "The Athenaeum" ("L'Athenaeum"), which was first published in August 1964 in *La Nouvelle Revue Française*. Earlier that year, in May 1964, Blanchot had published the essay "Interruption" ("L'Interruption") in the same review, in which he proposes to distinguish between an interruption that corresponds to a "dialectical exigency" and an interruption linked to a "non-dialectical exigency."[36] In the essay "The Athenaeum," this distinction appears again when Blanchot conceives of a tendency of Friedrich Schlegel's fragments "to refuse the opening that the fragmentary exigency [*l'exigence fragmentaire*] represents; an exigency that does not exclude [*exclut*] totality, but goes beyond [*dépasse*] it" (*IC*, 359).[37] To exclude means to will the dialectical system, even if one thinks the fragmentary interruption as the impossibility of the system. To go beyond or exceed is to think the interruption of the absolute *as* interruption without remaining within the thinking of the system. Blanchot thus opposes Schlegel's tendency to think the fragment as a dialectical exigency. Insofar as the fragmentary exigency is the demand of the dialectical understood as effecting actuality (*Wirklichkeit*), it is the pure literary will of the fragmentary production by which literature emerges as a dialectical absolute. But, it is also possible to understand this fragmentary exigency to indicate the very interruption of the dialectical Subject.

In the written conversation "Noli Me Frangere," Nancy and Lacoue-Labarthe address the possibility that Blanchot's fragmentary exigency is not "Schlegel's fragmentary *will*," that is, "the very will to Work," but an exigency that "exceeds the work, because that exigency exceeds the will."[38] In this understanding, the fragmentary exigency is not the romantic will to system but the indication of the *unthought* of Romanticism, which is the very concern of *The Literary Absolute*. But what is this unthought? In order to understand what this unthought is in *The Literary Absolute*, it is necessary to see how Nancy and Lacoue-Labarthe's analysis relies on Blanchot's essay "The Athenaeum."

In "The Athenaeum," this unthought emerges as what Blanchot calls "the non-romantic essence of romanticism" (*IC*, 357), which he finds is expressed in Novalis's short text, *Monologue* (*Monolog*, 1798).[39] For Blanchot, as we will see, it is the writer who cannot not-write intransitively that constitutes this non-romantic essence of Romanticism. Blanchot cites Novalis's proposition: "I am a writer by vocation, since only a writer is inhabited by language" (*IC*, 357), that is to say, "pressured to speak by speech itself" (*IC*, 357). Novalis indicates that this subject pressured to speak is a subject who must speak: "What would it be like though if I had to speak? [*Wie, wenn ich aber reden müßte?*]"[40] Novalis names this subject who must write the "born writer,"[41] and he understands the language that inhabits the writer to be an *intransitive* language: "One can only marvel at the ridiculous mistake that people make when they think—that they speak for the sake of things. The particular quality of language, the fact that it is concerned only with itself, is known to no one."[42] The subject who is pressured to speak by speech itself is the subject who cannot not-write, and this is the subject who apparently must write intransitively (without concern for things). But the question is how one is to understand intransitivity? What does it mean that language is concerned only with itself? Is this the self-reference of a pure subjectivity or the interruption of the Subject?

In the essay "The Athenaeum," in relation to his own reading of Novalis, Blanchot proposes,

> One can indeed say that in these texts we find expressed the non-romantic essence of romanticism …: that to write is to make (of) speech (a) work [*œuvre*], but that this work is an unworking [*désœuvrement*]; that to speak poetically is to make possible a non-transitive speech [*une parole non transitive*] whose task is not to say things (not to disappear in what it signifies), but to say (itself) in letting (itself) say, yet without taking itself as the new object of this language without object [*ce langage sans objet*]. (*IC*, 357)

Blanchot understands the writer who cannot not-write intransitively as the non-romantic essence of Romanticism. This understanding indicates the ambiguity of intransitivity. From Blanchot's perspective, romantic intransitivity tends to appear as the fragmentary interruption that is solely the reconstitution of the Subject. But, at the same time, the romantic fragment points to an understanding of intransitivity as the interruption of the dialectic, which constitutes the non-romantic essence of Romanticism. Blanchot's writer is a writer who must write but who does not write this or that work but writes intransitively (without object) such that the work unworks itself. For Blanchot, the act of writing does not take itself as a new object but is the pure interruption of *désœuvrement* (worklessness, unworking, inoperativity). In Chapter 5, I will come back to how this subject who cannot not-write intransitively emerges in Blanchot's thought. But, in Blanchot's reading of the *Athenaeum*, it is already visible how the writer who cannot not-write intransitively, the paradigm of writerly necessity, emerges as that which produces unworking.

This paradigm also appears in *The Literary Absolute*, insofar as Nancy and Lacoue-Labarthe propose that we should understand the unthought of

Romanticism as *désœuvrement* (unworking). This happens at the end of the chapter on "The Fragment." Nancy and Lacoue-Labarthe write,

> Within the romantic work, there is interruption and dissemination of the romantic work, and this in fact is not readable in the work itself, even and especially not when the fragment, *Witz*, and chaos are privileged. Rather, according to another term of Blanchot, it is readable in the *unworking* [désœuvrement], never named and still less thought, that insinuates itself throughout the interstices of the romantic work. Unworking is not incompletion, for as we have seen incompletion completes itself and is the fragment as such; unworking is nothing, only the interruption of the fragment. (*LA*, 57/80)

This is a decisive paragraph in *The Literary Absolute*. The romantic thinking of the literary absolute confirms the thinking of the Subject. In the *Athenaeum*, the fragment emerges as the absolute operation. Since *Witz* remains a form of absolute knowing, *Witz* conceals the unthought of the literary absolute. But this unthought of Romanticism is then the interruption of the fragment: unworking. The literary absolute is the absolute thesis, the *Setzung*, the position, but this positing also exposes itself *as* positing.[43] Even if the literary absolute, as it arises out of German Idealism, remains strictly within "the era of the Subject" (*LA*, 16), Nancy and Lacoue-Labarthe nevertheless claim that the unthought of the romantic work interrupts the dialectic. With allusion to Derrida, there is "dissemination," interruption, of the work, the "resistance" or "impossibility of reducing a text as such to its effects of meaning, content, thesis, or theme."[44] Nancy and Lacoue-Labarthe thus conceive the fragment as that which produces the dialectic of the living Subject and at the same time interrupts this dialectical production.

With reference to Blanchot's concept of *désœuvrement*, Nancy and Lacoue-Labarthe understand the unthought of Romanticism as the inoperativity of the work. It is this *unthought that is the horizon* of Nancy and Lacoue-Labarthe's *philosophical* investigation. But, at this point, the paradigm of writerly necessity also emerges as precisely the *unthought horizon* of Nancy and Lacoue-Labarthe's investigation insofar as it is Blanchot's short exposition of unworking that makes possible Nancy and Lacoue-Labarthe's identification of the literary absolute. It is thus the paradigm of writerly necessity, the subject who cannot not-write intransitively, which embodies the unthought non-romantic essence of Romanticism. This subject, which is nothing but an act of writing intransitively, poses the question of literature as the question of how to understand intransitivity: is it the negativity of the Subject or the pure interruption of the Subject? Does intransitivity in fact refer to an act of writing without object, or does it conceal that the act of writing takes itself as the new "object"? This question of intransitivity emerges as the question of literature, which is the concern of the philosophical study of *The Literary Absolute*. But the question remains how we are to approach this unthought non-romantic essence of Romanticism? How does this subject who cannot not-write intransitively emerge? How could we understand the question of literature?

Hölderlin and the Literary Absolute

A significant trace of the disjunction of the (non)-romantic is visible in Blanchot's essay when, in an ambiguous gesture, he deploys Hölderlin as an example of the "excess" (*IC*, 353) of Romanticism only to emphasize, in a note, "But it must immediately be added: Hölderlin does not belong to romanticism; he is not part of any constellation" (*IC*, 461, note 1). This equivocal gesture is moreover addressed by Nancy and Lacoue-Labarthe in a note where they add, "It would be a long and difficult task to specify the place Hölderlin occupied or the role he played in the genesis of romanticism and idealism" (*LA*, 131, note 4). In fact, to return to *The Literary Absolute*, Hölderlin is always in the *margins* of Nancy and Lacoue-Labarthe's investigation into the inauguration of literature as absolute in the *Athenaeum*. On the one hand, Hölderlin arises as the "mute presence" (*LA*, 28) behind the "System-Programme" ("Das älteste Systemprogramm des deutschen Idealismus," 1795/96)[45] found among Hegel's papers (see *LA*, 131, note 4) but supposedly composed by Schelling "under the direct influence of Hölderlin" (*LA*, 27). Nancy and Lacoue-Labarthe address this "System-Programme" since it "introduces, within the philosophical, a distance from the philosophical" (*LA*, 29), and the task of approaching Romanticism can be undertaken "only by means of the 'philosophical path'" (*LA*, 29) insofar as the question of literature exposes a philosophical crisis.[46] On the other hand, even if Hölderlin's poetic gesture, as Heidegger notes (cited by Nancy and Lacoue-Labarthe), "remains completely outside of the metaphysics of German Idealism" (*ST*, 190; see *LA*, 28), and the relation of Hölderlin's theoretical work with the dialectic is at least ambiguous (as we shall see), "Hölderlin did in fact," as Nancy and Lacoue-Labarthe say and which had already been undisputedly confirmed by Dieter Henrich,[47] "participate in the genesis of German idealism (and thereby in a certain genesis of romanticism)" (*LA*, 28). However, when Nancy and Lacoue-Labarthe try to show why exactly the *Athenaeum* embodies the inauguration of literature as *Work in progress*, they do it by opposing the Romantics to Hölderlin. As we have seen, this happens in the first chapter on "The Fragment," which is nevertheless concerned "with the initial proximity of the romantics and Hölderlin" (*LA*, 133, note 1).

According to Nancy and Lacoue-Labarthe, the proximity between the Romantics and Hölderlin consists in their common insistence that purely "theoretical completion is impossible" (*LA*, 48), and that the system can only be attained by unifying philosophy and poetry.[48] Hölderlin does not belong to Romanticism as such, and he is only a figure in the margins of *The Literary Absolute*. But even if, or perhaps because, he does not belong to the Romantic constellation, Hölderlin also functions in *The Literary Absolute* as an exemplary exclusion that is included as that which is unthought in Romanticism. As I will argue, Hölderlin emerges as a name that designates the interruption of the dialectic. In this respect, Heidegger's reading of Hölderlin is significant for Nancy and Lacoue-Labarthe. For Heidegger, Hölderlin emerges as "*the poet's poet* [der Dichter des Dichters]."[49] Hölderlin's poetic work marks the "essence of poetry [*Wesen der Dichtung*]"[50] insofar as this *Dichtung* "anticipates a historical time [*geschichtliche Zeit*]"[51] in which Being becomes transparent to itself. The question for Heidegger is whether Hölderlin embodies the dialectical literary Subject or the very disappearance of the Subject in which the withdrawal of Being manifests itself. In *Identity and Difference*, Heidegger himself contrasts his own thinking with Hegel's thinking of the absolute Concept. Against the movement of *Aufhebung* in which Being emerges as the identity of beings, Heidegger aims to think "Being with respect to its difference from beings. ... For us, formulated in a preliminary fashion, the matter of thinking is the difference *as* difference."[52] Heidegger aims to accomplish a "step back" by which difference *as* difference becomes visible as the manifestation of the withdrawal: "the destiny of the withdrawing concealment of perdurance [*das Geschick der sich entziehenden Verbergung des Austrags*]."[53] This would then be the historical time that could never be reduced to "*one* epoch in the history of the clearing of 'Being.'"[54] The question implicit in the question of literature is precisely whether a "historical time" is possible in which the dialectical metaphysics of philosophy and literature is left behind. For Heidegger, Hölderlin is not suspended in the (romantic) "self-contemplation [*Selbstbespiegelung*]" of form without "worldly content [*Weltfülle*]" but "poetically thinks through to the ground and center of being [*Mitte des Seins*]."[55]

Let me reread the paragraph in which Nancy and Lacoue-Labarthe contrast the Romantics with Hölderlin:

> Yet unlike Hölderlin, and much closer to idealism, the romantics simultaneously postulate the motifs of a present, accomplished [*effectué*] infinite in a work that the logic of the fragment stubbornly summarizes within the contours of its ideal, and as a corollary to this, the potential infinite in itself *as* the actuality of the work. (*LA*, 48)

The romantic fragment arises within the entire problematic of the will to system. The fragmentary "progression" *and* the fragmentary "ideal" constitute the literary absolute as *Work in Progress*. This conceptualization of the literary absolute remains strictly within the metaphysics of the Subject. This is the reason why Nancy and Lacoue-Labarthe can write that the Romantics are closer to Idealism than Hölderlin. As Lacoue-Labarthe thus writes in the essay "The Caesura of the Speculative" ("La Césure du spéculatif," 1978), to which Nancy and Lacoue-Labarthe refer in *The Literary Absolute* (*LA*, 131–2, note 4), Hölderlin's theoretical work "always lacks a principle of [dialectic-speculative] resolution" ("CS," 230).[56] The romantic fragments present the system, the absolute, as the *actual* work-thing, even if this absolute is a *small* work that interrupts itself. The Romantics are thus closer to the speculative truth than Hölderlin whose work interrupts the dialectical Work and therefore cannot be integrated into German Idealism. Such is the logic of this paragraph of *The Literary Absolute*.

But, while we should without a doubt be careful not simply to identify the romantic fragment with Hölderlin's writings, this supposed difference between the Romantics and Hölderlin is at the very least ambiguous since, as we have seen, Nancy and Lacoue-Labarthe have themselves claimed that *unworking* is the true *unthought* of the Romantics. They might thus claim that the thought of the Romantics constitutes a dialectic of the Subject produced absolutely, but the *unthought* of Romanticism must then necessarily consist in the interruption of this dialectic (unworking). This complicates of course the relation between the Romantics and Hölderlin significantly, and it becomes even more equivocal when we read in Lacoue-Labarthe's essay (which is no doubt exact on this point) that the "theory put forward in Hölderlin—and this would apply to more than just those texts which are usually classified as such—is, through and through, speculative. At least ... it can always be interpreted in this way" ("CS," 226). Lacoue-Labarthe thus understands Hölderlin's theoretical texts to *think* a non-dialectical interruption not intentionally but *despite* their dialectical thought. I will call this interruption the *unthought* of Hölderlin:

> For even if Hölderlin, using all the means available to him, and to the point of exhausting his dialectical resources (the text [*Der Grund zum Empedokles*], indeed, loses itself and fails to close with a result of any kind), strives to think the dramatic figure as a means or a mediation for the paradoxically adequate expression of the author or the subject, this dialectical starting device, constantly reengaged, always lacks a principle of resolution. ("CS," 230)

The Romantics think the dialectical Subject absolutely, but the unthought of Romanticism is unworking, the interruption of the dialectic and, in proximity, Hölderlin's thought is dialectical "through and through," but this thought always includes its unthought in which it becomes visible that dialectical resolution is impossible. Following Lacoue-Labarthe's own argument from "The Caesura of the Speculative," the distinction between the *Athenaeum* and Hölderlin is thus not so much between different concepts of the absolute, as Nancy and Lacoue-Labarthe claim in *The Literary*

Absolute; rather, if we are to attend to the event of the emergence of the literary absolute, unworking arises as the unthought of both the *Athenaeum* and Hölderlin, insofar as unworking, without further specifications, is the very interruption of the dialectical Subject. But to this extent Hölderlin's place in the inauguration of the literary absolute remains obscure. However, Nancy and Lacoue-Labarthe's final focus on this "Hölderlin" is not on how up and until the *Athenaeum* he played *some* role but on how he arises in the shadow of Romanticism as *the literary Subject* per se, fragmentation embodied in the "mad" poet:

> And surely nowhere else than in the shadow of romanticism could our modernity have thought of relating to literature even the supposedly most external accidents of its history: beginning, for example, with Novalis's death or Hölderlin's madness. These exemplary fragmentations—now "ontological" and no longer simply "literary"—have established for us (romanticism itself has compelled us to establish) the very character of literature; they have determined the entirety of our "literary criticism." (*LA*, 116)

As exemplary fragmentations, Hölderlin's madness and Novalis's death have received ontological status. They have been established as a part of the being of literature by later critical history (the "us" in the quote), Nancy and Lacoue-Labarthe write, as we were forced to do this by the event, literature *as* absolute, which made this "us" possible. This assessment remains plausible but also incomplete insofar as, as we have seen, a certain writerly subject who cannot not-write is the horizon for Nancy and Lacoue-Labarthe's identification of the literary absolute. Indeed, in order to understand not only how something like "madness" can assume ontological status with respect to literature but also how literature can emerge *as* absolute, it is necessary to explore how the literary absolute emerges for a subject who writes. I therefore turn to Hölderlin's writings, which are a testimony to how the literary absolute produces the necessity to write intransitively.

3

The Born Poet

The Emergence of the Subject
Who Cannot Not-Write

How does the paradigm of writerly necessity emerge? A letter from Hölderlin written on July 10, 1797, addressed to his friend Christian Ludwig Neuffer, bears witness to an event that constitutes a hiatus in Hölderlin's biography: "so you are not reduced to nothing if you are not a poet [*so bist Du nicht vernichtet, wenn Du nicht Dichter bist*]. For me, every other possibility [*alles Mögliche*], anything else I could do, is ruined [*verlaidet*]" (*EL*, 89/6:1, 244). The poet's words contain a triple negation that yields an affirmation: "You are *not* ... *nothing* ... if you are *not* a poet," the poet writes in order to say that "I" (Hölderlin) am nothing if I am not a poet. The subject writes that, in order to be, he cannot not-be a poet since every other possibility is ruined. This testimony to writerly necessity can be dated (July 1797); however, its sense as an event ("1797") transcends its actualization as a discursive occurrence with a prescribed date since the testimony means precisely that Hölderlin is a subject who *always already* must write. In the essay fragment "The Ground for 'Empedocles' " ("Grund zum Empedokles," 1799),[1] Hölderlin writes that Empedocles "seems indeed born to be a poet [*zum Dichter geboren*]" (*ET*, 55/4:1, 156). For Hölderlin, the event of writerly necessity produces himself as a "born poet." The event emerges as a historical (and biographical) a priori, which has always already made the poet's life possible but which appears only a posteriori. His birth as a poet ("1797") is retroactively marked as his birth *tout court* (1770). Before 1797 Hölderlin could thus still write to Friedrich Immanuel Niethammer (February 24, 1796), "Philosophy is once again almost my only occupation" (*EL*, 67). After 1797 he writes a letter to Neuffer (November 12, 1798) in which he assesses "philosophy" to be "a hospital where poets afflicted as I am may find honourable refuge" (*EL*, 109).

It is visible in both the letters and the essay fragments that after "1797" Hölderlin still thinks in philosophical terms; however, as I will show, in these writings philosophy emerges precisely *as* poetology (*Poetologie*), that is, as a concern for (his own) literary production. In fact, as Hölderlin's writings bear out, from "1797" onward the poet will begin to understand his daily life as such from the perspective that he cannot not-write literature. As Hölderlin writes to his mother from Bad Homburg (January 1799), the poet is now convinced that "every art [*Kunst*] requires a man's whole life [*ein ganzes Menschenleben*]" (*EL*, 127/6:1, 311). According to Hölderlin, "Everything an apprentice learns must be learnt in relation to his art if he wants to develop his disposition to it and not end up stifling it" (*EL*, 127). Around a half year later, in a letter (July 1799) to his sister Heinrike Breunlin, Hölderlin describes how he has arranged himself in a "couple of nice [*hübsche*] little rooms" with "books and papers," and "a little table by the window," where he feels most at home, *wo ich eigentlich zu Hauße bin* (*EL*, 157–8/6:1, 352). It is at this table by the window that, he says, *mein Wesen treibe* (*EL*, 157–8/6:1, 352): It is at this table that the poet can write but thus also literally here his being or essence (*Wesen*) "practises itself," moves itself, floats, drifts (*treiben*).

But, as he notes in a letter to his friend Neuffer (December 1799), the problem is that "it is almost impossible to live from writing [*Schriftstellerei*] alone if you don't want to be too much at the service of others and sacrifice your reputation for the sake of your livelihood" (*EL*, 170/6:1, 379). Since the poet feels that his very essence is to be a poet and that he thus must write so as to be, this problem of employment makes the poet unhappy: "It is almost as if no happiness costs more dear than being a writer, especially a poet [*Dichter*]" (*EL*, 170/6:1, 379). For Hölderlin, his studies, the occasional tutoring jobs, and the arrangements of his working space that situates his daily habits are all thought in terms of providing the most beneficial conditions for his practice of writing poetry. The event of writerly necessity produces a gap between 1796 and 1798 in Hölderlin's life, since this event ("1797") reconfigures this very life so as to produce it as a literary life. For the subject who cannot not-write, it is not possible to distinguish between life and literature since the poet's life depends on the very act of writing literature. Furthermore, for later literary history, Hölderlin as the "born poet" is first born after this event ("1797") insofar as this event retroactively transforms Hölderlin's birth into a *poet's* birth ("1770"). The letter of 1797 is a testimony to Hölderlin's birth as a subject who must write literature.

The Subject Who Cannot Not-Write Intransitively

Hölderlin emerges as the subject who cannot not-write literature since it is not possible for Hölderlin to distinguish between life and writing. But why is this necessity to write a necessity to write *intransitively*? In his "Remarks on 'Oedipus' " ("Anmerkungen zum Oedipus," 1803),[2] Hölderlin writes that the problem of poetry is that it lacks "reliability" since it is not given as a sensuous thing but as that which is indeterminate: "Among mankind, one has to make sure with every thing [*jedem Dinge*] that it is Something [*Etwas*], i.e., that it is recognizable [*erkennbar*] in the medium [*moyen*] of its appearance, that the way in which it is delimited [*bedingt*] can be determined and taught" (*ET*, 101/5, 195). Literature is comparable to the absolute monarchy that Hölderlin addresses in a letter to Isak von Sinclair (December 24, 1798): "But then it is a good thing, and even the first condition of all life and of all forms of organisation, that no force is monarchic in heaven and earth. Absolute monarchy will always cancel itself out, because it has no object; in the strict sense it has never existed" (*EL*, 117). The literary absolute "cancels itself out" since it cannot instantiate itself as a given object; rather, this absolute cannot even be said to exist as *something* in time and space given to the pure forms of sensible intuition. Because literature has arisen *as* absolute for Hölderlin, not as a *concept* of the literary absolute, but as his born *essence*, literature determines life. But, since literature is an absolute that interrupts its actuality, the literary work can never appear as a spatiotemporal object. This is the reason why Hölderlin writes in a letter to his stepbrother Karl Gok that we do not live in a poet's climate (early 1798): "Many a man has already perished who was made to be a poet [*der zum Dichter gemacht war*]. We do not live in a climate for poets [*Dichterklima*]" (*EL*, 98/6:1, 264; translation modified). As the qualification "who was made to be a poet" indicates, this remark only becomes intelligible within the horizon of writerly necessity as a subject position in which the literary absolute subsists. The literary absolute is a paradigm that produces a life in which this very life is at stake in writing. For Hölderlin, the literary absolute has become the essence of his very being as a subject produced by writerly necessity. Hölderlin has emerged as a subject who *cannot* write a work precisely because he *cannot not-write* the pure intransitive absence of work.

It is this paradigm that informs that which Hölderlin calls the lack of the work in a letter to Neuffer (November 12, 1798): "I cry like a child when I everywhere feel how my work [*Darstellungen*] is lacking [*fehlt*] in this or that respect and yet I cannot extricate myself from the poetic labyrinth [*poëtischen Irren*] I'm wandering about in" (*EL*, 108/6:1, 289). Hölderlin indicates the reason for this work's lack: "I shun the common and ordinary aspects of real life too much" (*EL*, 109). Life is the poet's concern: "Life in poetry [*Das Lebendige in der Poësie*] is what now occupies my thoughts and senses more than anything else" (*EL*, 108/6:1, 289). For Hölderlin, in terms of the work to be written, this concern for life in poetry implies the question of how to present the pure in the impure:

Purity [*Das Reine*] can only be presented [*darstellen*] in impurity [*Unreinen*] and if you try to render fineness [*das Edle*] without coarseness [*Gemeines*] it will appear entirely unnatural [*Allerunnatürlichste*] and incongruous, and this for the good reason that fineness itself, when it occurs [*zur Äußerung kommt*], bears the colour of the fate in which it arose [*die Farbe des Schiksaals trägt, unter dem es entstand*]; and beauty, when it appears in reality, necessarily assumes a form from the circumstances in which it emerges which is not natural to it and which only becomes its natural form when it is taken together with the very conditions which of necessity gave it the form it has. (*EL*, 109–10/6:1, 290; translation modified)

In this letter, Hölderlin postulates the possibility that pure "beauty" can assume its "natural form" as impure insofar as it is "taken together" with the necessary conditions that gave rise to the pure *as* impure. Before attending to Hölderlin's solution to how the pure absolute can be presented in the impure actuality, we should understand the condition of the problem itself. It is precisely because the pure absolute is *not* given as impure actuality from the outset for Hölderlin that the problem of *Darstellung* can arise as a problem at all. In opposition to Hegel's speculative idealism but in proximity to the *Athenaeum*, Hölderlin experiences that the absolute is without actuality. Since literature is absolute for Hölderlin, writing must be a pure writing, but insofar as the pure absolute is not actuality from the outset, literature can only be absolutely. Like the romantic fragment, Hölderlin's work must *be* in its *not being there*. If the work is to appear, then it must be the absence of work.

The Problem of Pure Writing in Hölderlin's Theoretical Texts

The problem of how to think a pure writing occupies Hölderlin in the essay fragment "On the Operations of the Poetic Spirit" ("Über die Verfahrungsweise des poëtischen Geistes," 1800).[3] In this text, the "significance [*Bedeutung*]" that lends poetry its "truth [*Wahrheit*]" lies between "the expression (the presentation [*der Darstellung*]) and the free idealistic treatment" (*ET*, 66/4:1, 245). In synonymic terms, the expression and the ideal is the relation between the *impure* "sensuous subject matter, that which is actually pronounced in the poem [*sinnlichen Stoffe, dem eigentlich ausgesprochenen im Gedichte*]" (*ET*, 65/4:1, 244) and the *pure* "spirit, the idealistic treatment [*dem Geiste, der idealischen Behandlung*]" (*ET*, 65/4:1, 244). My intention here is not to analyze this essay so as to attend to Hölderlin's enigmatic solution; rather, my aim is to draw out the problem *as* a problem and to examine in what way, for Hölderlin, there emerges a truth of literature that is different than the speculative truth.[4]

In order to examine this truth of literature, I will go back to Lacoue-Labarthe's "The Caesura of the Speculative" in which he attends to the motif of the (non)-dialectical interruption: "For Hölderlin," Lacoue-Labarthe writes, "rather, all things considered, art was a means of gaining access to truth—provided, obviously, that we not understand truth here in the speculative sense (if this is possible)" ("CS," 223).[5] In Hölderlin's theoretical writings, the dialectical production never resolves itself; rather, Lacoue-Labarthe writes, the truth of this production is always its suspension:

The act of suspension [*La mise en suspens*] is this: quite simply, the incessant repetition of the engaging of the dialectical process in the— never changing—form of *the closer it is, the more distant it is; the more dissimilar it is, the more adequate it is; the more interior it is, the more exterior it is*. In short, the maximum of appropriation (for the perpetual comparison here originates in a movement of passing to the limit, and proceeds necessarily from a logic of excess—of the superlative) is the maximum of disappropriation, and conversely. ("CS," 230/63)

For Lacoue-Labarthe, the act of suspension produces a "truth" that is nonspeculative. In "On the Operations of the Poetic Spirit," this act manifests itself in the "significance" that makes up (*gibt*) the truth of literature. This significance thus consists in its being suspended between that which separates and that which unifies. Hölderlin writes,

It [the significance of the poem] is the spiritual-sensuous, the formal-material of the poem; and if the idealistic treatment is more unifying in its metaphor, its transition [and] its episodes, whereas its expression, the presentation in its characters, their passions, their individualities, are more separating, then the significance rests between the two; it is characterised by being everywhere opposed to itself. (*ET*, 66)

Hölderlin construes this significance as produced by an operation in which there is a forward–backward moving suspension between a pure spirit (the absolute) and a detected sign, which is also understood as "the organ by which the spirit is comprised" (*ET*, 69). Hölderlin writes, "The operation [of the poetic spirit] which gives the poem its significance, is merely the transition from the pure [*Reinen*] to what is to be detected [*Aufzufindenden*] as well as backward from the latter to the pure" (*ET*, 68/4:1, 248). This is how the animation of life takes place: "The pure, conflicting as such with the organ, is present to itself in this very organ and only thus becomes a living one" (*ET*, 69). It is visible in these theoretical writings how Hölderlin aims to solve the problem of presenting the pure in the impure. But my concern here is not this theoretical solution to a problem but the paradigm that turns this question of the relation between the pure and the impure into a problem in the first place. Since the paradigm of writerly necessity emerges as Hölderlin's very essence, the literary absolute is for him not simply a concept of literature but also the experience that one must write in order to live because Being is at stake in writing. But how is Being then at stake in literary writing? This is the question.

"The Question of Literature"

The concern of Nancy and Lacoue-Labarthe's philosophical study of Romanticism is the "question of literature." But what is signified by this question? They write in *The Literary Absolute*, "What then is in question? Quite simply the question itself: what is literature?" (*LA*, 83). It is the question itself—the question *what is literature?*—that is in question. In "Literature and the Right to Death," Blanchot writes, "Let us suppose that literature begins at the moment when literature becomes a question" (*WF*, 300). He adds, "It has been noted with amazement that the question 'What is literature?' ['*Qu'est-ce que la littérature?*'] has received only meaningless answers [*réponses insignifiantes*]. But what is even stranger is that something about the very form of such a question takes away all its seriousness" (*WF*, 302/294). Literature is a question, but the question of literature is apparently not the question *what is literature?* since this question has only produced meaningless answers.[6] We should indeed be "amazed" by this issue insofar as this question of *whatness* is the fundamental form of metaphysical questioning. As Heidegger says in *The Essence of Human Freedom* (*Vom Wesen der menschlichen Freiheit*, 1982), first delivered as a lecture course at the University of Freiburg in 1930, the question *what are beings?* is the "traditional leading question of philosophy."[7] For Blanchot, the question of *ti estin*, the question of *what* literature *is*, of *whatness*, is meaningless with respect to literature. But what is even more "strange" apparently is the issue that "the very form of such a question takes away all seriousness." Why?

If literature cannot be determined by its *whatness*, it is not possible to define the being-literature of literature, its essence, which is also its being *present*.[8] Heidegger thus identifies the meaning of Beingness in Aristotle as *ousia*, essence, "the sense of constant presence."[9] The essence is *to ti esti*, literally "the what it is." As a translation of the Greek *ousia*, the Latin *substance* then has the character of a "constant presence."[10] Within the paradigm of writerly necessity in which literature emerges as absolute, literature thus becomes the question of (its own) Being. Literature arises as the withdrawal of presence. Derrida paradigmatically proposes,[11] "Before having a philosophical content, before being or bearing such and such a 'thesis,' literary experience, writing or reading, is a 'philosophical' experience which is neutralized or neutralizing insofar as it allows one to think the thesis; it is a nonthetic experience of the thesis."[12] The proposition that literary experience suspends the *thesis* (from Greek via Latin), the placing, the positing, the proposition, the *Setzung*—this proposition here constitutes the truth of literature. Literature emerges as the question of Being, which means that it is not certain that something like literature exists.[13] But what is such a proposition supposed to signify? The question is what the philosophic-historical conditions are that make it possible to think *literature* as the interruption of thetic Being. In the first instance, insofar as the literary absolute emerges in the *Athenaeum* and in Hölderlin's thought, this is a question of how the understanding of the Being of literature relates to Kant's thought and Hegel's thought of Being.

In the first *Critique*, Kant understands "*Being* [Sein]" as "merely the positing of a thing [*bloß die Position eines Dinges*]" (*CR*, A598/B626).[14] Being is "merely" positing; it is the pure existence of a *thing*, which is not expressed in predicates, since such predicates presuppose the copula "is" as that which "posits the predicate *in relation* to the subject" (*CR*, A598–9/B626–7). In its logical sense, Being is the mere positing of the subject–predicate relation, which means that Being can never be stated in a proposition, since every proposition presupposes Being (the logical copula). In his essay "Kant's Thesis about Being" ("Kants These über das Sein," 1962), Heidegger shows how Being as positing also has the sense of the pure synthesis of the Subject by which it relates to objects.[15] Being is not simply the copula presupposed in the subject–predicate relation but Kant's self-identical transcendental unity of apperception. Being is the pure synthesis of the Kantian Subject, which makes experience of objects possible.

Hegel transposes this understanding of Being as *thesis* into the dialectical system of the self-relating negativity. This negativity is the "perfectly transparent"[16] self-movement, which completes itself as the absolute Concept or *Idea* that "alone is *being* [Sein], imperishable *life*, *self-knowing truth*, and is *all truth*."[17] Hegel's speculative Concept produces "an absolute *liberation* [Befreiung] for which there is no longer any immediate determination that is not equally *posited* [gesetzt] and itself Concept [*Begriff*]."[18] This speculative positing must always already posit itself in order to have been posited and always already have posited itself insofar as it *is* posited actuality. The absolute is an unconditioned positing, which by definition is without presupposition; however, the speculative absolute must thus presuppose itself, its own mediation, in its positing. The self-relating negativity must always already have begun.[19]

From the perspective of speculative dialectic, the literary absolute is precisely the concept of an absolute that has not always already begun but interrupts its own coming into being. The literary absolute does not posit itself as the speculative absolute; rather, it interrupts its own unconditioned positing. The literary absolute cannot posit itself, and it can therefore not be defined in the form of a proposition (*S is P*) since literature is not a subject relating to predicates. For Blanchot, as we have seen, the very form of the question *what is literature?* is meaningless since literature is the interruption of every positing.[20]

The unthought of Romanticism thus indicates literature as the suspension of thetic Being, literature as the appearance of the disappearance of everything, since it is merely the manifestation of the withdrawal of Being. Nancy and Lacoue-Labarthe's study concerns the unthought of the *Athenaeum* in which the spiraling dialectic of the literary Subject also conceals the unthought of Romanticism as the very interruption of the dialectical Subject. Derrida says, "It is this experience of nothing-ing of nothing that interests our desire under the name of literature. Experience of Being, nothing less, nothing more, on the edge of metaphysics, literature perhaps stands on the edge of everything, almost beyond everything, including itself."[21] For such thinkers as Blanchot, Derrida, Nancy, and Lacoue-Labarthe, literature presents the possibility of a non-dialectical experience, the possibility of a writing that points beyond not only philosophy but also literature itself.[22] But the question is then whether literary intransitivity is this interruption of thetic Being or simply the self-reference of thetic Being suspended in its abstract dialectic. Literature is the question of literature; however, this thought is precisely what we are questioning—not so as to argue against it but to understand how literature became its own question. Today, in the year 2020, this understanding of literature appears almost as a truism. However, my question is: How is it possible to understand literature as the question of literature?

I have argued that it is possible because the literary absolute emerges as a paradigm of writerly necessity. It is thus within the horizon of an act of pure intransitive writing that literature arises as the question of whether intransitivity is the self-reference of thetic Being or that which interrupts thetic Being. Let me retrace my investigation in order to show how the paradigm of writerly necessity emerges as the subject position that makes it possible to pose this question of literature. Within the Kantian "moment," literature emerges as the name for a form of writing a priori. This form of writing is supposed to take place prior to any actual written objects since it would constitute an act of intransitive writing: a pure act of writing that is not simply given as an object in time and space insofar as it would first make any actual space-time possible. The question of literature is the following: How is writing a priori possible? From the perspective of Hegel's speculative system, this is the question of how to produce that which Heidegger shows to be an understanding of Being as *thetic* Being: An absolute positing that as dialectical knowing is not relative to any particular knowledge but is absolute knowing presenting itself *as* actuality. But within the horizon of Blanchot's thought of *désœuvrement*, this question of literature is read as the question of the interruption of thetic Being. In his essay on the *Athenaeum*, Blanchot thus appropriates Novalis's subject who cannot not-write literature. The truth of literature depends on the answer to this question: Does *intransitivity* indicate the Subject's self-reference or the interruption of the Subject?

For Novalis, language is a self-referential form that is concerned only with itself. For Blanchot, language indicates not the Subject's self-reference but the very interruption of any thinking of the Subject. It is this Blanchotian interpretation of the romantic writer that governs Nancy and Lacoue-Labarthe's investigation of the concept of the literary absolute. They identify the question of literature as the unthought horizon of Romanticism. This question of literature is the question of how to understand *intransitive writing*: whether literature, as writing a priori, is the pure Subject or the withdrawal of the Subject. But that which is then unthought in this question is the act of writing itself: The "born poet" who writes cannot be separated from this pure act of writing, but this act then also shows itself to be produced by a necessity to write. Hölderlin emerges in the position of this act of writing intransitively in which the writer's life is at stake. In order to occupy the position of this act of writing, the writer must be a subject who cannot not-write literature. We are yet to examine the enunciative positions of the act of intransitive writing. But in my analysis of Hölderlin, I hope to have shown that the literary absolute emerges as the condition of the subject who cannot not-write intransitively. This subject, who is nothing but an act of writing, constitutes the paradigm of writerly necessity. To pose the question of literature is thus possible because the literary absolute emerges as a paradigm of writerly necessity. It is within the horizon of a pure act of intransitive writing that literature can arise as that which interrupts thetic Being. And this act of writing is linked to the "born" poet's necessity to write. The subject who writes intransitively is the subject who cannot not-write literature.

Hölderlin and the Romantics

It should now be visible how literature is absolute and how the paradigm of writerly necessity emerges as a subject who cannot not-write intransitively. The unthought of the *Athenaeum* is unworking in which thetic Being is in question. However, in his later writings, Nancy tends to forget this *unthought* of romantic fragmentation that is addressed in *The Literary Absolute*:[23] Whereas the *Athenaeum* presents a spiraling or "mirroring" dialectic that only radicalizes the metaphysical thinking of the Subject (see *LA*, 121), Hölderlin apparently presents an alternating poetic suspension of the dialectical Subject. But such a proposition neglects that this very ambiguity between the dialectical Subject and the interruption of this Subject is *inherent* to the literary absolute, which is also to say that it concerns both

Hölderlin and the *Athenaeum* insofar as they are involved in the emergence of the question of literature.

In terms of the romantic *thought*, the literary absolute is nothing but the Subject, but it is so in the ambiguous sense of the system *absolutely*. From a Hegelian perspective, this means that the literary absolute is "abstract" since it lacks actuality. For Hegel, the romantic Subject is an artist "to whom no content of consciousness appears as absolute" (*A*, 65). This is the reason for Hegel's critique of romantic irony, which he understands as the transposition into art of Fichte's absolute I (*Ich*) in which "every content is negated" (*A*, 64). It is striking how Hegel's allocation of Novalis in the subject position of the romantic Subject echoes Hölderlin's position when Hölderlin attempts to deal with the problem of the finite pollution of the infinite. According to Hegel, Novalis's romantic longing means that he entered "a spiritual decline. This is a longing which will not let itself go in actual action and production, because it is frightened of being polluted by contact with finitude, although all the same it has a sense of the deficiency of this abstraction" (*A*, 160). It is precisely such an anxiety of pollution, of the "impure," which Hölderlin identifies as his main poetic fault. But, as we have seen, it is also this "fault" that makes it possible for Lacoue-Labarthe to demarcate a "truth" within Hölderlin's theoretical texts that differs from the dialectic of speculative thought. The lack of (speculative) resolution produces a literary truth of unworking. In terms of the *unthought* of the Romantics, the literary absolute is thus the interruption of the dialectic.

The question is how we are to understand the thought of intransitivity: Is literary intransitivity the self-reference of an abstract Subjectivity that never coincides with its content? Or is intransitivity the very interruption of the dialectical Subject that affirms the absence of work without negation? The interruption of the literary absolute points in both directions: toward an infinitization of the metaphysics of the Subject and toward the unthought literary truth of unworking by which the disappearance of the dialectical Subject appears. From this perspective, Hegel's *dialectic* indicates that the interruption of literature is an abstraction and Hölderlin's concept of the *caesura* indicates the possibility of nonspeculative truth. The answer to this question of literature is suspended in the ambiguity of how one should understand intransitivity.

Threshold

I have argued that the literary absolute emerges as the paradigm of writerly necessity: the subject who cannot not-write intransitively. I claim that there is an irreducible link between the essence of the writer (the necessity to write) and unworking (the act of writing intransitively). Since intransitivity as the interruption of the Subject is always already linked to the "essence" of the Subject, it is never possible to confirm the truth of literature as unworking. Thus, even if intransitivity for Blanchot indicates the unworking of the Subject, this interruption is intrinsically linked to the subject who cannot not-write literature. The question of literature therefore emerges as the suspension of any answer to the following question: Is intransitivity the self-reference of the Subject or the interruption of the Subject?

In the first part, I have aimed to show this link between the necessity to write and the act of writing intransitively. Insofar as the paradigm of writerly necessity has never been transparent, the "essence" of the subject who cannot not-write intransitively has never been visible. Therefore, I will argue, the *historicity* of literature has been concealed, that is, the historical conditions of the possibility of posing the question of literature. I will now retrace the emergence of the paradigm of writerly necessity, which we have seen arising out of the problem of philosophical presentation.

1. *Literature emerges as a priori writing.* We see the modern concept of literature arises out of the Kantian problematic of how to present philosophy. The Kantian Subject cannot present itself to itself. Moreover, from a Kantian perspective, the thought of an absolute (intransitive) writing remains a fiction insofar as the absolute can never become an object of knowledge. The object is only given for the transcendental Subject who makes possible objectivity by holding before itself a spatiotemporal horizon. The finite transcendental Subject can never present its own unconditional condition of possibility. Literature will thus be the name for the fiction of a pure a priori writing that could make philosophy into a pure science.

2. *Literature emerges as absolute.* For the Romantics, literature is the solution to the problem of presenting the absolute Subject. Literature is the operation by which the absolute presents itself. But the literary absolute is not the speculative absolute in which the absolute is the self-presentation of actuality; rather, the literary absolute interrupts its own presentation. From the perspective of Hegelian dialectic, this means that the (romantic) literary absolute is an abstract Subject, which lacks any positive content. It is the fiction of a pure absolute, but this absolute is without actuality. But, from the perspective of Blanchot's conceptualization of unworking, this interruption of the literary absolute is also the possibility of a non-dialectical truth.

3. *Literature emerges as the question of literature.* The question of literature is not the question *what is literature?* but a question that puts this form of questioning in question. Literature is the question of (its own) Being. For Kant, Being is *thetic* Being. Insofar as literature emerges as absolute, literature does not exist as a

spatiotemporal object for a subject but puts into question this very subject–object relation. For Blanchot, literature is the suspension of thetic Being. In literature, it is thus the very "is" that is in question. For Blanchot, this is the "truth" of literature. Literary theory can therefore proclaim that the question *what is literature?* is without sense, since it is the very *whatness*, the essence of Being, which is in question. There is no answer to the question *what is literature?* because literature is not a positive entity. Literature does not subsist as *something* but emerges as the very (im)possibility of any subject–object relation. The question of literature can thus initially be formulated as the following question: Does something like literature exist? Is it possible to write literature a priori? Is a pure writing possible? Is it possible to write intransitively? But insofar as literature emerges as intransitivity, the question of literature is the following: Does intransitivity indicate the self-reference of the Subject or the interruption of the Subject? Literature does not provide an answer to this question; rather, from this perspective, literature is the suspension of an answer to the question of intransitivity.

4. *Since literature is absolute, there is a necessity to write intransitively.* For the subject who cannot not-write ("Hölderlin"), literature is absolute. When literature is absolute for a subject, literature is the unconditioned that conditions the possibilities and limitations of life. In order to live, the subject produced by writerly necessity must write literature. But what is literature? Literature is the fiction of a pure intransitive writing. Since the literary absolute interrupts actuality, there is thus no positive work to write but only the absence of work. Writerly necessity produces a subject who cannot not-write the pure intransitive absence of work.

5. *Life and writing coincide for the subject who cannot not-write.* Since the subject who cannot not-write literature must write intransitively, this writer occupies a position of suspension between a necessity and an impossibility. This subject cannot not-write, but this does not mean that the subject can write; rather, this subject cannot write a work. For the subject who cannot not-write, it is not simply the work that depends on his operation; on the contrary, his very being also depends on the operativity of the work. In the paradigm of writerly necessity, it is not possible to distinguish between operativity and operation, between Being and action, between Being and having-to-be, between life and writing, between writer and work.

The following question remains: What place is left vacant by the *death* (interruption) of the Subject? Is this death always the self-relating negativity of the speculative Concept, or is there a non-dialectical experience of literature? This is the question of how writerly necessity produces the Subject as the question of its own intransitive interruption. The literary absolute constitutes the return of the Subject. The Subject will not disappear before literature has disappeared (as absolute), and this disappearance must be different than the "disappearance" that only constitutes the most essential manifestation of literature: disappearance as the very (re)appearance of literature. We must thus interrogate the space of inoperativity. But first we must understand the ambiguity of the literary absolute, which consists in the issue that it is the very essence of the Subject (the necessity to write) that produces its own disappearance (the absence of Subject-Work) insofar as the literary subject must write intransitively. In Blanchot's formula, "'Where is literature going?' … literature is going toward itself, toward its essence, which is disappearance."[24] Within the paradigm of writerly necessity, this disappearance only signifies the *return* of the abyss of the Subject (the essence of writerly necessity) since the mode of appearance of the literary act of writing is precisely disappearance (intransitivity). But how does this literary act of writing function?

PART TWO

The Paradigm of Writerly Necessity

4

Between the Subject and Language

Hölderlin in Foucault's Early Thought

My concern in the second part of this archaeology is the question of how writerly necessity produces the literary Subject. What is indicated by the intransitive interruption of the Subject insofar as this interruption is itself the production of the (disappearing) Subject? What are the positions of enunciation that are possible within the paradigm of writerly necessity? The paradigm of writerly necessity emerges between the subject who writes and the intransitive work to be written. In the 1960s, Foucault locates "literature" in this position between the Subject and intransitive language, and I therefore turn to Foucault's early works in order to make an initial delimitation of the paradigm of writerly necessity.

For Foucault, the investigation of the emergence of literature is linked to such writers as Hölderlin, Antonin Artaud, Stéphane Mallarmé, Marquis de Sade, and to his own archaeology of madness that appeared in the first French edition in 1961 as *Folie et déraison. Histoire de la folie à l'âge classique* (*Madness and Unreason: History of Madness in the Classical Age*). Ian Hacking has noted that the subtitle has become the main title in the second edition: *Histoire de la folie à l'âge classique* (1972).[1] In the 1961 version, in distinguishing *déraison* from *folie*, Foucault retained the possibility to think madness in its purity, which he nevertheless from the very beginning in 1961 excludes as an actual possibility: "a madness whose wild state can never be reconstituted; but in the absence of that inaccessible primitive purity, the structural study must go back to that decision that both bound and separated reason and madness."[2] In the 1961 preface, Foucault thus introduced pure madness only to deem such purity inaccessible, but in the second edition of 1972 this first preface has been replaced by a new preface, which does not address the question of madness in its "wild state."[3] Foucault has abandoned the thought of an inaccessible purity, but the *History of Madness* still concerns an experience of "unreason," which relates to that "decision" that binds and separates reason and madness.

In the *History of Madness*, Foucault locates Hölderlin in "the moment of unreason" that can never be understood "from a positivist conception of madness."[4] A year later, in "The Father's 'No' " ("Le 'Non' du père," 1962), a review published in *Critique* of Jean Laplanche's *Hölderlin and the Question of the Father* (*Hölderlin et la question du père*, 1961), Foucault allocates "a unique and exemplary position [*une place unique et exemplaire*]" (*AM*, 19/231) to Hölderlin, with reference to the emergence of literature and madness as the limit-manifestations of that which he understands as the modern epistemic configuration:[5] "He [Hölderlin] forged and manifested the link between a work and the absence of a work, between the flight of the gods and the perdition of language" (*AM*, 19). For Foucault, Hölderlin manifests not only the link between the work and the absence of work, and between literature and madness, but also the link between the finitude of man and the intransitivity of language.[6]

As I hope to have shown in the previous part, Hölderlin occupies the paradigmatic position of the subject who cannot not-write literature. In this chapter my questions are the following: What is the relation between man (the Subject) and language (intransitivity)? What place does literature occupy in Foucault's thought? What is the relation between literature and madness?

Literature: The Subject and Language

In 1966, Foucault publishes *The Order of Things* (*Les Mots et les choses*) in which he undertakes an archaeological description of the so-called "*episteme* of Western culture" (*OT*, xxiv). Foucault understands the episteme as an epistemological field that functions as the condition of possibility of knowledge (*connaissance*) in a historical epoch (see *OT*, xxiii–xxiv). But in "The Subject and Power," originally published in English as an appendix to Hubert Dreyfus and Paul Rabinow's *Michel Foucault: Beyond Structuralism and Hermeneutics* (1982), Foucault retrospectively readjusted the main focus of this earlier work when he said, "The goal of my work during the last twenty years … has been to create a history of the different modes by which, in our culture, human beings are made subjects."[7] From this later perspective, the focus in *The Order of Things* is on how a historical a priori produces modes of subjectivity. The question is how discursive positions produce certain possibilities and limitations for the living beings that occupy such positions. Even if this retrospective focus is only implicit in the earlier works, it is indeed visible in *The Order of Things* when Foucault conceives the "modern" mode of Being as a hiatus between "man" and "the being of language," between the Subject and intransitivity.

Foucault claims that the subject position in which we exist and talk is situated at the point at which "man" and "language" exclude each other: "The right to conceive both of the being of language and of the being of man may be forever excluded; there may be, as it were, an inerasable hiatus at that point (precisely that hiatus in which we exist and talk)" (*OT*, 369). This "hiatus" is our mode of Being since man and language cannot coexist; however, according to Foucault, it is also this incompatibility that produces the position in which we live as speaking beings. Even if these two functions are thus mutually exclusive, they are also irreducibly linked: "He [man] was constituted only when language, having been situated within representation and, as it were, dissolved in it, freed itself from that situation at the cost of its own fragmentation" (*OT*, 421).

For Foucault, the figure of "man" emerged only at the point when language appeared not as representation but as the interruption of the Subject. Foucault traces this co-emergence of man and language to the beginning of the nineteenth century (see *OT*, xxiv). For Foucault, this is the beginning of the "modern age" that replaces the historical a priori of the "Classical age" that itself emerges "roughly half-way through the seventeenth century" (OT, xxiv) when the a priori of the "Renaissance" disappears. According to Foucault, the twofold happening of the disappearance of man and the appearance of language indicates the possibility of an event that would reconfigure our Modernity:

> If this same language is now emerging with greater and greater insistence in a unity that we ought to think but cannot as yet do so, is this not the sign that the whole of this configuration is now about to topple, and that man is in the process of perishing as the being of language continues to shine ever brighter upon our horizon? (*OT*, 421)

The concern for such an event is not arbitrary; rather, the possibility of an event that would reconfigure the contemporary "historical *a priori*" (*OT*, xxiii) so as to make possible new modes of knowing is the ultimate perspective of Foucault's archaeological investigation. Foucault's concern is thus that the discourse that governs history has itself emerged *in* this history, which means that this discourse could also disappear. For Foucault, the task of archaeology is to show not only how "the modern *episteme*" (*OT*, 419) arises but also to display its possible dispersion. This entails that the historian must be concerned with a historical "discontinuity," which Foucault presents as a thought of "the outside":

> Generally speaking, what does it mean, no longer being able to think a certain thought? Or to introduce a new thought? Discontinuity—the fact

> that within the space of a few years a culture sometimes ceases to think as it had been thinking up till then and begins to think other things in a new way—probably begins with an erosion from outside, from that space which is, for thought, on the other side, but in which it has never ceased to think from the very beginning. (*OT*, 56)

Discontinuity is here understood as the gap between two modes of thought. It signifies a change of the historical conditions of the possibilities of thought. These conditions are that which give rise to a given spatiotemporal horizon, which determines what it is possible to think and what it is not possible to think in a given culture. Foucault proposes that this discontinuity, the transformation of the conditions of thought, emerges from the "outside." This outside is comprehended as the other of thought that thinking has nevertheless never ceased to think. It is the unthought of thought.

Literature: The Thought of Contingency

But what is the "outside" as the unthought of thought? The answer to this question will manifest what place literature occupies in Foucault's thought.[8] Discontinuity emerges from the "outside." In *The Archaeology of Knowledge* (*L'Archéologie du savoir*, 1969), Foucault writes that the aim of archaeology is to analyze the discontinuity of history:

> My aim was to analyse this history [i.e. our own history of thought], in the discontinuity that no teleology would reduce in advance; to map it in a dispersion that no pre-established horizon would embrace; to allow it to be deployed in an anonymity on which no transcendental constitution would impose the form of the subject; to open it up to a temporality that would not promise the return of any dawn.[9]

The horizon of archaeology is thus a temporality in which the teleological necessity of the (Hegelian) absolute Subject is replaced by the contingency of the emergence and dispersion of any forms of Subjectivity. For Foucault, "Continuous history is the indispensable correlative of the founding function of the subject: ... In this system, time is conceived in terms of totalization and revolutions are never more than moments of consciousness."[10] The absolute Subject is the consciousness in which contingency can never be thought as such. For Foucault, the concern of archaeology is to think the unthought of thought, the "outside," which delimits any thought of the Subject. But this "outside" is thus nothing but contingency itself.

Archaeology is a thinking of the "outside" as the thought that things could be otherwise than they are: a thinking of the contingency of a given historical a priori. It is from this perspective that we should understand

Foucault's statement from *The Order of Things* that "literature is appearing more and more as that which must be thought" (*OT*, 49). Like archaeology, literature for Foucault is a discourse that manifests the contingency of the a priori. In an essay on Blanchot's thought entitled "The Thought of the Outside" ("La Pensée du dehors"), published in *Critique* in 1966, Foucault thus conceives literature as a thought of the "outside":[11]

> It is a widely held belief that modern literature is characterized by a doubling-back that enables it to designate itself; this self-reference supposedly allows it both to interiorize to the extreme (to state nothing but itself) and to manifest itself in the shimmering sign of its distant existence. In fact, the event that gave rise to what we call "literature" in the strict sense is only superficially an interiorization [*intériorisation*]; it is far more a question of a passage to the "outside" ["*dehors*"] [...]. The "subject" of literature (what speaks in it and what it speaks about) is less language in its positivity than the void that language takes as its space when it articulates itself in the nakedness of "I speak." (*AM*, 148–9/548)

Foucault's distinction here between literature as a question of interiorization and exteriorization concerns the "truth" of literature, which we have seen emerge in the paradigm of writerly necessity: whether literature is the self-referential reflecting back of the (romantic) Subject or the very interruption of the dialectical Subject. In both cases, literature appears as an intransitive language. But, on the one hand, literature embodies the (abstract) form without content in which linguistic self-reference never actualizes itself in a positive content but takes itself as an object. On the other hand, literature is the very disappearance of the form–content relation, insofar as intransitive language is the locus of the contingency of the Subject. For Foucault, the truth of literature is its interruption of the dialectical Subject, and this interruption is the thought of the "outside."[12] Similar to the thought of archaeology, this literary thought of the outside manifests the dispersion of the Subject (see *AM*, 150). There is thus a fundamental link for Foucault between archaeology and literature: This link is the possibility of contingency as the suspension of thetic Being.[13]

Literature as Counter-Discourse: Between the Subject and Language

In "The Thought of the Outside," Foucault presents literature as a discourse on contingency, which is situated at the limit of the modern historical a priori. Literature manifests the possibility of an event in which the Subject disperses and in which such an interruption of the self-conscious ego entails the reconfiguration of history. Foucault is concerned with how we can "gain access" (*AM*, 149) to such an event in the modern period: "We are standing on the edge of an abyss that had long been invisible: the being of language only appears for itself with the disappearance of the subject" (*AM*, 149). Foucault thus construes the subject position between the unity of man (the Subject) and the intransitivity of language as an abyss.

Since to think this abyss is the very task of archaeology, and literature is the manifestation of this abyss, literature is for Foucault nothing but a "counter-discourse" (*OT*, 48).[14] This counter-discourse is a discourse that discloses the possible disappearance of the modern episteme. But, at the same time, Foucault will maintain that literature has itself arisen *in* this episteme (cf. *OT*, 418). The conceptualization of literature as a counter-discourse will therefore never mean that literature is outside the contemporary historical a priori; rather, for Foucault, literature has arisen in the modern epistemic configuration as a function of this configuration, a function, which nevertheless displays the contingency of this episteme.

Foucault construes the emergence of literature in the modern age as something alike the appearance of a remnant from the historical a priori of the Renaissance in which "the signification of signs did not exist" (*OT*, 48). Foucault writes, "'Literature', as it was constituted and so designed on the threshold of the modern age, manifests, at a time when it was least expected, the reappearance, of the living being of language" (*OT*, 48). Literature is "this language that says nothing, [but] is never silent" (*OT*, 333). It is "fragmented" language that "speaks truly" (*OT*, 333) because it is concerned less with its signification than with the withdrawal of representation. According to Foucault, the being of language appears in literature in a similar way to how language appeared in the Renaissance as "fragmented nature" (*OT*, 39) in which language was a part of the "world-wide dissemination of similitudes and signatures" (*OT*, 39). But literature is a modern phenomenon since, contrary to the Renaissance, there is no longer "that primary, that absolutely initial, word upon which the infinite movement of discourse was founded and by which it was limited; henceforth, language was to grow with no point of departure, no end, and no promise" (*OT*, 49). In the modern age, there is no God that every signature reveals, no Absolute, which secures a historical teleology. Rather, literature as the language that "speaks truly" indicates the contingency of history. In the modern age, language manifests its own fragmentation: Literature appears as the questioning of Modernity insofar as the modern age is the age of the Subject. But, for Foucault, language is nevertheless intrinsically related to the Subject. In a posthumously published notebook from the 1880s, Friedrich Nietzsche poses the question of "who speaks?" now that "belief in God has vanished."[15] With reference to a "distance"[16] between Nietzsche's question *who speaks?* and Mallarmé's reply that it is language itself that speaks, Foucault comments,

What relation is there between language [*langage*] and being [*l'être*], and is it really to being that language is always addressed—at least, language that speaks truly [*parle vraiment*]? What, then, is this language that says nothing, is never silent, and is called "literature"?)—it is quite possible that all these questions are presented today in the distance that was never crossed between Nietzsche's question and Mallarmé's reply. (*OT*, 333/317)

For Foucault, the question of literature presents itself as the hiatus between language and the Subject. From the beginning of the nineteenth century (the modern age), language is not only the dispersion of the Subject insofar as language excludes man; the linguistic ability is also located in "the active subject" (*OT*, 316), since like "action, language expresses a profound will to something" (*OT*, 316). For Foucault, literature is precisely the language that speaks truly because it is not the operative will but the interruption of the Subject.

With reference to Blanchot's theme of *désœuvrement* and the absence of work, and similar to Nancy and Lacoue-Labarthe, Foucault understands literature as a possibility to unwork the dialectic. But, in the space of a few pages of *The Order of Things*, Foucault will nevertheless insist, in an ambiguous way, that literature is not a sign of an imminent end of Modernity, even if it manifests the end of man. On the one hand, Foucault writes that the fact that "in literature as well as in formal reflection, the question of language is being posed, prove no doubt that man is in the process of disappearing" (*OT*, 420). But, on the other hand, the fact that "literature in our day is fascinated by the being of language is neither the sign of an imminent end nor proof of a radicalization: it is a phenomenon whose necessity has its roots in a vast configuration in which the whole structure of our thought and our knowledge is traced" (*OT*, 418). It is possible that the reason for this ambiguity is the position of literature between the Subject and language. Even if literature indicates the linguistic interruption of the Subject, it is always possible that this interruption is only the locus of the negative work of the Subject. But, for Foucault, literature nevertheless presents itself as a counter-discourse that must be thought since it displays the disappearance of the Subject: Even though literature is itself a function in the epistemic configuration, literature is the locus of the intransitivity of language that interrupts Being understood as positing. This is moreover the reason why Foucault links literature to madness, which for Foucault is a form of the absence of work. Madness thus concerns the very question of intransitivity, which emerges within the paradigm of writerly necessity. In order to make this visible, I turn to the question of what the relation is between literature and madness in Foucault's early works.

The Absence of Work: Literature and Madness

Whereas Foucault understands *The Order of Things* as "the history of the Same,"[17] his earlier archaeology, the *History of Madness*, is "the history of the Other—of that which, for a given culture, is at once interior and foreign, therefore to be excluded (so as to exorcize the interior danger) but by being shut away (in order to reduce its otherness)" (*OT*, xxvi).[18] According to Foucault, in the classical age (the seventeenth and eighteenth century), what he understands as the Renaissance experience of "unreasonable Reason, or reasoned Unreason" becomes impossible: "While *man* can still go mad, *thought*, as the sovereign exercise carried out by a subject seeking the truth, can no longer be devoid of reason."[19] Foucault perceives this exclusion of "unreasonable reason" in the classical age to be an ethical decision. In the classical age, a "space of confinement" is invented in the "imaginary geometry" of a "morality that was both an anticipation of the torments of eternal damnation and an attempt to bring the patient back to health."[20] Foucault describes how this space of confinement not only excludes "mad" subjects but also constitutes certain practices and regulations.[21] In the modern age (from the end of the eighteenth century), the exclusion of madness from reason, the impossibility of experiencing reasoned unreason, "was no longer an ethical exclusion, but a distance that had already been granted."[22] In the modern age, reason does not need to exclude madness but only to recognize itself as exterior to it. Madness has become the scientific object of medical perception.

For Foucault, to write this history of madness is to write "a history of *limits*," which is the history of the limits of culture, "the very birth of its [a culture's] history."[23] Since contingency marks this "birth" of history, there is "a strange proximity between madness and literature":[24] Both madness and literature thus display the limit of the possible in modern discourse and the possibility of contingency. In his early review concerned with Hölderlin, "The Father's 'No,'" Foucault writes, "The dissolution of a work in madness, this void to which poetic speech is drawn as to its self-destruction, is what authorizes the text of a language common to both. These are not abstractions, but historical relationships that our culture must examine if it hopes to find itself" (*AM*, 18). For Foucault, there is a determinate historical relationship between madness and literature. As we recall, in the 1961 preface Foucault wrote, "The structural study must go back to that decision that both bound and separated reason and madness."[25] This decision is the exclusion of unreason, which Foucault understands in Modernity to be the very "difference" that opens up the space in which reason and madness become possible: "Why is it not possible to remain in the difference that is unreason? Why is it that unreason always has to separate from itself, fascinated in the delirium of the sensible and trapped in the retreat that is madness?"[26] For Foucault, it is precisely this almost impossible space of unreason that Hölderlin occupies. But in Modernity this space must be "abolished no sooner than it is measured, in the vertigo of the sensible or the confinement of madness."[27] The space of unreason is nothing but the historical contingency that produces itself as the difference between reason and madness.

But Foucault can therefore also understand the difference between reason and madness in the modern age to conceal unreason *as* reason's moment of emergence. In the *History of Madness*, Foucault thus claims that the unthought of Modernity is "madness" insofar as madness is both the truth of the Subject and manifests this Subject's possible disappearance: "If madness in the modern world has a meaning other than being a night in the face of the light of truth, if, in the depths of the language that it speaks, what is at stake is the truth of man, and of a truth that precedes it, founds it and has the power to destroy it, then that truth is only available to man in the disaster of madness."[28] Madness speaks a language in which the "truth" of the Subject manifests itself. Madness points to unreason as the difference that separates reason and madness.

With reference to such writers as Artaud and Hölderlin, Foucault notes in *The History of Madness*, "*Where there is an œuvre, there is no madness*: and yet madness is contemporaneous with the œuvre, as it is the harbinger of the time of its truth."[29] Madness interrupts the work of reason, so there is no madness when there is a work. But, since the "truth" of literature is the pure act of intransitive writing (the absence of work), Foucault can say that madness inaugurates the truth of the work precisely because madness announces the absence of the (literary) work. Similarly to literature, madness indicates the absence of work that is the very interruption of the Subject.[30]

Foucault and Blanchot: Literature, Madness, and the Outside

During the 1960s, Foucault and Blanchot had an ongoing conversation in the pages of *La Nouvelle Revue Française* and *Critique*. In 1961, Blanchot reviews Foucault's *History of Madness*, a history that itself implicitly relates to Blanchot's reading of Hölderlin in the early essay "Madness *par excellence*" ("La Folie par excellence," 1951). In 1962, Foucault touches on this reading by Blanchot in the review of Jean Laplance's *Hölderlin and the Question of the Father* (*Hölderlin et la question du père*, 1961) and in 1966 appears Foucault's essay "The Thought of the Outside" ("La Pensée du dehors"), which is concerned with Blanchot.[31] For Foucault and Blanchot, their common concern is the possibility of a non-dialectical experience, an experience of the "outside," which indicates the interruption of the Subject.

For Foucault, Blanchot's literary thought is paradigmatic for the possibility of thinking contingency insofar as Foucault conceives Blanchot's thought to be "that thought [of the outside] itself" (*AM*, 151). Literature emerges as this thought of contingency within the paradigm of writerly necessity; however, the question is still how this paradigm should be delimited and thus how contingency emerges as the utmost possibility of literature. For Foucault, Blanchot's discourse is an exemplary literary form of thinking since this discourse investigates the limit space of the modern age in which there emerges a link between madness and literature. In the essay "The Father's 'No,'" Foucault understands Blanchot's discourse to place itself between literature and madness in the conjunction *and*:

> But a discourse (similar to Blanchot's) that places itself within the grammatical posture of the "and" that joins madness *and* an artistic work, a discourse that investigates this indivisible unity and concerns itself with the space created when these two are joined, is necessarily an interrogation of the Limit, understood as the line where madness becomes, in a precise sense, a perceptual rupture. (*AM*, 18)

For Foucault, both literature and madness manifest the discontinuity of history, the possibility of contingent "rupture." In his review of the *History of Madness*, Blanchot addresses Foucault's understanding of madness as a limit experience: "We have to ask ourselves if it is true that literature and art might be able to entertain these limit-experiences and thus, beyond culture, pave the way for a relation with what culture rejects: a speech of borders, the outside of writing" (*IC*, 196). For Blanchot, Foucault's work on madness is a way to question the "limits" of our history and thus displays the interruption of thetic Being comprehended as reason (see *IC*, 196). Blanchot understands madness to be excluded by reason as "*the impossible* itself" (*IC*, 199). If madness is the suspension of thetic Being, then madness is precisely that which the Subject can never think insofar as this Subject is absolute positing. But, for Blanchot, madness and literature are thus also forms of the absence of work that provide access to the question of inoperativity. To think the absence of work is to think a non-dialectical experience:

> If madness has a language, and if it is even nothing but language, would this language not send us back (as does literature, although at another level) to one of the problems with which our time is dramatically concerned when it seeks to keep together the demands of dialectical discourse and the existence of a non-dialectical language, or, more precisely, a non-dialectical experience of language? (*IC*, 201)

In order to investigate further how madness emerges in relation to literature, and how literature emerges as a non-dialectical experience of language, I will turn to Blanchot's *The Space of Literature*. It is already visible *that* the Subject and language delimit the paradigm of writerly necessity, but in the next chapter on Blanchot my aim is to show *how* these figures delimit this paradigm and thus what positions of enunciation that are possible when an individual occupies the position of a subject who cannot not-write literature.

5

The Paradigm of
Writerly Necessity

The Subjectivation of the Literary Absolute

For Nancy and Lacoue-Labarthe, the romantic project is "that brief, intense, and brilliant *moment of writing* (not quite two years and hundreds of pages)" (*LA*, 7), which concern the *conceptualization* of the literary absolute. But the question remains how the literary absolute subsists as an embedded "moment of writing": How does writerly necessity simultaneously produce the dialectic of the Subject and the interruption of this very dialectic? In order to make this visible, I argue, it is necessary to expose the literary absolute as a paradigm. The literary absolute is not simply the modern *concept* of literature but emerges as the *paradigm* of writerly necessity. The question is now how the subjectivation of the literary absolute takes place by which this absolute itself subsists as the "essence" of a subject who cannot not-write intransitively. This is the question of how the literary Subject produces its own death. This death can either signify the self-relating negativity of the dialectic or the interruption of the dialectic. In order to expose the space of this "death," I will examine the positions of enunciation that a subject must occupy in order to write literature. In Foucault's words from *The Archaeology of Knowledge*, "In the proposed analysis, instead of referring back to *the* synthesis or *the* unifying function of *a* subject, the various enunciative modalities manifest his dispersion. To the various statuses, the various sites, the various positions that he can occupy or be given when making a discourse."[1] My concern is what positions the writer must occupy in order to be a subject who cannot not-write intransitively. In order to examine these enunciative positions, I turn to Blanchot's *The Space of Literature* (*L'Espace littéraire*, 1955). This work was Blanchot's fourth collection of essays, which was based on writings that he had published in the *Nouvelle Revue Française* and *Critique* during the previous four years.[2]

I will read Blanchot as a cartographer of writerly necessity who exposes how the paradigm appears as the writer who cannot not-write intransitively.[3] My aim is here analytical rather than exegetical: The question is to map the enunciative position of the paradigm of writerly necessity. In *The Space of Literature*, Blanchot writes, "Formerly, art was able to coexist with other absolute demands" (*SL*, 213), suggesting that, at the end of the eighteenth century, literature emerges as absolute for at least one (other paradigmatic) subject: "Hölderlin about whom it would not be enough to say that his fate was linked to poetry's, for he had no existence at all except in and for poetry" (*SL*, 213). When the literary absolute emerges as the paradigmatic condition for a subject, writing constitutes this subject's very life.

Blanchot conceives of the act of writing as an interaction between a hand that *cannot not-write* (necessity) and a hand that *can not-write* (contingency). According to Blanchot, the mastery of the subject who must write subsists in the ability to not-write: "The writer's mastery is not in the hand that writes, the 'sick' hand that never lets the pencil go—that can't let it go [...]. Mastery always characterizes the other hand, the one that doesn't write and is capable of intervening at the right moment to seize the pencil and put it aside" (*SL*, 25). With a notable exception, the critical reception of Blanchot has mainly focused on this interruption of writing:[4] the theme of *désœuvrement* (unworking, inoperativity, worklessness), which indicates the suspension of the Hegelian dialectic.[5] Regarding this concept of *désœuvrement*, several critical works on Blanchot highlight the question of "influence." Emmanuel Levinas's concept of the *il y a*, often in relation to Martin Heidegger's *es gibt*, is thus often perceived in the critical literature to condition Blanchot's concept of literature as an abyssal opening of Being (the withdrawal of "there is"). Simon Critchley's reading of Blanchot in *Very Little ... Almost Nothing* is here exemplary insofar as he claims that Levinas's thought of "the *il y a* is a kind of primal or primitive scene in Blanchot's work, something to which it keeps returning as its secret, its unstable point of origin, *as the origin of the artwork*."[6] But the question remains how we are to understand this act of writing produced by a necessity to write. Even if we thus make this claim regarding Levinas "influence" on Blanchot, such a focus on influence can never explain how it is possible "legitimately" to rename the *il y a* with the name of "literature." It can never manifest how such a proposition with respect to literature can be "true." To show how this is possible is the task of an archaeology of writerly necessity. I will argue that there is an irreducible link between the necessity to write and unworking, which Blanchot understands to be an intransitive act of writing.[7] It is thus the paradigm of writerly necessity that conditions Blanchot's understanding of literature as unworking. The paradigm of writerly necessity manifests a series of dialectical moments, but the question of literature also introduces the interruption of the dialectic into the paradigm. With reference to Blanchot's text, I have named these moments: *man—dying—death doubled*. My aim is now to examine these enunciative positions.

The Enunciative Positions of Writerly Necessity

Blanchot gives the name "humanism" to the position in which *man* appears as the writer who cannot not-write literature. Writerly necessity here functions as the Subject's essence, since the literary "truth" of unworking is hidden from the writerly subject at this point: "Art seeks to become the presence of art, but that it does so initially by offering to man a means of self-recognition, of self-fulfilment. At this stage, art is what we call humanistic" (*SL*, 218). For Blanchot, this "stage" indicates, on the one hand, "the modesty of its [art's] useful manifestations" and, on the other, a "useless pride in being pure essence" (*SL*, 218). Art is subordinated to the artist's apparent "true" nature: The subject "becomes the one who creates, the creator, but always, nonetheless, man the creator—creation at the level of man, of man understood as the ability to produce and to act, as the will to exert power, whose true nature is revealed by commitment to goals, by thought's need of objects in order to find its way" (*SL*, 218). Writerly necessity appears as the necessity to be, as an origin, which constitutes the writer as a subject who cannot not-write. The writer therefore construes himself as Sovereign. He exists as the guarantor of the literary work and writes so as not to die, since not only does the work depend on the subject's life, but his life also depends on the presence of the work. But, for Blanchot, the work therefore becomes death rendered vain since the writer attempts to affirm the absolute work: "To write in order not to die, to entrust oneself to the survival of the work: this motive is apparently what keeps the artist at his task. Genius confronts death; the work is death rendered vain" (*SL*, 94).

For Blanchot, this writerly Subject, the "Genius," is a modern phenomenon since, with reference to Hegel's *Lectures on Aesthetics* (*Vorlesungen über die Ästhetik*, 1818–29),[8] it is linked to the fact that art appears as aesthetic enjoyment. At this stage, Hegel's judgment on art as "a thing of the past" (*A*, 11) remains valid, since art cannot accommodate the absolute. Blanchot writes, "Art, useless [*inutile*] to the world where only effectiveness [*efficace*] counts, is also useless to itself" (*SL*, 215/285). For Hegel, "the form of art has ceased to be the supreme need of the spirit" (*A*, 103), since philosophy supersedes art as the essential unveiling of truth. Art is no longer the true manifestation of the absolute but available for "not just immediate enjoyment [*unmittelbaren Genuß*] but our judgement [*Urteil*] also" (*A*, 11/I:25–6). For

Blanchot, however, this uselessness of art as the unveiling of truth points to art as a thing of the future: Literature is not effective actuality but the inoperative interruption of the Work.

Blanchot will therefore say that the literary work is an empty demand that demands nothing, an imperative of a pure necessity to write since life is at stake. It is a purely impersonal demand in which there can be no essence, no whatness, of the work:

> The work requires of the writer that he lose everything he might construe as his own "nature," that he lose all character and that, ceasing to be linked to others and to himself by the decision which makes him an "I," he becomes the empty place where the impersonal affirmation emerges. This is a requirement which is no requirement at all, for it demands nothing; it has no content. It does not oblige anyone to anything; it is only the air one has to breathe, the void on which one has to get a footing, daylight worn thin where the faces one loves best become invisible. (*SL*, 55–6)

This paragraph points to the next "moment" of the dialectic of writerly necessity—*dying*—which I will address now. Writerly necessity is the subject's essence, but it is thus an essence that takes the form of a necessity to erase itself *as* essence since it is a necessity to write intransitively. The subject position of man's death emerges in which this absence (of the Subject) is disclosed as the Subject's "essence." But, as such, this essence (death) is still construed as the act *of* the Subject. "To write so as not to die" therefore becomes "to write so as to die," but only because it is first an avoidance of death. The act of writing implies the death of the Subject, but only because this death is required by writerly necessity as the essence of this Subject. It is the erasure of an "I" that does not imply the Subject's disappearance since it is precisely this Subject whose necessity produces its own erasure. Writerly necessity excludes itself as essence but makes possible its own *essential* realization *as* erasure. The movement from the Subject to the erased Subject is, on the one hand, the death of man, but on the other hand, the appearance of the voice of man's absence: "The tone is not the writer's voice, but the intimacy of the silence he imposes upon the word" (*SL*, 27). The subject who writes so as not to die is also the erased subject who writes so as to die, and this erased essence produces itself as the Subject's *dying*. At this "moment," the literary truth of unworking remains concealed, insofar as the dialectic of the Subject reproduces itself as man's interminable dying. This dying is an incessant interrupted constitution in which the interruption solely signifies the very reconstitution of the Subject.[9]

But, according to Blanchot, the literary truth of unworking is the disappearance of the Subject as such. In Blanchot's terms, the postulation that literature is the question of its own Being thus means that not only man but also the thinking of self-referential language might disappear. It is not solely man's givenness but moreover man's death that is at stake in literature. The literary absolute, subsisting as the paradigm of writerly necessity, manifests its own contingency: The ultimate possibility of the literary absolute, which is also its limit, is the possibility that this paradigm itself disappears as that which constitutes a writerly life in which this life is itself at risk in writing. Blanchot can therefore say that it is not only a subject but (thetic) Being that is in danger in the literary work:

> In the poem it is not any particular individual who risks himself alone, or a particular mind that is exposed to the touch and the burn of darkness. The risk is more essential. It is the danger of dangers by which, each time, the essence of language is radically placed in doubt. To risk language [*langage*]: this is one of the forms of this risk. To risk being [*l'être*]—the word uttered when absence is spoken, and which the work pronounces by pronouncing the word *beginning*—this is the other form of the risk. In the work of art, being is risked. (*SL*, 238–9/320)

It is not just *a* subject (a particular writer), neither man nor language (as functions in a historical configuration of the literary absolute), but the relation of the Subject to intransitivity that is at risk (the paradigmatic configuration as such). It is the very paradigm of writerly necessity that might disappear.

This disappearance points to the "moment" of *death doubled* (see *SL*, 104), which I will address now. This moment is however not a moment in the dialectic of writerly necessity but the interruption of the dialectic. Blanchot describes the difference between *a* subject and *the* Subject's disappearance as two forms of "death," which take place in two separate temporalities ("nights"). The "first night" (*SL*, 163) is the moment of the subject's *dying* in which writerly necessity erases itself as essence only to emerge as an essential erasure. This is a time of the writer's repeated *dying* in which he never dies: "There the incessant and uninterrupted reign—not the certainty of death achieved, but 'the eternal torments of Dying'" (*SL*, 119). In this night, writerly necessity arises as that which ruins every work because it means that no work can ever realize itself as an actual given object. The subject is situated between a "cannot not-write" and a "cannot write," between a necessity and an impossibility of writing.

In opposition to this first night, "the *other* night" (*SL*, 163) designates that death has come "to transform the fact of death" (*SL*, 146). It designates an impersonal death "which never comes and toward which I do not direct myself" (*SL*, 104). Death is here an event that utterly reconfigures the horizon of the literary as such since death is an interruption of the literary absolute. In Blanchot's terms, this *other* night is the night of art that is the time "when everything has disappeared in the night, 'everything has disappeared' appears" (*SL*, 163). It is thus the appearance of the disappearance of the literary absolute. The essence of literature is the essence of the subject who cannot not-write literature: It is literature as an intransitive writing. For Blanchot, intransitivity indicates itself as the very manifestation of the disappearance of literature. It is the interruption of thetic Being.[10]

Double Negativity

My aim in this chapter has been to show how the dialectic of writerly necessity takes place between the Subject and intransitivity. In the next chapter, I will examine how this dialectic emerges as an actual desiring subject (Hölderlin). But first I will address how there is a double negativity that produces the paradigm of writerly necessity.

Literature is the question of its own disappearance. For Blanchot, this disappearance is the visibility of the Subject's contingency, insofar as it is a pure affirmation: "This negation [impersonal death] only masks the more essential fact that in language at this point everything reverts to affirmation: in this language what denies affirms. For this language speaks as absence [...]. The poet is he who hears a language which makes nothing heard" (*SL*, 51). In this claim that literature consists in a negation turned into a pure affirmation, Blanchot attends to literature as a non-dialectical experience of language. Literature as a pure affirmation, nothingness itself, is an interruption of the dialectical Subject produced by writerly necessity: "The time of time's absence is not dialectical. In this time what appears is the fact that nothing appears. What appears is the being deep within being's absence" (*SL*, 30).

This "absence of Being" concerns the interruption of the dialectical Subject, which makes visible a double negativity of the paradigm of writerly necessity. On the one hand, from the point of view of the constituted paradigmatic subject who writes, writerly necessity is a lack (the inability to not-write literature), which always already constitutes the writer *as* subject. Literature is an intransitive language, which can only indicate itself in discourse but never be represented as an object by the subject. On the other hand, from the perspective of writerly necessity as the constitutive paradigm, the literary absolute is that which produces a writerly life but itself first emerges *as* a condition of life in its instantiation as the essence of the writerly subject. The literary absolute is not a substance that preexists a writerly subject; rather, the instantiation of the literary absolute, as that which makes this subject possible, is the emergence of a condition (writerly necessity) that *was never there* before its retroactive emergence *as* condition. In this sense, it is first through the emergence of the literary absolute *as* a condition that the very lack (of the Subject) is produced by which the literary absolute constitutes itself. The dialectical negativity of the literary absolute thus conceals its historical contingency, which consists in its aporetic retroactive constitution. The paradigm of writerly necessity constitutes itself as the Subject who cannot not-write intransitively; however, this paradigm has thus itself emerged *in* history *as* a condition subsisting as this Subject.

It is from this perspective that we should understand Blanchot's proposal that the act of writing consists in the interaction of two hands: It is thus precisely the inability to not-write (necessity) that is also the inability to write any actual work (impossibility) that, exposing itself as the ability to not-write (contingency), produces the ability to write (possibility) the absence of work.[11] Insofar as the literary absolute constitutes the "truth" of literature, the act of writing sustains itself in the movement from writerly necessity (cannot not-write/cannot write) to the erasure of this necessity (can not-write/can write) by which the contingency of this act of writing becomes visible. With reference to Blanchot, to approach this contingency is then also to think "the mastery that consists in the power to stop writing" (*SL*, 25). It is to open up for an altogether different "literary future" in which literature is not anymore the reenacting of the same act of writing that affirms that the Subject has died; rather, the contingency of writerly necessity exposes itself. With respect to literature, this is the philosophical task of the future: to think the contingency by which a different (literary) future becomes possible. The question is how to expose the inoperative space of literature. But this does not hide the issue that literature emerges as absolute for subjects who cannot not-write intransitively. The names "Hölderlin" and "Rimbaud" thus still function as traces of an a priori that to this day not only governs the comprehension of the "truth" of literature but also indicates the "end" of literature.

6

The Writer Who Cannot Not-Desire to Write

The Desiring Subject

Writerly necessity constitutes a subject who cannot not-write intransitively: The subject must not write any work as an actual object-thing but the absence of work. Here I will be concerned with how the literary absolute produces a psychic form: How this subject who must write emerges as an actual desiring being, in other words, as a writer who cannot not-desire to write. My exposition of what I am calling the subject who cannot not-desire to write is a restaging of the dialectic of the subject that is visible in the sequence I drew out from Blanchot: man—dying—death doubled. This writer who cannot not-desire to write desires not *this* or *that* literary work but the *act of writing*. Now, this move to consider the desire of the subject who cannot not-write seems to me to call for a turn to psychoanalysis. Accordingly, in order to delimit the subject positions of this desiring writer, I will examine this writer in Lacanian terms. I will aim to show that the subject who cannot not-write literature is constituted by an essential lack, which corresponds to the lack of the subject that is conceptualized in Jacques Lacan's theoretical transposition of Sigmund Freud's insights. My aim is thus to examine the subject who cannot not-desire to write literature in order to understand how the paradigm of writerly necessity emerges as a process of subjectivation (as a relation between subject and object). Since the Subject is itself contingent, the essential lack of the literary Subject is thus a constitution that has arisen in history and could disappear in the future. But the question is then how this Subject emerges as a writer who cannot not-desire to write literature.

Double Negativity

The literary Subject's desire is not simply a desire *of* language, of the signifier, but a desire *for* the signifier, a desire for language itself. It is a desire for the taking place of language; for the locus of writing, which constitutes the essence of the writer who must write. The literary absolute only subsists as a paradigm of writerly necessity because the literary Subject *is* the "failure of its own actualization."[1] The subject writes literature but, since literature is nothing but the absence of work, the subject fails, and this failure *is* the literary Subject insofar as its dialectic is at work. This can also be expressed by saying that the literary Subject is the overlap of two lacks. In Lacan's terms, these two lacks are the lack of a particular subject and the inherent lack in the Other that constitutes the symbolic of this subject. In terms of the paradigm of writerly necessity, these two lacks are the lack of the subject who must write and the inherent void of the paradigm itself as the signifying frame. The literary absolute constitutes a *split* subject that cannot represent its own essence to itself since writerly necessity first makes possible the very Being of the subject and thus constitutes any possibility of literary representation. But the paradigm of writerly necessity is then also itself retrospectively actualized *as* the subject's very condition. It is not only the subject that is constituted by a lack in its inability to not-write that literary work that is impossible to write. The literary absolute is itself contingent on its actualization as writerly necessity: as the essence of the literary subject, an essence, which is nothing but the pure necessity to write.

The contingency of the literary absolute is thus the mark of its historicity: The paradigm is an a priori condition inscribed a posteriori in literary history as the point of emergence of this history.[2] But this contingency is concealed in writerly necessity, which appears for the subject as a condition that could not be otherwise: The subject must not only live in order to write but also write so as to live. Writerly necessity limits the subject in the sense that a lack constitutes Being, but it is thus also this very lack that makes the subject come into being as a writer. This lack of ability to not-write is the condition of possibility for this subject. The *ich muß* is a discursive place that produces not only the literary subject's limits but also his or hers possibilities. In order to investigate this subject who cannot not-desire to write, I will examine the paradigmatic example of Hölderlin.

Since the event of "1797," Hölderlin is always already a subject who cannot not-write literature.[3] In a letter to his stepbrother Karl Gok (Frankfurt, February 12, 1798), Hölderlin speaks of his desire to write: "Do you know the root [*Wurzel*] of all my trouble [*Übels*]? I want to live for the art that is my heart's desire [*Ich möchte der Kunst leben, an der mein Herz hängt*], and am forced to shift for a living in the world [*muß mich herumarbeiten unter den Menschen*], making me often so weary, weary of life [*lebensmüde*]" (*EL*, 98; *SA* 6:1, 264). The writer is divided between *I* (*Ich*) and *my* (*mein*), between the subject of enunciation and the subject of statement. The writer desires to *live art*; he has lost his heart to art, "*I* want to live for *my* heart's desire." *My* heart's desire is a mode of being; it is *to be* the locus of the subject as signifier. Hölderlin's *I* (ego) desires this position of the pure signifier: *my* heart's desire. It is a desire for the very taking place of language.[4] It is a desire for the act of writing, for the impossible literary "object," which is impossible because literature is the very suspension of the relation between a knowing subject and an object of knowledge.

The Subject and the Work

The paradigm of writerly necessity arises as the co-emergence of a split literary subject and an impossible literary object. The ego (Hölderlin's "*I*") who cannot not-desire to write emerges in an imaginary relation to its "*objet a* cause of desire."[5] The object is the correlate to the subject, but it is an impossible object that can never be actualized.[6] According to Slavoj Žižek, the very relation of the barred subject and *objet a* can itself be understood as a "doubly inscribed entity" that is both surplus and lack:[7]

> In other words, as soon as the symbolic order emerges, a minimal difference is introduced between a structural place and the element that occupies or fills out this place: an element is always logically preceded by the place in the structure it fills out. The two series, therefore, can also be described as the "empty" formal structure (signifier) and the series of elements filling out the empty places in the structure (signified). From this perspective, the paradox consists in the fact that the two series never overlap: we always encounter an entity that is simultaneously (with regard to the structure) an empty, unoccupied place and (with regard to the elements) a rapidly moving, elusive object, an occupant without a place.[8]

Insofar as the literary absolute is the symbolic order for the writer, writerly necessity inscribes the relation of subject–*objet a* in its production.[9] Writerly necessity produces a subject who must write intransitively (without object), which is also to say that not only is the subject's Being a pure signifier without signified that is always already occluded in discourse (the essence of writerly necessity is only a purely formal necessity to erase itself as essence), but the literary object is also always lacking with respect to discourse insofar as literature is the absence of work. Moreover, this lack of the object indicates nothing but the very inconsistency of the paradigm itself: It is not simply that writerly necessity is a subjective contingency, which eludes the literary absolute in the sense that an empirical subject would not be able to be totalized in an absolute. Rather, this contingency of writerly necessity is inherent to the literary absolute itself. The absolute is itself contingent insofar as its paradigmatic a priori status is only inscribed retroactively in history as the paradigm of writerly necessity.[10] The question is then whether the *objet a*, the absence of the literary work, is an interruption that indicates the interruption of the dialectic (unworking), or whether it is nothing but the inherent self-relating negativity of the dialectic itself at work.

Within the paradigm of writerly necessity, the literary absolute appears as the incessant dialectic of an *act of writing* that fails and, in its failure, produces the very absence (of work), which the literary Subject *is*. I have described this production in Blanchot's terms and will here explicate them in Lacanian terminology in order to describe the writer as a desiring subject. My aim is to examine how a subject (Hölderlin) who cannot not-desire to write emerges as a neurotic, perverse, and psychotic writerly subject. Lacan understands the neurotic, the perverse, and the psychotic to be different formal structures of how subjects relate to language. With reference to Blanchot, I will argue that there is a correlation between, respectively, *man* and *the neurotic*, *dying* and *the pervert*, and *madness* and *the psychotic*. First, I investigate how a neurotic structure forms the writer and how the intransitivity of language is hidden from the writer at the same time as it is the cause of his desire. Second, I examine the writer as a perverse subject who conceals the lack of the symbolic of literature but also exposes his own constitutive lack. Third, I consider the position of the psychotic subject, and I introduce a subject position into Lacanian theory that is neither neurotic nor perverse (nor psychotic) but a form of *death doubled* (Blanchot) in which the writer appropriates *jouissance insofar as it is lacking*. These Lacanian terms should enable us to understand how the subject who cannot not-write literature emerges as a desiring being in actual space-time. I therefore focus on a finite, particular subject—Hölderlin—so as to examine how the paradigm of writerly necessity produces an experience of writing that involves pleasure and suffering and in which the act of writing literature appears to be a matter of life and death for the subject who writes.

The Incessant Dying: The Neurotic Subject

The neurotic structure forms the writer in such a way that the lack of the Other (language) is hidden from the subject at the same time as this lack is the cause of his desire (*objet a*). The neurotic writer, the desiring ego, unknowingly refuses to acknowledge the castration that constitutes him. This means that not only the writer's own emergence as a subject is fundamentally barred for the ego, but that the contingency of the paradigm of writerly necessity remains concealed. For the neurotic writer, *objet a* is intrinsically related to his ego because it performs an imaginary function.

This object-cause of desire thus makes his fantasy function as a protection from *jouissance* by fixating desire in its constant metonymical deferral.[11] The neurotic writer can never attain what he desires (literature) because desire is always "the *desire for something else*" (*E*, 431): The literary work is never *there* but always interrupts its actuality. In the seminar *The Four Fundamental Concepts of Psychoanalysis* (*Les Quatre concepts fondamentaux de la psychanalyse*, 1973), first delivered in 1964 at the Ecole Normale Supérieure in Paris, Lacan defines the *objet a* as "something from which the subject, in order to constitute itself, has separated itself off as organ. This serves as a symbol of the lack, that is to say, of the phallus, not as such, but in so far as it is lacking."[12] *Objet a* is the symbol of the phallus *in so far as it is lacking*; it is the void in which the neurotic poet sustains himself as desiring in his fantasy. The writer's fantasy sustains his literary actuality by indefinitely withholding the literary subject's dissolution as a subject.[13] According to Lacan, this dissolution is the "point of aphanisis, assumed to lie in $ [the barred subject]" (*E*, 654). Insofar as the neurotic subject correlates with the subject position of "man" (Blanchot), this fantasy consists in the imagination of an *absolute* work. But, as Žižek notes, the implied notion of fantasy as the representation of the realization of desire is at least ambiguous since "in the fantasy-scene the desire is not fulfilled, 'satisfied', but constituted (given its objects, and so on)—*through fantasy, we learn 'how to desire'*."[14] The fantasy not only protects the subject but also sustains the production of desire; however, this desire is the Other's desire that does not maintain the writer's pleasure since desire is always deferred. The subject writes this or that (literary) work, which can only disappoint him because he desires the very *act of writing*: the lack of the paradigm of writerly necessity that makes his agency possible.

In Hölderlin's letter to Neuffer (July 10, 1797) in which the writer bears witness to the a priori event that constitutes him as a writer who cannot not-write literature, the desire of the writer exposes itself. Hölderlin writes that a radical change has taken place in his life:

To tell the truth I think I was more balanced than I am now, with a better judgment of myself and others, when I was 22 and still lived with you, my dear Neuffer. Oh, give me back my youth! I am torn apart by love and hate. But vague utterances of this kind are only going to frustrate you. And for that reason I would do better to keep quiet. You too have been happier than you are. But you have peace and quiet [*Ruhe*]. And without that life is no better than death [*Und ohne sie ist alles Leben so gut, wie der Tod*]. That's what I want too, dear friend, peace and quiet. You say that for some time now you have left your harp hanging on the wall as you put it [*Du hast die Harfe, wie Du schreibst, eine Zeit lang an der Wand hängen gehabt*]. That's all right too, if you can do it without pangs of conscience [*Gewissensbisse*]. And your sense of yourself reposes on other appropriate activities, so you are not reduced to nothing if you are not a poet. For me, every other possibility, anything else I could do, is ruined, and nothing delights me except when from time to time I allow myself, in the heat of the moment, to be pleased by a few lines written down in the excitement of invention. But you yourself know how fleeting that pleasure [*Lust*] is. (*EL*, 89–90/6:1, 243–4)

I have already discussed the last part of this passage, but I will now examine Hölderlin's letter from the perspective of psychoanalysis. In the first instance, we should note the experience of the law of the pleasure principle, which commands one to *enjoy as little as possible*.[15] Hölderlin writes that he desires peace and quietness in his life, something, which his existence as a poet will not allow him. This makes him mention "death" (*Tod*), a possibility, which cannot be neglected insofar as the poet cannot not-write literature and thus supposedly cannot attain peace. Whenever Hölderlin does not write he feels guilty, but writing also provides the poet with his only pleasure, which is however only temporary. With reference to Freud, it is possible to identify this ambivalent relation to poetry as a testimony to a fundamental *melancholy* characterized by "an object-loss which is withdrawn from consciousness."[16] Insofar as writerly necessity produces the writer, it is the coincidence of the loss of ability to not-write (intransitively) with the loss of ability to write (transitively), which forms the writer's melancholy. The writer is suspended between a necessity to write and an impossibility of writing. Writerly necessity produces the writer as a desiring being, as a living being who desires his own Being, which is intransitive language.

The poet thus desires life only because life is the lost literary work that sustains the poet's life as a *writerly* life. In order to live, the writer must write, since writerly necessity constitutes his subjectivity, but it is also this necessity to write the impossible work that threatens the subject. Insofar as Hölderlin desires to live, he desires poetry, which he cannot live without, but poetry is also the lack of being where his very life is at stake. Intransitivity is not a desire to write any work but a desire for the very lack of work. Intransitivity is the limit that the poet "is": It is thus the writer's own writerly essence, which threatens him with dissolution. Insofar as literature is always already lost, this constitutive loss is thus not a loss of a love object but the loss of the very ability to love.[17] The writer's melancholia signals a constitutive loss that both sustains and disrupts the act of writing, which makes up the writer's Being.

Hölderlin's sense of guilt is marked by his superego that judges and constrains the writer. Located within the symbolic, the superego is concordant with the law of the signifier but, simultaneously, transgresses the law because it functions as a tyrannical imperative:[18] "The super-ego has a relation to the law, and is at the same time a senseless law, going so far as to become a failure to recognise [*méconnaissance*] the law."[19] For the writer, the law is reduced to "the *You must*, which is speech deprived of all its meaning."[20]

For the neurotic writer, the law shows itself in a double form. On the one hand, the law is the superego that obligates the poet to write, commands that *you must write*. But, on the other hand, the law is the law of the pleasure principle that commands one to *enjoy as little as possible*. The law is thus not only an imperative but also a pact: It is the regulation of desire by law. To the extent that the writer ego wishes a peaceful life, the lack of unpleasant tensions, the pleasure principle is his law. The law constitutes the writer as desiring; but, at the same time, as the law produces desire, a desire that is always deferred, the command of the law (*to enjoy as little as possible*) also produces the potential for its own destruction, since the writer's desire can never be satisfied.

The writer who desires poetry experiences the impossibility of writing (transitively) since the desire is always deferred because it is desire for *desire* itself. Since the writer must write, he cannot withdraw his libido from the literary thing without risking his life as a subject. But, following Freud, when the love object is not withdrawn, the libido is internalized toward the writer's own ego insofar as a narcissistic identification takes place between the writer's *I* (ego) and literature (object). Freud writes, "In this way an object-loss was transformed into an ego-loss and the conflict between the ego and the loved person into a cleavage between the critical activity of the ego and the ego as altered by identification."[21] This identification produces the ambivalence of the writer's love of literature. It is the state of being "torn apart by love and hate" (*EL*, 89),[22] since the failure of every actual literary work is the failure of the subject's very Being.

Hölderlin's contemplation of suicide ("death") can be seen from the perspective of the sadism that emerges when, through the narcissistic identification, the destruction of literature (the object) entails the perishing of the writer's own ego.[23] But Hölderlin also writes about the excitement of invention, the pleasure of writing, arising "in the heat of the moment." In Freudian terms, it is the tendency of melancholia to turn into mania when the writer experiences the triumph of writing what appears as literature.[24] But this mania can indeed only be "fleeting" since this or that work can never *be* desire itself: language as such. The writer who cannot not-write intransitively can never reach the locus of writing: the absolute work in its purity.[25]

This subject is thus a writer who must write but who never can write any literary work, which could satisfy his desire. This subject writes *absolutely*, which means that he can never fully actualize himself *as* a writer in a work, but must fail to write an absolute work since his very essence *is* this failure of writing transitively. The melancholic writer desires his own death (suicide) since an absence (of work) constitutes his very desiring being.[26] But, insofar as the writer does not approach this death, he reproduces himself in the incessant locus of *dying* (as we saw in the discussion of Blanchot).

One Lack Visible: The Perverse Subject

The writer desires not to write this or that work but the very act of writing. The problem with any literary work is that it is an object, whereas the poet desires precisely to write intransitively (without object). The poet desires *to be* literature: to place himself in the very negativity by which he is constituted as a split subject. As a neurotic, the poet turns his face away from the risk of death, "when the opportunity to acquire mastery is offered to him in a struggle for pure prestige" (*E*, 259). The neurotic poet accepts his *dying* condition as a desiring ego. Rather than pursuing the anticipated enjoyment, the neurotic poet abandons *jouissance* in the hope that he will receive such enjoyment without a struggle to death (see *E*, 259). But, Hölderlin considers death in the letter to Neuffer (July 10, 1797). And, in a later letter (December 4, 1801), the poet writes that he now pursues death, the path of *jouissance*: "It is god-forsaken and madness to look for a path out of all danger—there exists no plant to remedy death" (*EL*, 209).

In Lacan's words, the poet recognizes "that this being has never been anything more than his own construction [*oeuvre*] in the imaginary and that this construction undercuts all certainty in him" (*E*, 207). The poet decides to accept death as a possibility, and he thus risks his life because without peace it is no life anymore. The writer is on the path of death in order to become the symbol of the being of language. The neurotic writer emerged into the symbolic through the renunciation of the "evil"[27] *jouissance*, but this writer vanishes as a subject. The writer dies.

This death is not the zero point of the writer's biological life but of his subject position as the dying "man": "The death instinct essentially expresses the limit of the subject's historical function" (*E*, 261–2). It is disappearance of the writer as the *neurotic* writer who refuses to acknowledge his own lack. The writer appropriates his impossible possibility: "man's death." He displays his own lack and perishes as a neurotic only to emerge in the position of the pervert. Like the pervert Alcibiades in Lacan's analysis in "The Subversion of the Subject and the Dialectic of Desire in the Freudian Unconscious" ("Subversion du sujet et dialectique du désir dans l'inconscient freudien," 1960), the writer exhibits his own "object as castrated, ... flaunts the fact that he is imbued with desire" (*E*, 699). The writer is the "epitome of desirousness, and a man who pursues jouissance as far as possible" (*E*, 700). The writer thus makes himself the instrument of the Other's *jouissance*. He realizes himself as *objet a* by satisfying the Other's will to castrate him (see *E*, 697–700). The writer makes himself visible as a split subject.

In a letter to his mother (Bordeaux, January 28, 1802), Hölderlin presents himself as "someone reborn" (*EL*, 211). He is a writer who displays his essential finitude, the lack, which produces his life:

> These last few days I have been walking in nothing but fine spring weather, but not long before, high up in the snowy hills of the fearful Auvergne, in storms and wilderness, the nights icy-cold and a loaded pistol beside me in the rough beds—I prayed a prayer then that was the best of my whole life and that I shall never forget. [...] I am now hardened through and through, initiated as you could wish. I think I shall remain so, in the main. Fearing nothing and enduring a good deal. (*EL*, 211)

This letter was written after Hölderlin's long walk from Nürtingen in Germany to Bordeaux in France during the winter of 1801–2. During this walk, suicide was a constant possibility. In Bordeaux, he was to work as a tutor for the children of consul Meyer, living in the palace of the consul on Allées de Tourny.[28] In the letter to his mother, Hölderlin notes, "My accommodation is almost too grand [*Fast wohn' ich zu herrlich*]" (EL, 211/6:1, 430). After the long walk, "out of danger" (*EL*, 211), Hölderlin conceives himself as someone reborn. But by the summer of 1802, Hölderlin is back in Germany again. There are no letters from this period in which Hölderlin returned from France; however, in November 1802 from Nürtingen, Hölderlin writes, "The violent element, the fire of the sky, and the quiet of the people, their life in the open and their straitenedness and contentment, stirred me continually, and as one says of heroes I can probably say of myself: that Apollo has struck me" (*EL*, 213). Even if Hölderlin exposes his essential lack, he also conceals the essential lack of the paradigm of writerly necessity. For Hölderlin, literature (Apollo) still constitutes his life, which thus coincides with an act of writing.

In Lacanian terms, Hölderlin is the perverse writer who protects himself. Even if the perverse writer exhibits his own lack, "this does not mean that the pervert's unconscious is right out in the open. He, too, defends himself in his desire in his own way. For desire is a defense, a defense against going beyond a limit in jouissance" (*E*, 699). Having risked death, the perverse writer makes visible his own constituting split by positioning himself in the symbol of the locus of writing intransitively (in the *objet a*). But, at the same time, the writer projects onto literature "the ideal of the perfect Master" (*E*, 700). The writer refuses to acknowledge the Other's lack: Hölderlin refuses to acknowledge the fictional character of Apollo. The poet succeeds in *being*, as *objet a*, the symbol of the act of writing. The poet *lets himself be written*, but only because he has appropriated the Other as the locus of the signifier without admitting that "there is no Other of the Other" (*E*, 693). The writer refuses to acknowledge that there is "a lack inherent in the Other's very function as the treasure trove of signifiers" (*E*, 693). Lacan describes this lack inherent in the Other in linguistic terms: "No authoritative statement has any other guarantee here than its very enunciation, since it would be pointless for the statement to seek it in another signifier, which could in no way appear outside that locus" (*E*, 688). Since every signifier represents the subject to another signifier there is no beyond of signification, there is no statement, which can represent language *as such*, the being of language.

The Double Lack Visible: Between Madness and Contingency

The perverse writer protects himself by refusing the Other's inherent lack. He manifests his own lack but hides the lack of the Other. For the perverse writer, the contingency of the paradigm of writerly necessity is thus not visible as that which constitutes his subject position. The writer's desire is a desire constituted by negation; but, insofar as the truth of literature is unworking, the writer anticipates a position without dialectical negation. The writer anticipates the impossible enjoyment of *jouissance*.

The concept of this impossible enjoyment displays itself in the paradoxical relation of the *law* to itself, which I will explicate here. The law of the pleasure principle is encapsulated in the imperative of *enjoy as little as possible*. It is thus built on the exclusion of *jouissance*; it constitutes its regulation of desire on the basis of a prohibition. But besides being the imperative of the law, this law moreover produces the very means to transgress itself through the superego's tyrannical imperative of *you must*. The law thus produces the path to *jouissance*, the prohibition by which the law has constituted itself. But the impossible pain of pleasure, *jouissance*, then shows itself as that which *was never* possible to achieve at any point in history anyway. Lacan can thus speak of the subject as that which is *almost naturally barred*: "It is not the Law itself that bars the subject's access to jouissance—it simply makes a barred subject out of an almost natural barrier" (*E*, 696). The ultimate pleasure is impossible to access; this pleasure does not exist, since pleasure itself sets the limit to *jouissance*: "Pain, like pleasure, nevertheless comes to an end—when the subject passes out" (*E*, 653). The subject who anticipates *jouissance* as the ultimate pleasure that is denied to him by law is in fact not capable of experiencing this painful pleasure. As the moment of orgasmic climax, *jouissance* thus designates the subject's dissolution as subject. The prohibition *jouissance* is an exclusion by which the law of language is founded but which was never there in the first place. As that which never was, *jouissance* is thus paradoxically what is removed in the locus of negation.[29]

For the writer to appropriate *jouissance* as that which never was, it would mean for him *to go on the path of jouissance insofar as it is lacking*.[30] On the one hand, the writer would then not attempt to conceal his own lack as a neurotic. On the other hand, the writer would also not maintain the perverse function, which hides the inherent lack of the Other. Rather, the writer would expose the contingency of the paradigm of writerly necessity. To expose *jouissance* insofar as it is lacking means to display the double negation of the paradigm of writerly necessity. To show that the exclusion on which the law of the paradigm of writerly necessity is constituted first emerges *as* exclusion through the retroactive constitution of the paradigmatic law itself.

This path can lead to "madness" that, as the absence of work, discloses the contingency of the paradigm.[31] The question of Hölderlin's "madness" is intrinsic to the reception of the "public image" of this poet, which in the nineteenth century overshadows the critical understanding of Hölderlin's literary production.[32] During the "time of madness" from 1807 until his death in 1843, Hölderlin lives in the later named *Hölderlinturm* in Tübingen in which the poet receives many visitors. Henning Bothe traces how the "topos of the 'feminine', seraphic Hölderlin"[33] arises in the nineteenth century as a concern for the "mad" poet's "pureness" (*Reinheit*), which means that Hölderlin at the beginning of the twentieth century has become the *allegorical personification of poetry itself*.[34] During the twentieth century, from the categorization of Hölderlin's literary work under the category of "poetry of the asylum" and Wilhelm Lange's (1909)[35] psychiatric diagnosis of Hölderlin to Pierre Bertaux's claim (1978) that Hölderlin was in fact never "mad" (*geisteskrank*),[36] the question of "madness" has occupied the (biographical-oriented) critical reception of Hölderlin.[37]

In *Hölderlin and the Question of the Father* (*Hölderlin et la question du père*, 1961), Jean Laplanche attempts to reexamine the relation between life and work by "listening to and making more explicit the poetic utterance of madness."[38] Laplanche's concern is the apparent "enigma" that Hölderlin could at the same time be "mad" and a "poet."[39] In order to establish the emergence of the poet's madness, rather than attending to Hölderlin's "character traits,"[40] Laplanche examines the "interpersonal constellations"[41] so as to investigate "Hölderlin's relationships with love objects."[42] With reference to Lacan, Laplanche identifies psychotic "foreclosure" as the fact that the position of the law of the signifier remained vacant: "The father as promoter of the Law, the 'Name of the Father,' was never admitted into the subject's system of significations."[43] Laplanche adds, "This is what accounts for the feeling of a lack almost impossible to fill that one experiences in the presence of schizophrenia. It suggests that the origin of this lack is to be sought in the most primal relationship of the child with language."[44] Laplanche convincingly shows how Friedrich Schiller emerges in "the *position of the father*"[45] for Hölderlin between 1794 and 1795. For Hölderlin, Schiller is an absolute "all-powerful object,"[46] "the very image of totality and perfection."[47] According to Laplanche, during the Homburg years (September 1798 to June 1800), Schiller vanishes from this object-position:[48] "One would search in vain in Hölderlin's circle for a real person who would have the function that Schiller had."[49] What has happened between 1795 and 1798?

Literature has become absolute for Hölderlin since the event of "1797." Hölderlin's love object has emerged as the impossible "object" of intransitive language. Literature is embodied in the very act of writing, which coincides with the interruption of thetic Being. Laplanche never considers that Hölderlin's love object during the Homburg years is not any "person" but intransitive language itself. Laplanche thus also rejects Blanchot's thesis from the essay "Madness *par excellence*" ("La Folie par excellence," 1951) in which Blanchot writes, "It is the realization of the true [poetic essence] which, at a certain point and in spite of him [Hölderlin], demands of his personal reason that it becomes pure impersonal transparency whence there is no return."[50] Blanchot's thesis is however correct if we identify the paradigm of writerly necessity as the production of what Blanchot calls "the truth and affirmation of the poetic essence" in which "pure language"[51] manifests itself. Since the paradigm produces a subject who cannot not-write intransitively, the literary "essence" demands that the writerly subject vanishes in the pure intransitive language. In terms of psychotic foreclosure (madness), we can understand this vanishing as the exclusion of the writer from every intelligible enunciative position within the paradigm of writerly necessity, which itself disappears and becomes transparent as the contingent signifier-frame that sustains the symbolic for the writer. Insofar as intransitivity indicates the interruption of the Subject, it thus manifests the possible disappearance of the paradigm of writerly necessity.

Blanchot identifies Hölderlin's words from "Mnemosyne" (1803?) as "the last word" from the "heart of madness":[52]

A sign we are, without meaning
Without pain we are and have nearly
Lost our language in foreign lands.

[*Ein Zeichen sind wir, deutungslos*
Schmerzlos sind wir und haben fast
Die Sprache in der Fremde verloren.][53]

Hölderlin's madness emerges as the poet's mute sign: the intransitive language. Insofar as "madness" is indeed the manifestation of this absence of work, it is also the exposition of the contingency of the literary absolute. The writer who displays *jouissance* insofar as it is lacking exposes the double negation of the paradigm of writerly necessity. Like the voice in the last stanza of Hölderlin's "The Poet's Vocation" ["Dichterberuf," 1800–1], this writer thus "fearlessly" evokes the possibility of the absence in the Other:

Fearless yet, if he must, man stands, and lonely
Before God, simplicity protects him, no
Weapon he needs, nor subterfuge
[So long as,] Till God's being not there helps him.

[*Furchtlos bleibt aber, so er es muß, der Mann*
Einsam vor Gott, es schützet die Einfalt ihn,
Und keiner Waffen brauchts und keiner
Listen, so lange, bis Gottes Fehl hilft.][54]

In the locus of his vocation, the poet needs no protecting tools because simplicity keeps him safe.[55] In this place, which never was, the writer who cannot not-desire to write exposes not only his own essential lack but also the Other's inherent lack. The double negativity of the paradigm of writerly necessity is visible. In fact, this double lack is not just visible; rather, the lack helps for a period of time indicated by "so long as" (*so lange*), or the lack is going to help in the future indicated by the conjunction "until" (*bis*).

Insofar as the literary subject is produced by writerly necessity, the inconsistency of the paradigm (the lack inherent in the Other) is *yet* to help since such an aid would mean that the paradigm has already disappeared. The act of writing sustains itself in the movement from writerly necessity (cannot not-write/cannot write) to the erasure of this necessity (can not-write/can write) by which the contingency of this act of writing becomes visible. To approach this contingency is then also to secure the place "that never was," which the writer "never left" in order to expose its nonnecessary habitual status. On the one hand, this place "never was" since it is nothing but the lack by which the paradigm produces itself. On the other hand, the writer "never left" this place insofar as the double negativity of writerly necessity thus produces his very Being.

To expose the double negativity of the paradigm of writerly necessity is to make the contingency of the literary absolute visible. It is the inability to not-write (necessity) intransitively that is also the inability to write an actual work (impossibility), which, exposing itself as the ability to not-write (contingency), produces the ability to write (possibility) the absence of work. For the writer to "return" to the place that never was and that he never left is to transform the *cannot not-write intransitively* into a *can not-write intransitively* by which one *can not-write* and thus *can write*. But does this "can write" imply a form of *transitive* or a form of *intransitive* writing? What are we to understand by an *ability* to write the *absence* of work? The absence of work appears to indicate an altogether different "literary future" in which *jouissance* would not be the exclusion that grounds the law of the signifier (the literary paradigm). Rather, it would indicate the interruption of thetic Being and as such the very exposition of positing by which a different writing becomes possible.

Threshold

The paradigm of writerly necessity constitutes a subject who cannot not-write intransitively. This paradigm delimits a space in which a limited number of positions are possible between the Subject and language. My concern in this second part has been with questions around the meaning of the "death of the Subject" and with how this "death" emerges as the very "essence" of the Subject that must erase itself. I propose now to retrace this emergence of the death of the Subject in order to elucidate how this emergence manifests itself as the question whether this "death" is the negativity of the Subject's dialectic or the interruption of thetic Being.

1. *The paradigm of writerly necessity emerges between the Subject and language.* Foucault shows how "man" and "language" emerge in the modern age as a relation between the Subject and intransitivity. Blanchot in turn shows how an act of writing emerges between the modalities of necessity (cannot not-write) and contingency (can not-write). For the subject who cannot not-write, the essence of "man" is nothing but the necessity to write literature, while the truth of literature is precisely the intransitive language in which the contingency of "essence" manifests itself.

2. *Literature emerges as that which must be thought because it is the thought of contingency.* For Foucault, to think the intransitivity of language is to think the dispersion of the Subject. Insofar as literature instantiates intransitive language, to think literature is to think the contingency of the Subject. Literature is a "counter-discourse" because it is a discourse that emerges within the modern constellation between the Subject and language and at the same time exposes the possible disappearance of this constellation.

3. *Literature and madness are non-dialectical experiences.* In the paradigm of writerly necessity, the truth of literature emerges as the absence of work since the subject cannot not-write intransitively. For Foucault, literature and madness are therefore both experiences at the limit of Modernity since madness is itself the absence of work. For Foucault, Hölderlin manifest the link between literature and madness. This understanding of Hölderlin is possible because Hölderlin emerges as a paradigm of writerly necessity.

4. *The paradigm of writerly necessity produces a limited number of subject positions of enunciation.* The Subject who cannot not-write is not a unitary absolute; rather, the paradigm manifests the dispersion of the Subject in different subject positions between the Subject's essence and language as the vanishing of essence. The

subject who cannot not-write literature emerges as: (a) The Subject's essence, thetic Being, in which the subject cannot not-write the absolute work. (b) The death of the Subject in which the essence emerges as an incessant repositing of thetic Being. The subject must write but can never write any (transitive) work; rather, the Subject only affirms its own negativity, its death. (c) The interruption of thetic Being. The subject who cannot not-write intransitively manifests the contingency of the paradigm of writerly necessity and thus the contingency of his own essential necessity to write. This exposition takes place either in the position of "madness" in which the subject is not anymore intelligible within the paradigm of writerly necessity or in the position of "contingency" in which the writer retains the ability to not-write (the absence of work) at the very moment this subject writes.

5. *The paradigm of writerly necessity emerges as the subject who cannot not-desire to write literature.* The subject who cannot not-desire to write desires the very act of writing. This subject emerges in positions that correspond to *man*, *dying*, and *death doubled*: (a) The neurotic subject is the writer who conceals both the fact that writerly necessity is not an essence given "at birth" and that the Subject's truth of literature is the absence of work. This subject hides both his own constitutive lack and the lack of the literary absolute. (b) The perverse subject is the writer who conceals the lack of the literary absolute but exposes his own constitutive lack. For the perverse subject, to write is still to write the absolute work. (c) The psychotic ("mad") subject is the writer who manifests the absence of work as the disappearance of the Subject. But unless this subject appropriates *jouissance* insofar as it is lacking, this subject also excludes himself from the intelligibility of the paradigm of writerly necessity. To appropriate *jouissance* insofar as it is lacking means to expose the double negativity of the paradigm of writerly necessity and thus the contingency of this paradigm.

The paradigm of writerly necessity thus delimits certain positions between the Subject and language. Moreover, even if this paradigm (re)posits thetic Being, it also exposes the interruption of positing and the dispersion of the Subject. But how does this paradigm of writerly necessity constitute the "truth" of literature? What forms of "truth" correlate to the different enunciative positions of the paradigm of writerly necessity? How do the criteria of modern literary criticism emerge within the paradigm of writerly necessity? These questions are the concern in the third part of my archaeology of literary theory.

PART THREE

Literary Criticism

7

The Author (Sincerity)

Sincerity: The Primary Criterion of Literature in the Nineteenth Century

Since the emergence of the literary absolute at the end of the eighteenth century, the paradigm of writerly necessity functions as the condition of literary "truth." But how does writerly necessity constitute the truth of literary criticism? During the last two hundred years, the literary criteria have changed radically from the theme of authenticity and the concept of sincerity to the theme of the death of the author and the thought of intransitivity. Since authenticity implies the sincere author and the thought of intransitivity indicates the death of the author, these themes appear to be mutually exclusive. However, as we shall see, they both instantiate the paradigm of writerly necessity. The question is now how the criterion of sincerity instantiates the paradigm of writerly necessity as its condition.

In *The Mirror and the Lamp* (1953), M. H. Abrams argues that the focus of literary criticism radically changes at the beginning of the nineteenth century, "from imitation to expression."[1] This turn around 1800 means that poetry ceases to be thought in terms of an imitation of nature, as a mirror of the "world," and begins to be viewed as the expression of nature, that is to say, as the voice of the poet's "essence." As I. A. Richards writes, "Thus to be sincere is to act, feel and think in accordance with 'one's true nature,' and to be insincere is to act, feel or think in a contrary manner."[2] This turn is a fundamental shift in the very conditions of literary criticism, which moves away from a neoclassical rhetoric so as to focus on poetic authenticity. Abrams shows how the notion of *sincerity* as the apogee of expressive poetics "began in the early nineteenth century its career as the primary criterion, if not the *sine qua non*, of excellence in poetry."[3] From the beginning of the nineteenth century, the truth of poetry is no longer imitation but expression:

The first test any poem must pass is no longer, "Is it true to nature?" or "Is it appropriate to the requirements either of the best judges or the generality of mankind?" but a criterion looking in a different direction; namely "Is it sincere? Is it genuine? Does it match the intention, the feeling, and the actual state of mind of the poet while composing?"[4]

The externalization of the Subject's essential interiority means that, as Abrams notes, the poet *ex-presses* himself, in the etymological sense from Latin, "to press out," *ex-* meaning "out" and *pressāre* meaning "to press." Abrams's analysis of this expressive poetics concerns a variety of literary theorists: "We may notice that there are a limited number of assertions about poetry which turn up so persistently [in the nineteenth century], although in very different theoretical frames, that they may perhaps be called *the* romantic complex of ideas about poetry."[5] The core of this romantic complex consists, on the one hand, in an understanding of the "born poet" as "distinguished from other men particularly by his inheritance of an intense sensibility and a susceptibility to passion"[6] and, on the other hand, in the understanding of poetry as the genuine "expression or overflow of feeling."[7] For Abrams, an exemplary instance of this expressive poetics is John Stuart Mill's two essays from 1833: "What is Poetry?" and "The Two Kinds of Poetry."[8]

For Mill, the word "poetry" denotes the concept of literature insofar as poetry is "something which may exist in what is called prose as well as in verse."[9] In "What is Poetry?," Mill understands poetry to emerge not only as the essence of art as such but also as the mark of a fulfilled life: "To the mind, poetry is either nothing, or it is the better part of all art whatever, and of real life too."[10] Mill's concern is not to produce a new definition of poetry but to attempt "to clear up to them [mankind] the conception which they already attach to it [poetry]."[11] Mill is thus concerned with providing the *principle* of poetry that already guides the "actual employment of the term."[12] For Mill, the truth of poetry is to imitate the human Subject: "The truth of poetry is to paint the human soul truly."[13] This imitation is thus not a classical poetics in which poetry is the imitation of the external world but a romantic poetics in which poetry is the true expression of the human soul. For Mill, poetry is pure expression, an "act of utterance,"[14] which is not a means to an end but an end in itself. Poetry is not that which is said but the very act of enunciation situated within the Subject: "Poetry is not in the object itself, ... but in the [poet's] state of mind."[15]

Since Mill understands poetry as nothing but the pure act of sincere expression, everyone can in fact speak poetically. In "The Two Kinds of Poetry," Mill thus proposes, "All persons, even the most unimaginative, in moments of strong emotion, speak poetry."[16] But Mill nevertheless distinguishes between the subjects who are poets "by nature" and the subjects who are poets by "culture."[17] The natural poet has a constitution fit for poetry, but whereas this disposition is a condition for writing supreme poetry, it is not a *sufficient* condition. It only means that a "poetic aspect" determines the horizon within which objects emerges for the poet: "The poet of culture sees his object in prose, and describes it in poetry; the poet of nature actually sees it in poetry."[18] For this natural poet, poetry "is Feeling itself, employing Thought only as the medium of its utterance."[19] For this poet, feeling is nothing but the sincere act of enunciation, which must be expressed in a work but can never be identified with this object.

Poetry consists in the sincere strong emotion, which is not conveyed in the thoughtful propositions of a work but is only the very act of expression. This expression is thus sincere because the very *act* of expression testifies to the born poet's genuine need to express himself according to his "nature" as a poet. For the poet, *to be* sincere means to present oneself truthfully, which is also to say that the most sincere poet is the subject who must be nothing but a poet, the born poet, who by definition cannot not-express himself. For Mill, accordingly, "the poetic temperament" is constituted not by the subject who "wills to be" poetical but by the subject who "cannot help it."[20] For Mill, in opposition to the natural poet, the poet by culture ("Wordsworth") is the subject who can not-write and who appears to be able to stop writing poetry: "Did he [Wordsworth] will to dismiss poetry, he need never again, it might almost seem, have a poetical thought. He never seems *possessed* by a feeling; no emotion seems ever so strong as to have entire sway, for the time being, over the current of his thoughts."[21]

The sincerity of the act of writing thus lies in the issue that the writer must write. But this does not mean that the literary criticism of the nineteenth century neglects that which is expressed; rather, what is notable is that, whereas the actual expressed changes during the nineteenth century, the *act* of the sincere expression remains unquestioned. The paradigm of writerly necessity emerges in the writer's sincere need to express the poetic "soul," and this very act of enunciation remains widely unthought in Anglo-American literary criticism until the beginning of the twentieth century.

New Criticism: The Transposition of the Criterion of Sincerity

New Criticism dominated Anglo-American literary criticism during the first half of the twentieth century. Early figures that gave rise to this tradition are the English literary critics I. A. Richards (*Practical Criticism*, 1929) and William Empson (*Seven Types of Ambiguity*, 1930), but the "movement" received its name from the American critic John Crowe Ransom's book entitled *The New Criticism* (1941). The literary critics subsumed under the name *New Criticism* establish literature as a linguistic object that cannot be evaluated with reference to the author's intentions. Significant figures associated with this movement are also the American critics Cleanth Brooks, William K. Wimsatt, and Monroe C. Beardsley. My concern now is how the paradigm of writerly necessity emerges as the condition of New Criticism.

In their seminal essay "The Intentional Fallacy" (1946), Wimsatt and Beardsley argue that the "intention of the author is neither available nor desirable as a standard for judging the success of a work of literary art."[22] In the essay "The Affective Fallacy" (1949), they further reject a standard of criticism that relies on the "the psychological *causes* of the poem."[23] The criterion of the literary object cannot lie in an external source since a poem belongs neither to the authority of the author nor the reader but is "embodied in language."[24] In the cases in which external sources are relied upon, the concept of sincerity emerges as a criterion of critical evaluation. For the affective critic, the "sincerity of the critic becomes an issue, as for the intentionalist the sincerity of the poet."[25] But, for Wimsatt and Beardsley, the judgment on poetry can only depend on the unity of the literary work in which the positing of the work coincides with the posited propositions: "A poem can *be* only through its *meaning*—since its medium is words—yet it *is*, simply *is*, in the sense that we have no excuse for inquiring what part is intended or meant."[26] The criterion of the true literary work is that "all or most of what is said or implied [in a work] is relevant."[27] As Wimsatt writes in *The Verbal Icon*, the critic should search for the criterion of the poem as a "verbal object"[28] in the "unity and wholeness of a poem,"[29] which itself is nothing but "a fullness of actually presented meaning."[30] New Criticism thus decisively installs the literary work as the systematic unity of the Subject.

It is significant however that Wimsatt and Beardsley reject the possibility of equating "the passwords of the intentional school"[31] such as sincerity and authenticity with other "more precise axiological terms"[32] of evaluation such as integrity and unity. Insofar as the concept of "sincerity" implies that the work is evaluated from the perspective of the external sources (the author or the reader), this claim remains a valid assessment; however, this proposition also conceals the intrinsic relation between sincerity and the literary criterion of the unity of the work in literary criticism. I. A. Richards's *Practical Criticism* (1929) is a seminal source for the understanding of the unity of the literary work in New Criticism; however, when Richards critically examines the concept of sincerity as the expression of an author, he also explicitly transposes the concept of sincerity into the criterion of the unity of the literary work.[33] In his study, Richards documents that sincerity is still an unthought criterion of poetry for young literary students at the beginning of the twentieth century: "'Sincere' is a great favourite in its primitive unanalysed condition—we have the poem up before us and apply the test."[34] For Richards, this concept of sincerity still remains, moreover, the ultimate criterion of poetry: "Whatever it [sincerity] is, it is the quality we most insistently require in poetry. It is also the quality we most need as critics."[35] But the criterion entails an "uncomfortable problem" since it is "a word much used in criticism, but not often with any precise definition of its meaning."[36] Richards comes to the conclusion that sincerity "is obedience to that tendency which 'seeks' a more perfect order within the mind."[37] Sincerity is here not so much the sincere expression of an author as the general requirement of the systematic unity of the literary work.

For Wimsatt and Beardsley, Cleanth Brooks's criticism is an exemplary form of what is now called New Criticism.[38] In *Modern Poetry and the Tradition* (1939), Brooks however redirects the concept of sincerity in a way similar to Richards's transposition. Brooks thus opposes the notion of sincerity as the expression of the author's intention that excludes artificial "wit" only to introduce the concept of sincerity as the mark of the poem's integrity: "The test of his [the poet's] sincerity is to be measured by the integrity of tone which the poem achieves."[39] In opposition to the classic concept of sincerity in the expressive poetics, Brooks understands sincerity as a harmonious unity: "Sincerity ... reveals itself as an unwillingness to ignore the complexity of experience. The poet attempts to fuse the conflicting elements in a harmonious whole."[40]

Wimsatt and Beardsley are also content with T. S. Eliot's essay "Tradition and the Individual Talent" (1919), which shows "the right view of author psychology."[41] Eliot here proposes that the poet has no "'personality' to express";[42] rather, the impersonal work is itself "an expression of *significant* emotion, emotion which has its life in the poem and not in the history of the poet."[43] Eliot's literary criterion is thus not the author's sincere expression, but his valuation of expression of the literary work still entails the (sincere) "pressure" that manifests itself in the etymological sense of expression: "For it is not the 'greatness', the intensity, of the emotions, the components, but the intensity of the artistic process, the pressure, so to speak, under which the fusion takes place, that counts."[44]

In New Criticism, the sincere expression has not vanished as a criterion but is only displaced from the poet to the process of the harmonious work itself. The paradigm of writerly necessity emerges here as the expressive operation of the literary work.[45] For the New Critics, the work is the verbal object that installs itself as the linguistic unity of thetic Being. For Brooks, as he writes in *The Well Wrought Urn* (1947), this object is "a positive unity, not a negative; it represents not a residue but an achieved harmony."[46] This is the reason why Brooks insists that the so-called "heresy of paraphrase" distorts "the relation of the poem to its 'truth.' "[47] Insofar as the paraphrase of a literary work is mistaken for "what the poem *really* says,"[48] such a paraphrase must necessarily do "violence to the internal order of the poem itself."[49] But this literary unity thus retains the criterion of sincerity insofar as this concept is transposed from the external sources of the author and the reader into the absolute presence of the work itself. The paradigm of writerly necessity manifests itself as the verbal expression of the literary object, which for New Criticism constitutes the "truth" of literature.

8

The Death of the Author (Intransitivity)

From Sincerity to Intransitivity

In 1966 an international and interdisciplinary conference took place at the Johns Hopkins University that would radically change the environment of Anglo-American literary criticism. The speakers included such figures as Roland Barthes, Jean Hyppolite, Jacques Lacan, and Jacques Derrida who here presented the seminal "Structure, Sign, and Play in the Discourse of the Human Sciences" ("La Structure, le signe et le jeu dans le discours des sciences humaines"), which François Cusset notes became "the outstanding event of the conference."[1] Richard Macksey and Eugenio Donato, both professors at Johns Hopkins, organized the conference that was to introduce structuralism in the United States (in 1966 the translation of Claude Lévi-Strauss's *La Pensée sauvage* and a double issue of *Yale French Studies* devoted to structuralism also appeared).[2] But, rather than an introduction to structuralism, especially Derrida's paper was "a criticism of structuralism,"[3] as Derrida noted in the discussion with Hyppolite following this paper. The event marks the turn in the 1960s away from the approach to texts as structures to the thinking of the dispersion and dissemination of *texts*. This event will also mark the beginning of a turn in American literary criticism insofar as Derrida here met the literary critic Paul de Man who was later to become the major figure of "deconstructionism" in America.[4]

In 1967, a year after the conference at Johns Hopkins, Barthes's essay "The Death of the Author" appeared in an English translation by Richard Howard in the multimedia magazine of arts, *Aspen* (nos 5–6, 1967). The French version, "La Mort de l'auteur," was published the year after in the French magazine *Manteia* (no. 5, 1968). My concern here is how the paradigm of writerly necessity constitutes the "death" (intransitivity) of the author as the truth of literature. Barthes's seminal essay testifies to the shift in the twentieth century against the criterion of sincerity and away from a literary criticism that makes it its task to discover "the Author (or its hypostases: society, history, psyché, liberty) beneath the work."[5] Barthes instead emphasizes the truth of language as a signifying chain in which every signifier only refers to another signifier: "Did he [the writer] wish to *express himself*, he ought at least to know that the inner 'thing' he thinks to 'translate' is itself only a ready-formed dictionary, its word only explainable through other words, and so on indefinitely."[6] The theme of the death of the author marks the change in literary criticism from the "Subject" to "language" insofar as the focus turns from the expression of a supposed interiority to a radical exteriority.

For Barthes, the author is nothing but the very act of writing, which correlates to the linguistic category of the "shifter" developed by Roman Jakobson in the essay "Shifters, Verbal Categories, and the Russian Verb" (1957). According to Jakobson, the shifter can only be defined with reference to the instance of the discourse in which it emerges. Jakobson points to the personal pronoun as an exemplary shifter: "*I* means the person uttering *I*."[7] The shifter "I" is thus an empty sign insofar as it only obtains its meaning in a particular discourse with reference to the utterance of the subject "I." The shifter does not *represent* the subject; rather, in the French linguist Émile Benveniste's terms, it is an *indicator* of utterance.[8] In terms of the shifter, it is not a question of that which is said but of the very *act* of enunciation since the shifter refers to nothing but its own taking place. For Barthes, the author is in the position of the shifter, which means that "the author is absent"[9] since this position is "never more than the instance writing, just as *I* is nothing other than the instance saying *I*."[10] The author is nothing substantial but only the very act of writing in which language appears only to disappear.

In the earlier essay "Authors and Writers" ("Écrivains et écrivants," 1960), available in the collection *Essais critiques* (1964),[11] Barthes had already implicitly linked this intransitive act of writing to the writer who cannot not-write literature. Barthes here understands "the very substance of this literary discourse [from the sixteenth to the nineteenth century in France]"[12] to be linked to the "author" (*l'écrivain*) who "essentialize[s] himself"[13] in language. For the author, language constitutes his very being, which means that this subject must write intransitively:

Language [*La parole*] is neither an instrument nor a vehicle: it is a structure, as we increasingly suspect; but the author [*l'écrivain*] is the only man, by definition, to lose his own structure and that of the world in the structure of language. Yet this language is an (infinitely) labored substance; it is a little like a superlanguage—reality is never anything but a pretext for it (for the author, *to write* [écrire] is an intransitive verb).[14]

For this subject whose structure *is* language, life is at stake in the intransitive verb "to write." Barthes notes, "This is why so few authors renounce writing, for that is literally to kill themselves, to die to the being they have chosen; and if there are such authors, their silence echoes like an inexplicable conversion (Rimbaud)."[15] For Barthes, the truth of literature emerges as the subject who cannot not-write intransitively. The paradigm of writerly necessity arises as the author's death: It becomes the criterion of intransitivity, which also manifests itself in certain linguistic[16] and deconstructive readings.[17]

In "What Is an Author?" ("Qu'est-ce qu'un auteur?"), first published in 1969 in *Bulletin de la Société Française de Philosophie*,[18] Foucault interrogates this space produced by the death of the author. This death appears in the modern age as the incessant reactualization of the absence of work. Foucault notes that the disappearance of the author "has been a constantly recurring event" (*AM*, 209), which means that it is not enough "to repeat the empty affirmation that the author has disappeared" (*AM*, 209). Rather, we must "watch for the openings this disappearance uncovers" (*AM*, 209). The question is thus to examine and delimit the space of the author's death, which is the position of the writer who cannot not-write literature.

It is here not simply that the author apparently is no longer a hindrance for the proliferation of possibilities of meaning in texts. Several commentators understand the author's death to signify the possibility of such a multiplication of sense. Séan Burke is here exemplary:

> No longer reduced to a "single message," the text [Barthes's "The Death of the Author"] is opened to an unlimited variety of interpretations. It becomes, in short, irresponsible, a ceaseless braiding of differences in which any sense of "the truth of the text," its original meaning in the world, is overrun by untrammeled significative possibilities. This is the message—indeed the "single message"—of "The Death of the Author."[19]

It is a fact that Barthes and Foucault value the proliferation of meaning. Barthes states, "To give a text an Author is to impose a limit on that text, to furnish it with a final signified, to close the writing."[20] Foucault writes that the author is "the ideological figure by which one marks the manner in which we fear the proliferation of meaning" (*AM*, 222). However, the "meaning" of the author's death is not simply the proliferation of meaning but the loss of meaning, that is, the interruption of thetic Being, which means that every positing of sense is also the interruption of sense. Barthes explicitly writes that writing only posits meaning to evaporate meaning: "Writing ceaselessly posits meaning ceaselessly to evaporate it, carrying out a systematic exemption of meaning."[21] Foucault identifies writing not as an "interiority," as the self-reference of linguistic Subjectivity, but as an "unfolded exteriority" (*AM*, 206), as the disappearance of the Subject. The only reason why there can be a "proliferation of meaning" is because the Subject not only interrupts its own positing but also constantly (re)posits itself. The event of the author's death indicates however the possibility of a pure interruption of thetic Being in which there is not the proliferation of meaning but the withdrawal of meaning. But the "sense" of this withdrawal indeed remains an unthought of literature, which (literary) thought is still to think. Foucault identifies that a transition takes place in the modern age from the work as the author's expression to the work as the recurrent disappearance of the subject who writes intransitively:

> First of all, we can say that today's writing has freed itself from the theme of expression. ... In writing, the point is not to manifest or exalt the act of writing, nor is it to pin a subject within language; it is, rather, a question of creating a space into which the writing subject constantly disappears. ... Writing has become linked to sacrifice, even to the sacrifice of life: it is now a voluntary effacement that does not need to be represented in books, since it is brought about in the writer's very existence. (*AM*, 206)

For Foucault, the truth of literature is neither the author's expression nor the interior self-reference of an act of writing; rather, the subject who writes literature risks his life in writing since literature is the exterior manifestation of the interruption of the Subject. Foucault is thus aware that literary writing puts the writer's very life into question; however, Foucault's propositions regarding a "voluntary" effacement at the same time testifies to the forgetting of the paradigm of writerly necessity that conceals itself as the relation between the Subject and language. The reason why the Subject constantly disappears in writing is thus that the writer cannot not-write since the "essence" that this subject must express is nothing but the very interruption of any essence. The truth of literature emerges as the interruption of the Subject because the writer must write intransitively.

The Question of the Author's Death

The question is how we are to understand the death of the author. What does this death indicate? In order to address this question, I will now turn to Giorgio Agamben's essay "The Author as Gesture" ("L'autore come gesto," 2005), which is written as a response to Foucault's "What Is an Author?" In this essay, Agamben addresses the space of the absence of the author. He writes, "The author is not dead, but to position oneself as an author means occupying the place of a 'dead man.' An author-subject does exist, and yet he is attested to only through the traces of his absence."[22] Agamben poses the question: "What does it mean for an individual to occupy the place of a dead man, to leave his own traces in an empty place?"[23] According to Agamben, for the author to occupy this place means that "the author is present in the text only as a gesture that makes expression possible precisely by establishing a central emptiness within this expression."[24] The gesture is the condition of possibility of expression since this gesture produces a void within the expression. But how are we to understand this emptiness produced by the author as a gesture? How does this void function as the condition of possibility of expression?

In *Means without End* (*Mezzi senza fine*, 1996), Agamben understands the gesture as an "ethical" dimension of the being-in-language: "The gesture is, in this sense, communication of a communicability. It has precisely nothing to say because what it shows is the being-in-language of human beings as pure mediality."[25] The gesture is the pure transparency of being-in-language in which language is not the communication of this or that message but the communication of the very taking place of language. The gesture is "neither biographic experience nor impersonal event"[26] but takes place in the "intersection between life and art."[27] This proposition corresponds to Agamben's concept of gesture in "The Author as Gesture" in which gesture is understood as the "taking place"[28] of the poem, which is a place "neither in the text nor in the author (nor in the reader): it is in the gesture through which the author and reader put themselves into play in the text and, at the same time, are infinitely withdrawn from it."[29]

The gesture, in Agamben's schema, is thus the place of the author's death that lies at the intersection of life and art. It is the pure transparency of being-in-language.[30] But how are we to understand this being-in-language? In *Language and Death* (*Il linguaggio e la morte*, 1982), Agamben delimits the place and structure of negativity that can be understood to constitute the emptiness of the author's gesture. With reference to Hölderlin, Hegel, and Schelling's "System-Programme," Agamben is concerned with the possibility of a form of life ("ethics") that is not grounded in negativity: "So if truly, as we read in the opening pages of the *Oldest Systematic Program of German Idealism*, in the future all metaphysics must collapse into ethics, the very meaning of this 'collapse' remains, for us, the most difficult thing to construe" (*LD*, xiii). *Language and Death* concerns the connection between "the 'faculty' for language and the 'faculty' for death, inasmuch as they open for humanity the most proper dwelling place, reveal and disclose this same dwelling place as always already permeated by and founded in negativity" (*LD*, xii). Agamben's concern is to interrogate the relation of language and death in order to make visible how a form of life can be possible, which does not have its foundation in negativity.

Agamben addresses the place of negativity in Western metaphysics by focusing on Hegel's investigation of *das Diese nehmen* (taking-the-*This*) in the *Phenomenology* (*Phänomenologie des Geistes*, 1807) and Heidegger's analysis of *Dasein* (Being-the-*there*) in *Being and Time* (*Sein und Zeit*, 1927).

Agamben examines how the shifters *Diese* (this) and *Da* (there) introduce living beings into the negativity of the act of enunciation. Agamben writes,

> This negativity is grounded in the reference that the shifters *Da* and *Diese* make to the pure taking place of language, and distinct from that which, in this taking place, is formulated in linguistic propositions. This dimension [i.e. the negativity of the shifter]—which coincides with the concept of utterance in modern linguistics, but which, throughout the history of metaphysics, has always constituted the field of meaning of the word *being* [essere]—finds it[s] final foundation in a Voice. Every shifter is structured like a Voice. However, the Voice presupposed here is defined through a double negativity. On the one hand, it is in fact identified only as a removed voice, as a having-been of the natural *phoné*, and this removal constitutes the originary articulation (*arthron*, *gramma*) in which the passage from *phoné* to *logos* is carried out, from the living being to language. On the other hand, this Voice cannot be *spoken* by the discourse of which it *shows* the originary taking place. (*LD*, 84/104)

For Agamben, the shifter as the taking place of language corresponds to the understanding of thetic Being within the history of metaphysics. The shifter is not this or that linguistic expression but the very act of positing by which language takes place as an expression of something. The Being of metaphysics is not this or that being but the very positing of Being by which beings take place as this or that being. Agamben proposes that the linguistic category of the shifter and the metaphysical category of (thetic) Being both correlate to the structure of "Voice," which arises through a double negativity. On the one hand, this "Voice" is capitalized in order to distinguish it from the "voice" that is removed in order for language to take place. On the other hand, this taking place of the "Voice" never arrives in propositional discourse insofar as it only indicates itself as the foundation of such discourse. Discourse is thus possible only because the "Voice" is structured as a having-been "voice" that is nothing but negativity as such, and this negativity then produces the "Voice" as the foundation of discourse. But this foundation can thus never be expressed in this or that proposition of discourse since it is the very condition of possibility of discourse, which can indicate this condition only through the linguistic categories of shifters.[31]

There is here a double negativity, which correlates to the overlap of the two lacks that makes up the paradigmatic production of writerly necessity as the essence of a subject constituted by the literary absolute. The dialectical negativity produces the positing of the "absolute" condition, which was never there before its retroactive emergence as condition. Discourse only takes place through exclusion, but this exclusion did not take place before its emergence as a *having-been removed*. It is thus the retroactive emergence of discourse, which produces the very exclusion by which it is itself constituted.

Moreover, insofar as this exclusion is itself fabricated in this emergence *as* always already excluded, this exclusion of "voice" indicates the contingency of the dialectical production. My concern is now to address this contingency of the dialectic.

Life without Negation

Agamben focuses on this contingency of the dialectic. The question is whether it is possible to think being-in-language not as the negative production of Voice as the already having-been of voice but as the appropriation of the contingent negativity of language:

> What is a language without Voice, a word that is not grounded in any meaning? This is something that we must still learn to think. But with the disappearance of the Voice, that "essential relation" between language and death that dominates the history of metaphysics must also disappear. Man, as a speaking being, is no longer necessarily the mortal, he who has the "faculty for death" and is reaffirmed by death; nor, as a dying being, is he necessarily the speaker, he who has the "faculty for language" and is reaffirmed by this. To exist in language without being called there by any Voice, simply to die without being called by death, is, perhaps, the most abysmal experience; but this is precisely, for man, also his most *habitual* experience, his *ethos*, his dwelling, always already presented in the history of metaphysics as demonically divided into the living and language, nature and culture, ethics and logic, and therefore only attainable in the negative articulation of a Voice. (*LD*, 95–6)

This being-in-language in which language and death are not intrinsically linked is that which Agamben calls the "communication of a communicability" that, insofar as it arises as the intersection of art and life, is the subject position of the author *as* gesture. This position is an abyssal existence in language in which pure potentiality is preserved in life *as* potentiality, insofar as the contingency of this or that actualization is transparent. In terms of the paradigm of writerly necessity, this author is thus a subject who, having completed the dialectical movement produced by writerly necessity from the Subject to the death of the Subject, emerges from this death in the position of contingency in which it is possible to write the absence of work. For the author as gesture, it is possible to write not because of an inability to not-write but because writing constitutes a contingent habitual practice in which the necessity to write has become visible in its "could not be." This gesture of the author is thus a gesture exterior to the paradigm of writerly necessity, a gesture, which makes this paradigm transparent by exhibiting its contingency.

Insofar as the gesture is nothing but contingency itself, it manifests itself as the interruption of the dialectic of thetic Being. Agamben notes that Rilke's proposition from the eighth *Duino Elegy* regarding a *Nirgends ohne Nicht* (a "nowhere without no") could indicate "a negativity that is more originary than the not of the dialectic" (*LD*, 57). In *The Space of Literature*, Blanchot had already addressed this *Nirgends ohne Nicht* and a similar statement from a letter (January 6, 1923) in which Rilke proposes to read the word "death" without negation. As we have seen, Blanchot conceives this possibility of pure (affirmative) negativity as the non-dialectical interruption of speculative truth. Insofar as this pure interruption is withdrawn from the dialectical self-relating negativity, it constitutes for Blanchot the experience of art. I quote from *The Space of Literature*:

> To read the word death *without* negation is to withdraw from it the cutting edge of decision and the power to negate; it is to cut oneself off from possibility and the true, but also from death as true event. It is to surrender to the indistinct and the undetermined, to the emptiness anterior to events, where the end has all the heaviness of starting over. This experience is the experience of art. (*SL*, 242)

This pure negativity discloses the literary interruption as a suspension of the paradigmatic dialectic of literature. The interruption here is not negativity at work in the production of writerly necessity but the interruption of this production insofar as it is without negation.[32] For Agamben, it is the position of the author as gesture in which the relation between life and art, biography and impersonal event, becomes transparent. On the one hand, from the point of view of the subject who writes literature (the biographical experience), writerly necessity is that which always already constitutes the writer *as* subject. Writerly necessity emerges as the impossible limit of every possibility of the literary life insofar as it makes this life possible. On the other hand, from the perspective of the impossible object of literature (the impersonal event), the paradigm of writerly necessity is that which constitutes literary life but itself first emerges *as* condition retroactively as the "essence" of the born writer. To expose this double negativity, the contingency of the paradigm, is to approach the space of inoperativity.

9

The Politics of a priori Poetry

The Poetized: Life and Literature

The paradigm of writerly necessity constitutes a subject who cannot not-write literature, which means that this subject's very life is at risk in literary writing. I have argued that the paradigm of writerly necessity constitutes the truth of literature for literary criticism. Writerly necessity is the unthought of literary discourse precisely because it first makes possible the criteria of this discourse: from the thinking of the author's sincere expression and the absolute presence of the work to the emergence of the death of the author and the intransitivity of language.

What is noticeable is that in all these criteria the relation between literature and life emerges as the primary question of literary criticism. On the one hand, since life and writing coincide in this paradigm, it is possible to think of literature as the expression of biographical, social, or historical life, and it is possible to conceive the literary work as itself a form of living expression. On the other hand, it is possible to think of literature as intransitive language in which literature is defined negatively as completely separated from life[1] or to propose that life and literature are indistinct in the being of language.[2] The analysis of the paradigm of writerly necessity manifests that the *relation* between literature and life emerges as the essential question in literary criticism, insofar as the criteria of literature are sincerity and intransitivity. But the paradigm only delimits the space for what it is possible to write and what it is not possible to write insofar as literary criticism itself instantiates the paradigm by maintaining a certain truth with respect to the relation between life and literature.

My concern now will be with how Walter Benjamin's early reading of Hölderlin manifests the relation between literature and life. This will lead me to address how the question of a priori poetry, of intransitive writing, arises as a political question in Benjamin's thought. Benjamin's early essay

"Two Poems by Friedrich Hölderlin" ("Zwei Gedichte von Friedrich Hölderlin," 1914–15) is an attempt to develop a form of literary criticism in which "a judgment [*Urteil*], even if unprovable, can nonetheless be justified" (*SW*, 21/II:1, 108). This evaluation of poetry is to be based on the critical concept of *the poetized* (*das Gedichtete*), which Benjamin understands as a "limit-concept" (*SW*, 21) with respect to poetry and life.[3] I will argue that the novelty of Benjamin's form of literary criticism consists in its innovative instantiation of the paradigm of writerly necessity, which makes it possible for Benjamin to invent "the poetized" as a legitimate criterion of literature. On the one hand, my concern here is to see how the critical concept of the poetized instantiates the paradigm of writerly necessity. But, on the other hand, my focus is on how literature emerges as a political question of writing and reading that which was never written. I understand Benjamin's reading of Hölderlin to be an extraordinary event in the history of the paradigm of writerly necessity insofar it is possible to trace and delimit in his essay how a priori poetry can be grasped as a question of a politics that concerns the interruption of the dialectic. I therefore turn to Benjamin's reading of Hölderlin.

Benjamin proposes that one "could say that life is, in general, the poetized of poems" insofar as life is "not the individual life-mood of the artist [*Lebensstimmung des Künstlers*] but rather a life-context determined by art [*ein durch die Kunst bestimmter Lebenszusammenhang*]" (*SW*, 20/II:1, 107). The concept of the poetized entails that art constitutes life since poetry is a destiny that is moreover the law of Hölderlin's poetry: "We shall pursue life in poetry (*Leben im Gesange*), in the unwavering poetic destiny (*dichterischen Schicksal*) which is the law of Hölderlin's world, on the basis of its context of figures [*Gestaltzusammenhang*]" (*SW*, 26/II:1, 113). For Benjamin, Hölderlin emerges in the position of the born poet whose destiny is literature and Benjamin can therefore understand Hölderlin as a "significant example" in relation to the attempt to show "how the poetized creates the possibility of judging poetry" (*SW*, 20).[4]

Benjamin is however not concerned with this or that poem but with "pure" poetry. Using Kantian terminology, Benjamin understands his commentary on Hölderlin to be a form of "pure aesthetics [*reine Ästhetik*]" (*SW*, 18/II:1, 105),[5] which concerns a priori poetry in which there is thus no actual empirical work. The concept of the poetized concerns literature: "the a priori of the individual poem [*Apriori des einzelnen Gedichts*], that of the poem in general, or even that of other literary genres [*Dichtungsarten*] or of literature in general [*Dichtung überhaupt*]" (*SW*, 21/II:1, 108). For Benjamin, the truth of literature is the intransitive "work" prior to any possible experience of the entity of the work. The poetized is the domain of a priori poetry, which is never manifest in this or that poem since every poem is only a determinate configuration (*Gestalt*) of the poetized:

This sphere, which for every poem has a special configuration [*besondere Gestalt*], is characterised as the poetized [*das Gedichtete*]. In this sphere that peculiar domain containing the truth of the poem [*Wahrheit der Dichtung*] shall be opened up. This "truth," which the most serious artists so insistently claim for their creations, shall be understood as the objectivity [*Gegenständlichkeit*] of their production, as the fulfilment of the artistic task [*künstlerischen Aufgabe*] in each case. "Every work of art has in and of itself an a priori ideal, a necessity for being in the world" (Novalis) [*Jedes Kunstwerk hat ein Ideal a priori, eine Notwendigkeit bei sich, da zu sein*]. (*SW*, 18–19/II:1, 105–6)

Benjamin conceives the poetized as the domain for the "truth of the poem." He relates this truth to a proposition by Novalis, which Benjamin in his later dissertation on Romanticism will say is "in complete agreement" with a question that Ludovico poses in Schlegel's *Dialogue on Poetry* (1800, *Das Gespräch über die Poesie*): "Do you by chance consider it impossible to construct future poems a priori?" (*SW*, 158).[6] The literary truth that emerges in the domain of the poetized is literature as a priori poetry. But what is in question in this "truth"?

In a letter written by Benjamin to Martin Buber (July 1916) from the same period as his essay on Hölderlin (1914–15), Benjamin considers the appropriate form of journal writing to be a form of "objective" (*sachliche*) writing, which he finds in the journal of the Early German Romantics, the *Athenaeum*: "The only thing at issue is objective writing. Whether a journal will achieve it cannot be humanly foreseen, and probably not many journals have done so. But I am thinking of the *Athenaeum*."[7] For Benjamin, the *Athenaeum* manifests an objective writing that he understands in the letter as a "sober manner of writing [*nüchternen Schreibart*],"[8] which is also how he characterizes Hölderlin's later works in the essay "Two Poems by Friedrich Hölderlin" (see *SW*, 35). This sober writing consists not in "the transmission of [propositional] content"[9] but in an intransitive manner that is political because it concerns that which was refused and never said:

My concept of objective and, at the same time, highly political style and writing [*hochpolitischen Stils und Schreibens*] is this: to awaken interest in what was denied to the word [*hinzuführen auf das dem Wort versagte*]; only where this sphere of speechlessness [*Sphäre des Wortlosen*] reveals itself in unutterably pure night [*unsagbar reiner Nacht*] can the magic spark leap between the word and the motivating deed, where the unity of these two equally real entities resides. Only the intensive aiming of words into the core of intrinsic silence [*Verstummens*] is truly effective. I do not believe that there is any place where the word would be more distant from the divine [*Göttlichen*] than in "real" action. Thus, too, it is incapable of leading into the divine in any way other than through itself and its own purity.[10]

The objective writing is a pure writing in which it is not possible to distinguish between the word and the deed since the political act is to manifest that which was not said in what was said.[11] The sober form of writing is an intransitive writing that corresponds to the a priori poetry, which Benjamin aims to grasp with the concept of the poetized. This concept also concerns a political task. For Benjamin, the poetized is thus a limit-concept in relation to poetry since the poetized is "the potential existence of those [determinations] that are effectively present in the poem and others [… *das potentielle Dasein derjenigen, die im Gedicht aktuell vorhanden sind und andrer*]" (*SW*, 19/ II:1, 106; translation modified). The poetized is not only the potentiality of that which is actualized in this or that poem but also potentiality of "others." In order to grasp the truth of the actual poem, the poetized must dispose of other possible manifestations of itself: "In order to lead us to this highest degree of determination in the poem, the poetized must disregard [*Absehen*] certain determinations" (*SW*, 19/II:1, 106). It is necessary to look away from other possibilities; however, insofar as the poetized is not only the potentiality of this or that poem but also of "others," it is furthermore necessary to look away from the particular poem in order to grasp the poetized.[12] Benjamin's essay materializes itself within this tension of reading the actual poems in order to grasp the poetized and aiming to grasp the poetized in which the truth of literature is not the actual configuration (*Gestalt*) but a priori poetry. For Benjamin, the disclosure of a priori poetry concerns the political task of that which was never written, of that which never materialized itself in words but manifests itself in the actual poems as their truth. For Benjamin, literary criticism thus concerns the poetic destiny, which discloses the artistic task as a political task.

The Question of a priori Poetry

The question is then how the artistic task is a political task of reading and writing the intransitive work. In Benjamin's commentary, "The poetized will come to light as the precondition of the poem, as its inner form, as artistic task" (*SW*, 20). Benjamin will derive the poetized through an "aesthetic commentary" (*SW*, 18) on Hölderlin's "The Poet's Courage" ("Dichtermut") and "Timidity" ("Blödigkeit"), which are understood as two actual manifestations of the poetized. For Benjamin, the question is to what extent art determines life in the two versions in such a way that the truth of literature emerges as a priori poetry.

The main difference between the two manifestations is "a dislocation of the mythological" (*SW*, 28), which takes place in the second version

("Timidity"). In the first version ("The Poet's Courage"), the mythological sun god dissolves the figure of the poet and thereby obscures the concept of the poetized, which is reduced to partaking in the governing force of Greek mythology: "*ananke* reigns" (*SW*, 22), the goddess of destiny and necessity. "The Poet's Courage" (first version) concerns a destiny (*Schicksal*) that Benjamin understands to be "the death of the poet" (*SW*, 22); however, this death does not "flow out of a pure, structured context" (*SW*, 23), that is, the life context determined by art. For Benjamin, the first version bears witness to the fact that "the poetic law [*das dichterische Gesetz*] has not yet fulfilled itself in this Hölderlinian world" (*SW*, 24/II:1, 111). In "The Poet's Courage," destiny is not purely *literary* destiny; rather, the necessity is more grounded in Greek mythology than in the mythic unfolding of the poetized. In the second version, on the contrary, the "gods and the living are bound together in the destiny of the poet by ties of iron" (*SW*, 24). "Timidity" (second version) is a configuration of the poetized that transcends traditional Greek mythology since the poet and the people (*Volk*) are included in the poetic destiny (see *SW*, 28).

My question is not *whether* Benjamin's novel form of literary criticism can be "justified"; rather, I am concerned with the fact that Benjamin coins the critical concept of the poetized in order to write a form of literary criticism that should be able to be justified and that the concept of the poetized instantiates the paradigm of writerly necessity. In Benjamin's criticism, the truth of literature emerges as the poet's necessity to write intransitively insofar as the poetized is the life determined by art and art is a priori poetry. For Benjamin, sober writing is by definition a political practice. This practice of writing transforms the modalities of being: It is an intransitive writing that is the possibility of a pure passivity in which that which was never written retains itself *as* possibility.

In Benjamin's later theses on history written in 1940, the thought of the "others" that never materialize themselves into actual poems can be understood to emerge in the context of Benjamin's thinking of history as the "irretrievable image of the past which threatens to disappear in any present that does not recognize itself as intended in that image."[13] But a priori poetry is thus a pure image that was never transmitted from the past to the present as the manifestation of an actual work. In his theses on history, Benjamin writes that the "historical materialist" must dissociate himself from the "process of transmission as far as possible" since "a document is never free of barbarism, so barbarism taints the manner in which it was transmitted from one hand to another."[14] The early Benjamin investigates the poetized in order to investigate the "truth" of poetry as that which is *not* transmitted in what is transmitted. This truth is intransitive writing that by definition can never materialize itself in a work as an object given for a subject. The truth of literature as a priori poetry is thus something like the "secret index" by which the past is "referred to redemption,"[15] which

Benjamin understands in his theses on history to be "indissolubly" related to "happiness."[16] As Werner Hamacher shows, this happiness is only accessible as that which is already missed and never posited as an actual work.[17] It is such a status of having always already being missed, which means that Benjamin can conceive poetry a priori as a political act of writing. Since a priori poetry never "is," it is never a cultural transmission of barbarism but the intransitive and intransmissible that can only be grasped as lost. But this loss is thus not the loss of something but the loss that emerges *as loss* when poetry actualizes itself as a particular work. The loss of poetry emerges as the possibility of nonactualization at the moment that poetry materializes itself. The political truth of a priori poetry consists in its possibility as an image of the oppressed, of the others, which is excluded as the non-posited spacing in every positing. With the concept of the poetized, Benjamin aims to justify a judgment of the literary work. The criticism of poetry can only be justified if it concerns the intransitive writing as the interruption of positing. This is the intransmissible message that Benjamin transmits to present literary criticism. If it is not to vanish, this message must be recognized by the literary studies of the present.

For the early Benjamin, the most pressing task of future literary criticism was to investigate the poetized in order to make political change possible. My investigation however is concerned with the historical conditions of this political function of literature. The question is not only how to rethink literature as a political tool but also to understand how it is possible for Benjamin to think the truth of literature as a priori poetry. The task is not simply to rethink a politics of poetry but to consider what has made it possible to rethink the relation of poetry to life. Otherwise modern criticism will fail to consider the conditions of possibility of theory itself, which means that any act of resistance risks reiterating the conditions that made this resistance possible in the first place. In order to transform the conditions themselves, it is necessary to make visible what made them historically possible. The paradigm of writerly necessity is effectively that which makes it possible for Benjamin to think literature as a political practice of writing. For Benjamin, Hölderlin emerges as the exemplary poet whose life is determined by poetry and who must write intransitively.[18] In order to think intransitive writing as a political practice, it is thus necessary to make the paradigm of writerly necessity transparent to the present. It will then become possible to begin to think whether a form of intransitive writing can be rethought as a political practice.

Threshold

This archaeology of literary theory concerns not the absolute truth of the criteria of literature but how the notions of "sincerity" and "intransitivity" function as the true criteria of the evaluation of literature. The paradigm of writerly necessity is accordingly the condition of possibility of these criteria; however, these criteria themselves instantiate the paradigm as the horizon for saying something meaningful about the concept of literature. We are now able to retrace how the paradigm of writerly necessity emerges as the horizon for the "truth" of literature:

1. *The concept of "sincerity" emerges in the nineteenth century as the primary criterion of literature.* This criterion signifies literature as the expression of life. The subject (the Author) who cannot not-express himself writes "true" literature. In the twentieth century, the criterion of sincerity is transposed into the formalist truth of literature as the absolute work. This absolute work is not the expression of life but life itself insofar as it is only the "expression" of its fullness of "meaning." The criterion of sincerity thus emerges in the position of the Subject, which correlates to the position of *man* (Blanchot).

2. *The concept of "intransitivity" emerges in the twentieth century as the truth of literature.* This truth manifests itself as the question whether literature is the self-referential interiority of thetic Being or the very linguistic interruption of thetic Being. The death of the author corresponds to the position of *dying* (Blanchot). But, insofar as the truth of literature emerges as unworking, this death (intransitivity) also indicates the suspension of the dialectic of the paradigm of writerly necessity. Literature emerges as the possibility of a "truth" that is different than the speculative truth of the dialectic.

3. *In literary criticism, the paradigm of writerly necessity emerges as the question of the relation between life and writing.* The paradigm is the condition of the possibility to think literature as the sincere expression of life regardless of whether this life is the author's life or the life of the absolute work. It is the condition for thinking literature as separated from life insofar as literature is understood as linguistic intransitivity and life as the substance of the Subject. Moreover, the paradigm of writerly necessity makes it possible to think the co-belonging of life and literature on the level of linguistic being-in-language. These mutually excluding understandings of the relation between literature and life all have the paradigm of writerly necessity as the condition that constitutes the relation between life and writing as the essential literary relation between the subject and the work.

The paradigm of writerly necessity emerges as a subject who cannot not-write intransitively. This paradigm constitutes the horizon for the "truth" of literature, which instantiates itself in the criteria of literary criticism. However, the question remains how we are to understand the concept of *literary criticism*. This question concerns the position "the critic" occupies in relation to the writer who must write and how we are to understand the concept of literature as itself a *critical* concept. The concept of literature thus means that literature is theory itself. How are we to think this proposition? How does literature emerge as criticism?

PART FOUR

Aesthetics

10

Literature in the Age of Criticism

Hegel's Aesthetics: The Romantic Form without Content

For Hegel, "the development of our reason" in modern times means that we have moved "beyond the stage at which art is the supreme mode of our knowledge of the Absolute. The peculiar nature of artistic production and of works of art no longer fills our highest need" (*A*, 10). After the stage of Antiquity, art cannot anymore present the absolute, and therefore Hegel writes in a well-known formulation: "Art, considered in its highest vocation, is and remains for us a thing of the past" (*A*, 11).[1] Aesthetics, as the philosophy of spirit, is itself the completion of art that is to be known philosophically. Hegel writes, "The *philosophy* of art [*Die* Wissenschaft *der Kunst*] is therefore a greater need in our day than it was in days when art by itself as art yielded full satisfaction. Art invites us to intellectual consideration, and that not for the purpose of creating art again, but for knowing philosophically [*wissenschaftlich*] what art is" (*A*, 11/I, 25–26).[2]

According to Hegel, art emerges as the philosophical reflection on art, which means that art in itself is a thing of the past. Moreover, as a thing of the past, there is no future of art as the unveiling of the absolute (speculative) truth. Hegel's judgment on art concerns the question of the role of literature in the age of criticism since Hegel's judgment includes a critique of romanticism. In order to approach the question of literature as criticism, I therefore turn to Hegel's *Lectures on Aesthetics* (*Vorlesungen über die Ästhetik*, 1818–29)[3] in order to situate the paradigm of writerly necessity within a broader philosophic-historical context.

Hegel's *Aesthetics* concerns art as a formation of truth: art as a mode in which the absolute manifests itself at a certain point in (its dialectical) history.[4] According to Hegel, Antiquity is the historical point at which art manifests itself as the truth of the absolute. Classical art is the "harmonious unity of content and form" (A, 301). It is the essential totality of spirit and body. But, Antiquity is at the same time only one formation of art as the self-manifestation of the absolute. On the one hand, the "classical" (A, 301) form of art is thus preceded by the "symbolic" (A, 302) that manifests an actual work that lacks spirit (content without form): "As symbolic, artistic productions have not yet gained a form truly adequate to the spirit, because the spirit here is itself not yet inwardly clear to itself, as it would be if it were free spirit" (A, 352). On the other hand, the classical art form itself precedes the (Christianized) "*romantic* art-form" (A, 301–2) in which, from Hegel's perspective, "art reintroduces, in an opposite way from the symbolic, the separation of content and form" (A, 302). The romantic form of art presents itself as the internalized self-conscious spirit that lacks any actual work (form without content).[5]

As Peter Szondi notes in his lectures on Hegel's aesthetics, Hegel perceives the process of the spirit from a dual point of view.[6] The classical art form is succeeded by the romantic form of art, which from the perspective of aesthetics lacks the true beauty of the classical age but from the horizon of the philosophy of spirit is a step toward a higher consciousness that will overcome art altogether in the formations of religion and, finally, philosophy.[7] The classical form of art is thus the highest *art form* since it consists in the unification of form and content. As Szondi notes, this Hegelian classicism is not accidental but grounded *in der Sache selbst*, namely in the principal coincidence between Hegel's philosophical intention, dialectic as a process of the identity of identity and nonidentity, and the conceptualization of the classical art form as the unification of form and content.[8] In its essential classical appearance, art is the self-manifestation of the absolute as the coincidence of subject and object that is the essence of truth in general: "Truth is just the dissolving of opposition and, at that, not in the sense, as may be supposed, that the opposition and its two sides *do not exist at all*, but that they exist reconciled" (A, 55). For Hegel, this coincidence means that classical art, as the production of the absolute, manifested the truth of the Greeks and provided them with a dwelling: "In the case of the Greeks, art was the highest form in which the people represented the gods to themselves and gave themselves some awareness of truth" (A, 102). In this sense, classical art could never fail in its effects since its objective basis constituted the very content of a people (see A, 279): "The most fundamental thing is and remains immediate intelligibility; and actually all nations have insisted on what was to please them in a work of art, for they wanted to be at home in it, living and present in it" (A, 274).[9] In opposition to the classical work, the romantic form without content is an intransitive work that can never constitute the true dwelling for man. From a Hegelian perspective, the emergence of literature as criticism thus means that art as absolute is a thing of the past.

The Subject Positions of Art

In Hegel's aesthetics, it is visible how each of the forms of art (i.e., the symbolic, the classical, and the romantic) produces a certain subject position that constitutes an artist's being (see *A*, 438/II, 27). The symbolic subject must produce his own content, which is not *essentially* given to him. For the symbolic artist, there is no content that corresponds to his inner truth (his form), since the symbolic subject first of all lacks subjectivity: "Symbolic art tosses about in a thousand forms without being able to hit upon the plainly adequate one" (*A*, 439). The symbolic subject is the content without form. In contradistinction to the symbolic subject, the classical subject can find his own true art content in his age as such. As the self-manifestation of the absolute, art is the truth of Antiquity. For the classical subject, content and form coincide: "The content [*Inhalt*] is determinate and the free shape [*Gestalt*] is determined by the content itself and it belongs to it absolutely, so that the artist seems only to execute what is already cut and dried on its own account in essence [... *so daß der Künstler nur zu exekutieren scheint, was schon für sich dem Begriff nach fertig ist*]" (*A*, 439/II, 29).

In this instance, Hegel's classicism coincides with Hölderlin's presupposition in the *Remarks on "Oedipus"* in which Hölderlin states that modern works of art lack reliability in comparison to classical art. Hölderlin writes, "It will be good, in order to secure for today's poets a bourgeois existence—taking into account the difference of times and institutions—if we elevate poetry today to the *mechane* of the ancients" (*ET*, 101). For Hegel, to calculate how to produce an artwork is indeed possible in Antiquity. The classical subject lacks neither substantial content nor the technical capacity to produce his work. Classical production is "the free deed [*freie Tun*] of the clear-headed man who equally *knows* [weiß] what he wills and *can* [kann] accomplish what he wills [*will*]" (*A*, 438/II, 27). But, this is then not the case for the romantic Subject who lives in the age of the higher spirit. The romantic artist lives in the age of reflection that conditions the possibility of the production of art. Hegel writes,

> Now contrasted with the time in which the artist owing to his nationality and his period stands with the substance of his being within a specific world-view and its contents and forms of portrayal, we find an altogether opposed view which in its complete development is of importance only in most recent times. In our day, in the case of almost all peoples, criticism, the cultivation of reflection, and, in our German case, freedom of thought have mastered the artists too, and have made them, so to say, a *tabula*

rasa in respect of the material and the form of their productions, after the necessary particular stages of the romantic art-form have been traversed. Bondage to a particular subject-matter and a mode of portrayal suitable for this material alone are for artists today something past .... No content, no form, is any longer immediately identical with the inwardness, the nature, the unconscious substantial essence of the artist; every material may be indifferent to him if only it does not contradict the formal law of being simply beautiful and capable of artistic treatment. (*A*, 605)

For Hegel, the romantic Subject is the self-mirroring of itself, which means that any content remains contingent and that the Subject therefore lacks actuality for itself.[10] Hegel's romantic Subject is a pure form without content and this form constitutes the ironic life that Hegel understands to be the life of the genius who is indifferent toward any actualization of the work: "This virtuosity of an ironical artistic life apprehends itself as a divine creative genius for which anything and everything is only an unsubstantial creature, to which the creator, knowing himself to be disengaged and free from everything, is not bound" (*A*, 66).[11] The romantic genius is only one form of Hegel's concept of genius understood as *the ability to produce*. For Hegel, the concept of genius emerges in all the constituting forms of art (the symbolic, the classical, and the romantic) insofar as it is nothing but "the *general* ability for the true production of a work of art, as well as the energy to elaborate and complete it" (*A*, 283).

For Hegel, this ability is partly inborn (*angeboren*) as a natural gift (*Naturgabe*) in the form of intuition and feeling and partly conscious thought and technical skill developed through education. But, moreover, such a genius has a natural impulse and immediate need to give form to what he feels. The genius has an inborn necessity to produce:

> For the genuine artist has a *natural* impulse [natürlichen *Trieb*] and an immediate need [*das unmittelbare Bedürfnis*] to give form at once to everything that he feels and imagines. This process of formation is *his* way of feeling and seeing, and he finds it in himself without labour as the instrument proper and suited to him. ... And this gift for formation the artist does not possess merely as *theoretical* idea, imagination, and feeling, but also immediately as *practical* feeling, i.e., as a gift for actual execution [*Gabe wirklicher Ausführung*]. Both are bound together in the genuine artist. (*A*, 286/I, 369–70)

Genius and writerly necessity, the ability to write and the necessity to write, cannot be separated in the genuine artist. But, in Hegel, the romantic Subject thus instantiates the paradigm of writerly necessity insofar as the romantic Subject is situated in the position between a necessity and an impossibility, between the lack of ability to not-write and the lack of ability to write any actual work. Rereading Hegel's history of art from the perspective of writerly necessity, the symbolic subject's necessity to write would be a transitive ability to write an actual work, which however would lack the spiritual form of the Work. The classical subject's necessity to write would coincide perfectly with this artist's ability to write. It would be a necessity to write transitively: to write a Work as absolute presence. But from the perspective of the modern romantic reflection on art, the classical art form also marks a period that lacks irony. In the modern age, writerly necessity thus emerges as the necessity to write intransitively.

The Romantic Genius

The thought that genius and writerly necessity are united in the genuine artist is already visible in Early German Romanticism. For Friedrich Schlegel, the genius thus emerges as a subject who cannot not-write intransitively. In *Critical Fragment 69*, Schlegel reworks the Kantian concept of "genius" in order to propose a writer who is in possession of the higher spirit but lacks the letter. In §46 of the *Critique of the Power of Judgment* (*Kritik der Urteilskraft*, 1790), Kant defines genius as "the inborn predisposition of the mind (*ingenium*) *through which* nature gives the rule to art" (*CJ*, 186). For Kant, genius is "a *talent* for producing that [original work] for which no determinate rule can be given" (*CJ*, 186). Such a work must be *exemplary* (*CJ*, 186) in the sense that the work must serve others "as a standard or a rule for judging" (*CJ*, 187). This work cannot be described "scientifically" since it is *nature* (*CJ*, 187) itself that gives the rule to *beautiful art* (and not to science). The Paulinian distinction between spirit (*Geist*) and letter (*Buchstaben*) is at the center of §49 of Kant's aesthetics in which the spirit is defined as the animating principle, as "nothing other than the faculty for the presentation of *aesthetic ideas* [*das Vermögen der Darstellung* ästhetischer Ideen]" (*CJ*, 192/249). Kant understands the aesthetic idea as that which "no language fully attains or can make intelligible" (*CJ*, 192), since there is no determinate concept that is adequate to this idea. Insofar as the essence of art is precisely such an aesthetic idea, the spirit is the capability to produce art, "express what is unnameable [*das Unnennbare*]" (*CJ*, 195/254). In terms of the production of linguistic works of art, the spirit is the ability *to write* such works. As Kant makes clear in the beginning of the paragraph, the works of aesthetic ideas (art as such) are distinct from the "products [*Produkten*] ... without *spirit*, even though one finds nothing in them [the works without spirit] to criticize as far as taste is concerned. A poem can be quite pretty and elegant, but without *spirit*" (*CJ*, 191–2/249).

In opposition to Kant's example of a form of "poetry" that consists of letters, but which nevertheless lacks the spirit, F. Schlegel proposes a negative sense (*negative Sinn*) that "emerges when somebody possesses only the spirit and not the letter."[12] Schlegel understands these qualities of the negative feeling (spirit and letter) as, respectively, the "kernel"[13] (spirit) and "the material and formal requisites, the dry hard shell [letter] of productive genius."[14] As the core of the concept of genius, this negative sense arises "when one always must want to without being able to; when one always likes to hear, but never hears."[15] From such a subject who *must want* to produce, "we get pure tendencies, projects that are as wide as the blue sky, or, at the very best, outlines of fantasies."[16] Schlegel's negative feeling means that a subject cannot not-desire to produce but can nevertheless not produce since this subject possesses the spirit (the ability to produce per se) but lacks the letter (the ability to *actualize* his production in a work). As Schlegel writes in his unpublished notebooks from the time of the publication of *Critical Fragments* (*Kritische Fragmente*, 1797), even if the spirit is understood as *absolute capacity*,[17] this spirit nevertheless needs the "letter" in order to be a *work*.[18] The negative feeling constitutes a genius who has the absolute capacity to produce intransitively (without work).

In *Critical Fragment 69*, writerly necessity thus emerges as the paradoxical inner core of the genius who can write only the fragmentary absence of work. Writerly necessity is here the suspension between a necessity to write and an impossibility of writing, between the inability to not-write and the inability to write a work. The genius cannot not-write the absence of work. But, with respect to the judgment on the future of art, it all depends on how we are to conceive of such an absence of work (intransitivity). The necessity to write does not provide the genius with the ability to write the Work; rather, writerly necessity constitutes the *inability* to produce an actual work (in Hegel's terms) or the *ability* to produce the absence of work (in Blanchot's terms). In order to understand the difference between these evaluations, it is necessary to further examine the emergence of literature as criticism. This entails that we should also investigate the position of the literary critic in relation to the literary writer who cannot not-write intransitively. This will be the concern of the next chapter. What position does the critic occupy in the paradigm of writerly necessity?

11

The Critic

The Destruction of Aesthetics

If it is difficult for us today to think that there is a paradigm that produces subjects whose very life is at stake in writing, it is no doubt because literature—for us—*is* a thing of the past. For Modernity, the question is how it can be that there is such a writer whose life depends on the work, whereas from the perspective of Antiquity (as understood by Hegel), insofar as art unveiled truth, the question is rather how it can be that there are so few, if any, subjects whose lives depend on art. For Modernity, the question is how anyone could think that it would truly be a necessity for our survival that something so useless as art exists; for Antiquity, the question is how in the future there could exist a civilization that does not find its very truth in art. From the classical perspective, therefore, the question is not how writerly necessity is possible, but how it is possible that there is no necessity to read.

In *The Man without Content* (*L'uomo senza contenuto*, 1970), Agamben argues that there is a fundamental link between this modern writer whose life essentially depends on the work and this modern reader whose life is essentially indifferent to the work:

> For the one who creates it, art becomes an increasingly uncanny experience, with respect to which speaking of interest is at the very least a euphemism, because what is at stake seems to be not in any way the production of a beautiful work but instead the life and death of the author, or at least his or her spiritual health. To the increasing innocence of the spectator's experience in front of the beautiful object corresponds the increasing danger inherent in the artist's experience, for whom art's *promesse de bonheur* becomes the poison that contaminates and destroys his existence. (*MC*, 5)

For Agamben, the aesthetic relation between the artist and the critic manifests the end of art. Agamben conceives *The Man without Content* as a "*destruction* of aesthetics [distruzione *dell'estetica*]" (*MC*, 6/16). Like

Heidegger's *Destruktion* of metaphysics, this destruction of aesthetics aims to make the history of Being transparent to itself in order to grasp the withdrawal of Being.[1]

Agamben's destruction of aesthetics is thus an extension of Heidegger's destruction of metaphysics. In the *Introduction to Metaphysics* (*Einführung in die Metaphysik*, 1935), Heidegger argues that we must produce a new thinking of art guided by a fundamental grasping of the withdrawal of Being.[2] In the "Epilogue" to *The Origin of the Work of Art* (*Der Ursprung des Kunstwerkes*, 1935–6), Heidegger writes,

> But the question remains: Is art still an essential and necessary way in which that truth happens which is decisive for our historical existence, or is art no longer of this character? If, however, it is such no longer, then there remains the question as to why this is so. The truth of Hegel's judgment has not yet been decided; for behind this verdict there stands Western thought since the Greeks.[3]

The truth of Hegel's judgment on the end of art is still undecided. For Heidegger, aesthetics is however the sphere in which "art dies."[4] Aesthetics is the philosophical thought in which art becomes the "object [*Gegenstand*] of *aisthēsis*, of sensuous apprehension in the wide sense," an apprehension, which in Modernity emerges as "lived experience [*das Erleben*]."[5] The work of art as an aesthetic object (*Gegenstand*) is that which stands opposed (*gegen-stand*) to a subject. According to Heidegger, the subject–object relation is thus the foundation for aesthetics in which the relation between form and content is the fundamental conceptual schema, which does not mean that this schema "belongs originally to the domain of art and the artwork."[6] Agamben's destruction of aesthetics therefore concerns the question of how to think beyond "the aesthetic-metaphysical determination of the work as matter and form [*materia e forma*]" (*MC*, 98/149). Aesthetics is a configuration of the metaphysics of will in which thetic Being is the will of unity: "This metaphysics of the will has penetrated our conception of art to such an extent that even the most radical critiques of aesthetics have not questioned its founding principle, that is, the idea that art is the expression of the artist's creative will" (*MC*, 72). Agamben's destruction of aesthetics is thus a destruction of the metaphysics of will. He seeks to suspend the operativity of the dialectical work. But how does Agamben think beyond the sphere of aesthetics?

Art: The Interruption and the Form without Content

For Agamben, the proper mode of art is inoperativity. In *The Man without Content*, this mode is understood as an (Heideggerian) *epochē* explicitly in the form of a Hölderlinian *rhythm* that introduces "interruption" (*MC*, 99) into time: "the presence of an atemporal dimension in time" (*MC*, 99).[7] This rhythm of art "holds *epochally* [epocalmente] the essence of man, that is, gives him the gift both of being and of nothingness, both of the impulse in the free space of the work and of the impetus toward shadow and ruin" (*MC*, 100/151–2). For Agamben, art holds *epochally*. It suspends the judgment of the will; it is the interruption as a space of contingency ("the gift of both being and nothingness"), exterior to the thought of the metaphysics of will and the primacy of Being over nothingness. In his later thought, Agamben will reformulate this "gift of both being and nothingness" as the potentiality not only to be but also to not-be.[8] Art is thus the locus of inoperativity insofar as this inoperativity is understood as pure potentiality.[9] According to Agamben, this potentiality of art is however concealed in the age of criticism in which art emerges in the sphere of aesthetics. But how does aesthetics distort the truth of art?

Agamben agrees with Heidegger's non-Hegelian proposal that there is a future of art as the unveiling of truth; however, Agamben also appropriates Hegel's critique of romantic art. First of all, Agamben presupposes the Hegelian proposition that the artistic material is to be "the infinite and true element in his [the artist's] own consciousness" (*MC*, 35; *A*, 603). Agamben's evaluation of aesthetics is in fact an adaptation of Hegel's critique of the ironic romantic Subject. Agamben writes, "Fatally, the moment will come when this immediate unity of the artist's subjectivity with his material breaks" (*MC*, 35). For Agamben, the artist is "the man without content" (*MC*, 55) whose work can never actualize itself. For the subject who writes intransitively, "art is the annihilating entity that traverses all its contents without ever being able to attain a positive work, because it cannot identify with any content" (*MC*, 57). The reason for this inability of art to emerge as the actual work is the consequence of the Subject's pure creative-formal principle. As this principle, the paradigm of writerly necessity emerges as the artist who cannot not-produce.[10] Agamben writes,

> What the artist experiences in the work of art is, in fact, that artistic subjectivity is absolute essence, for which all subject matter is indifferent; however, the pure creative-formal principle, split from any content, is the absolute abstract inessence, which annihilates and dissolves every content in its continuous effort to transcend and actualize itself. If the artist now seeks his certainty in a particular content or faith, he is lying, because he knows that pure artistic subjectivity is the essence of everything; but if he seeks his reality in pure aesthetic subjectivity, he finds himself in the paradoxical condition of having to find his own essence precisely in the inessential, his content in what is mere form. His condition, then, is that of a radical split; and, outside of this split, everything is a lie. (*MC*, 54)

For Agamben, the artistic Subject's essence consists in a lack of essence. The paradigm of writerly necessity emerges as the necessity to erase itself as essence (intransitivity), which is also manifest in Agamben's claim that what is at stake in the work of art is "the life and death of the author" (*MC*, 5). In Blanchot's terms, the pure creative-formal principle means that the Subject cannot subsist as *man* (in an essential content) or as *dying* (in the inessential essence of form) since his "condition" is a "radical split."[11] In Agamben's Hegelian understanding of romantic irony, art is the form without content (see *MC*, 55). For Agamben, the romantic form of art dissolves the shared (classical) space in which men can dwell and find their truth. The *reflection* on art is the death of art since it leads to the ironic Subject's internalized consciousness, which never actualizes itself in a work. The artist occupies the subject position produced by writerly necessity. But what position does the critic then occupy?

The Critic

For Agamben, modern aesthetics is split between the (romantic) *Artist* whose very life is at risk in the artistic production and the (Kantian) *Spectator* who experiences the beautiful artwork with disinterested enjoyment. The romantic Subject, the form without content, corresponds to the figure of *the Critic* whose truth is his (in)essential alienation from art:

> So long as the artist lives in intimate unity with his material, the spectator sees in the work of art only his own faith and the highest truth of his being brought to art in the most necessary manner, and a problem of art as such cannot arise since art is precisely the shared space in which all men, artists and non-artists, come together in living unity. But once the creative subjectivity of the artist begins to place itself above his material and his production, like a playwright who freely puts his character on the scene, this shared concrete space of the work of art dissolves, and what the spectator sees in it is no longer something that he can immediately find again in his consciousness as his highest truth. Everything that the spectator can still find in the work of art is, now, mediated by aesthetic representation, which is itself, independently of any content, the supreme value and the most intimate truth that unfolds its power in the artwork itself and starting from the artwork itself. (*MC*, 36–7)

Agamben discerns the problem of aesthetics in the relation between the artist and the spectator. Specifically, Agamben understands "the destiny of Western art" (*MC*, 35) to correlate with the artist's change of relation with his work. But Agamben focuses more on the specific development of the critic in relation to the artist than on the artist as such. This critic emerges as "the figure of the *man of taste*" (*MC*, 13). According to Agamben, this figure is a novelty in the history of art insofar as "even in the sixteenth century there was no clear boundary between good and bad taste" (*MC*, 13).[12] Moreover, the emergence of the man of taste "calls into question the very status of the work of art" (*MC*, 14). This figure thus constitutes the nonartist as a pure passive spectator who, in opposition to the medieval Maecenas, does not take part in the production of the work; rather, for this spectator, the work of art becomes "merely an occasion to practice his good taste" (*MC*, 15). In the third *Critique*, Kant proposes that the judgment of taste must be without any interest in the existence of the "thing" (see *CJ*, 90–1).[13] In opposition to a writer whose very life is at stake in writing the literary "work," the judgment of taste requires the critic to be absolutely indifferent with respect to the existence of the literary work. For Agamben, therefore, the disinterested "aesthetic judgment" (*MC*, 15), the modern critical reflection on art, "begins necessarily with the forgetting of art" (*MC*, 43). Literary theory conceals the more original epochal interruption of the artwork: "Whatever criterion the critical judgment employs to measure the reality of the work—its linguistic structure, its historical dimension, the authenticity of the *Erlebnis* from which it has sprung, and so on—it will only have laid out, in place of a living body, an interminable skeleton of dead elements" (*MC*, 43). In correlation to the artist as the subject who negates this or that work, the reflective critic "leads art to its negation" (*MC*, 48) in which "art (our aesthetic idea of art) sustains itself and finds its reality" (*MC*, 48). The subject who writes literature here appears in a correlation to the subject who reflects on literature. But the true writer and true critic are at the same time diametrically opposite figures. The true writer is the subject who *cannot* not-write, which means that the writer's very life is at stake in writing. The true critic is the subject who *can* not-write, which means that the critic's life is indifferent to writing.

Literature as Criticism

For Agamben, on the one hand, there is the (Hegelian) fact that art itself has become critical reflection on art and, on the other hand, the (Heideggerian) hope that "art, at the furthest point of its destiny, makes visible its original project" (*MC*, 115). Romantic criticism is the forgetting of a more originary rhythm (interruption). For Agamben, following Hegel, it is the critical status of art that produces art as a thing of the past; however, in contradistinction to Hegel, Agamben conceives a future of art as the unveiling of truth. For Nancy and Lacoue-Labarthe, there is also a future of art as the interruption of the Subject; however, according to Nancy and Lacoue-Labarthe, it is precisely because literature arises as the romantic *concept* of literature that art can manifest itself as unworking. What is thought in Romanticism is the (modern) concept of literary theory: literature producing itself as theory. From the Hegelian perspective, criticism as the aesthetic judgment *on* art makes art into a thing of the past. But romantic criticism is not a reflective judgment on art but the reflection *of* literature itself as the form in which the literary absolute produces itself. Criticism is the ability to produce works. Nancy and Lacoue-Labarthe write, "Criticism itself must be, is expected to be, practical and productive, if not of works then at least of capacities to make work" (*LA*, 114). This capability is immanent to the work itself insofar as the operator is the operation (and vice versa).

Nancy and Lacoue-Labarthe here refer to Benjamin's dissertation in which Benjamin examines the romantic concept of criticism (see *LA*, 147, note 19). Benjamin shows how criticism is not the judgment on the work but the immanent reflection of the work itself. Criticism is the capability of the work to produce itself: "Criticism of a work is, rather, its reflection, which can only, as is self-evident, unfold the germ of the reflection that is immanent to the work" (*SW*, 159). The criterion of literature is thus also nothing but its "criticizability," its immanent possibility of being available for criticism, since criticism itself constitutes the truth of literature: "If a work can be criticized, then it is a work of art; otherwise it is not" (*SW*, 160). It is not the critic but the work of art that passes judgment on itself: "The critic does not pass judgment on the work; rather, art itself passes judgment" (*SW*, 161).[14] Or, we might say, the critic only passes judgment on the literary work insofar as the critic coincides with the form of criticism immanent to the work of art. Criticism coincides with (transcendental) poetry, the poetry of poetry, as the "reflection in the work of art itself" (*SW*, 170). Poetry is always already poetry *of* poetry that is poetry conscious of itself. Poetry is the expression of the absolute as reflection of reflection (see *SW*, 171). This reflection constitutes the romantic *Work in Progress*, which for Benjamin is not "an infinity of continuous advance" (*SW*, 126) but "a continuum of forms" (*SW*, 168) in which reflection is a "limitless capacity" since it turns "every prior reflection into the object of a subsequent reflection" (*SW*, 123).[15]

Criticism is the capacity of the immanent production of the work. Nancy and Lacoue-Labarthe can therefore write that Romanticism "inaugurates criticism as re-production, second and first, or twice the first production of the work, so to speak" (*LA*, 111). Benjamin notes, "In the theory of Romantic art one cannot avoid the paradox that criticism is valued more highly than works of art" (*SW*, 185). The literary Subject *is* the critical operation in which it is not possible to distinguish between life and work, operator and operation, poetry and criticism, potentiality and actuality. We reread in *The Literary Absolute*, "An epoch that begins with criticism is perhaps an epoch that begins (without beginning, for it is in suspense) with the supplement or with the *perfection* [parachèvement] of the work of art rather than with the completed [*achevée*] work of art" (*LA*, 110/382). As we have seen in Part 1, the epoch of criticism is the epoch of the supplement, of *writing*, but thus also the epoch of the loss of origin and the self-presence of the Work. Criticism manifests the ambiguity of literature as the absence of work.

Since literature *is* criticism itself, the *concept* of literature, it is the absence of the (literary) Work. It is therefore the *critical* character of literature that manifests the possibility of an art of the future *insofar* as criticism produces art as a thing of the past. Criticism, as the supplement of the Work, inaugurates the past of art as the unveiling of the absolute and the future of literature as the interruption of the absolute. The possibility of the future of art as inoperativity is thus the horizon of both *The Man without Content* and *The Literary Absolute*, but the evaluation of the critical character of literature in the age of criticism differs. For Agamben, reflection *on* art signifies intransitivity as the inability to actualize the work of art whereas for Nancy and Lacoue-Labarthe the reflection *of* art indicates the unthought possibility of literature as the absence of work.[16] But this difference in the evaluation of literature in the age of criticism reflects only the ambiguity inherent in the paradigm of writerly necessity.

This ambiguity manifests itself for the subject who writes, in the work to be written, and for the critic who evaluates the work. The true literary writer is the subject who cannot not-write, but this subject is thus either unable to write a (transitive) work or able to write an (intransitive) absence of work. The true literary work is the intransitive work that is either the form without content, the spirit that lacks actuality, or the interruption of thetic Being, the suspension of the dialectical Work. The true critic is the concealed writer whose essence is the literary work; however, this subject is either alienated from his own literary essence or he embodies an inessential contingency insofar as literature is nothing but criticism. For the writer, for the critic, and with respect to the literary work, intransitivity emerges as the unthought negativity that signifies both the reconstituting of the paradigm and the disappearance of the paradigm. In order to examine the possibility of thinking a literary future beyond the paradigm of writerly necessity, I now turn to the possibility that this paradigm produces when literature and criticism coincide: a subject who is at once writer and critic. The name is Roland Barthes.

12

To Write as an Intransitive Verb

The Sincere Critic

Agamben does not describe the novel manifestation of the critic who was to replace the man of taste from the end of the eighteenth century: the connoisseur. Perhaps the reason for this is that one of Agamben's cherished references in *The Man without Content*, Edgar Wind, had already examined this figure in *Art and Anarchy* (1963). The figure of the connoisseur is linked to the emergence of the phenomenon of originality as the principle by which the work excludes its possible reproducibility (see *MC*, 61). This figure whose importance grows in the nineteenth century is intrinsically linked to writerly necessity as the literary Subject's *sincere* need to express his essence. The connoisseur focuses on the traits of a work of art that reveal authenticity. In his lectures on aesthetics, Hegel identifies *der Kenner* as the replacement for the man of taste. In opposition to the man of taste, *der Kenner* is the connoisseur who can relate to the passions of the (romantic) genius:

> For when great passions and the movements of a profound soul are revealed, there is no longer any question of the finer distinctions of taste and its pedantic preoccupation [*Kleinigkeitskrämerei*] with individual details. It [i.e. taste] feels genius striding over such ground, and, retreating before its power, finds the place too hot for itself and knows not what to do with itself. (*A*, 34/I, 55)

Edgar Wind identifies the Italian Giovanni Morelli (1816–1891) as a connoisseur per se. Morelli's method marks the emergence of sincerity as a criterion of the truth of art in the nineteenth century. Wind indeed perceives Morelli as a product of the romantic thinking of the fragment.[1] But the Morellian method thus also simply carries the thinking of authenticity in art criticism to its logical conclusion.[2] Morelli's method is "to arrest, even to reverse, the normal aesthetic reaction"[3] insofar as the critic is not to experience a "general impression"[4] in the apprehension of an artwork but should focus on the idiosyncrasies that reveal the signature of the artist. The aim is thus to focus on apparent "irrelevant" features of the work where "the artist himself, no less than his imitator, is likely to relax in their execution; they are the places where he lets himself go, and for that reason they reveal him unmistakably."[5] In this method, we find the traces of the whole economy of authenticity. The truth of art lies in the criterion of sincerity insofar as the critic must examine the parts of the artwork in which the artist is likely to show his "true" self without any artificial performance. The work of art must be original (so that it cannot be reproduced), be created by an inspired artist (so that it is not a technician's labor but a gift from the Muse), and be the mark of the spontaneous artist who is the absolute origin of the work. In terms of literary criticism, Morelli's method marks the age of the author critic. In the twentieth century, the critic emerges in the position of the death of the author. My question is now how this later critic emerges as a subject who cannot not-write intransitively.

The Will to Write

At least two significant events in literary studies took place at the end of the year 1978. On the one hand, the publication in September 1978 of Nancy and Lacoue-Labarthe's *L'Absolu littéraire* (*The Literary Absolute*) in which the concern is the emergence of the question of literature in Early German Romanticism. On the other hand, the commencement of Roland Barthes's lecture course at the *Collège de France*, *La Préparation du roman* (*The Preparation of the Novel*) on December 2, 1978, which lasted until the beginning of 1980. In this late lecture course, Barthes is concerned with a *Vouloir-Écrire*, a will to write or a desire to write, which according to Barthes perhaps signifies an "attitude, drive, desire [*l'attitude, la pulsion, le désir*]" but overall is "insufficiently studied" (*PN*, 8/27). With this term, Barthes refers to Nancy and Lacoue-Labarthe's *The Literary Absolute* in which they, as we have seen, understand the journal of Early German Romanticism, the *Athenaeum* (1798–1800), to be a manifestation of "the will to system [*la volonté du système*]" (*LA*, 32/46). Barthes will in the session on December 1, 1979, link this will-to-write to *The Literary Absolute* and on December 8 designate his concern as "*Writing* as absolute" (*PN*, 148). In the session of February 23, 1980, Barthes will explicitly say that "the writer, such as I've tried to imagine him" is "someone who devotes himself to the *Literary Absolute*" (*PN*, 296). My question is how this will-to-write emerges as what the critic-writer Barthes understands as *a necessity to write* and how this necessity for him is linked to the question whether the act of writing is transitive or intransitive.[6]

For Barthes, the focus of the lecture course is a writerly subject (Barthes himself) who is situated at a "juncture" (*PN*, 3) that divides the life that came before and the life that is to come. The question for Barthes in this lecture series is the possibility of a new future, of a new life, which can only be a *writerly* life insofar as Barthes is *someone who writes*: "Now, for someone who writes, ... there can be no other *Vita Nova* (or so it seems to me) than the discovery of a new writing practice" (*PN*, 5). For Barthes, the will-to-write is "explicit" (*PN*, 9) in Rilke's *Letters to a Young Poet* insofar as these letters concern a necessity to write:

> The "essential" form of the Advice offered to a Writer ultimately concerns not the practice of writing but the very Will to Write: Writing as the *Telos* of a life = in answer to the question "Should I write? Continue to Write?" they all say (Flaubert, Kafka, Rilke): it's not a matter of a gift, of talent, but of *survival*: write, but only if you're absolutely convinced that, if you don't, you'll perish (what we call a *vocation* probably refers to this kind of survival). (*PN*, 280)

Rilke's letters written at the beginning of the twentieth century are addressed to the young poet who would be situated in a position of suspension between a "must" and a "cannot." The writer is *not able not to write* but nevertheless *not able to write*. The aim of Rilke's letters is precisely to address the question of how to manage this position between a necessity to write and an impossibility of writing. It is from this perspective that one should understand the notion of *patience* (*Geduld*) that is a recurrent theme in these letters. Rilke proposes to the young writer in the letter from Paris (February 17, 1903): "Nobody can advise you and help you, nobody. There is only one way. Go into yourself. ... This above all: ask yourself in your night's quietest hour: *must* I write?"[7] Barthes's course is an "intellectual narrative [*récit intellectuel*]" about "a man who's deliberating the best way to realize that desire [of writing], or that will [*volonté*], or indeed that *vocation*" (*PN*, 171/319). For Barthes, "writing *leads* [life]: poetically, transcendentally" (*PN*, 210). Writing is the transcendental condition of this life devoted to writing literature.

It is here possible to see the connection between Barthes's understanding of the Will-to-Write as a necessity to write and his assertion that the writer is someone who is devoted to the literary absolute. When literature emerges as absolute for a subject as the condition of this very subject's life, this subject is a writer who cannot not-write literature. Moreover, when literature is the condition that constitutes the subject's very desire, it is not possible for this subject to not-desire writing. Within the horizon of the literary absolute as an a priori condition, the desire of writing establishes this writerly life. The consequence is that it is not possible to distinguish between the writer and literature since the writer's very life depends on (the actualization of) the literary work. Barthes can therefore claim that the will-to-write delimits literary writing insofar as literature is "an order of knowledge where the product is indistinguishable from the production, the practice from the drive" (*PN*, 8–9). In Barthes's understanding of literary practice, the written work coincides with the act of writing as the will-to-write. Barthes says, "To say that you want to write—there, in fact, you have the very material of writing" (*PN*, 8). For Barthes, literature is thus situated at the indistinction between producer and production, between life and writing, between subject and work.

Barthes focus is thus "existential, not aesthetic" (*PN*, 283) since it concerns the "Desire to be," which for the writer Barthes is a "desire for language [*désir du langage*]" (*PN*, 302/551–2). For Barthes, the question is not to suspend writing but to interrupt the incessant will-to-write so as to make possible a new life. To think the verb *to write* anew concerns the possibility of inventing a new practice of writing in which there is no necessity to write, no desire of writing, which makes the interruption of writing impossible. Since literature is absolute for this writer, Barthes's lecture course concerns the interruption of the desire for literature that coincides with the interruption of literature as absolute. We should pay attention to the implicit transposition of the will-to-write that takes place here: Nancy and Lacoue-Labarthe's study concerns the *concept* of the literary absolute as the *living System* (*LA*, 34), whereas Barthes's lectures concern *the system that is alive* as the writer who must write literature. For Barthes, the literary absolute is not simply a concept of the absolute but embedded in the writer who must write. This *transposition* of the literary absolute as a concept into that which constitutes an actual living being is the condition of Barthes's investigation into the will-to-write.

Intransitive Writing

Barthes understands himself as someone who is devoted to the literary absolute: Literature has emerged as the absolute condition of the subject's life. Barthes emerges in the position of the critic who coincides with the subject who cannot not-write intransitively.[8] At the beginning of the second session (December 9, 1978), Barthes presents the horizon for his practice of writing as the question whether to write is an intransitive or transitive verb: "For a long time I thought that there was a *Will-to-Write* [*Vouloir-Écrire*] in itself: *To Write*, intransitive verb—now I'm less sure. Perhaps to will to write = to will to write something → To Will-to-Write + Object" (*PN*, 10/31–2). In the paper "To Write: Intransitive Verb?" ("Écrire, verbe intransitif?," 1966), delivered at the conference at Johns Hopkins University around twelve years earlier,[9] Barthes posed the question whether the modern act of writing indicates *to write* as an intransitive verb, or whether this intransitivity conceals an act of writing that takes this act itself as its object. In either case, Barthes understood the transformation of the verb *to write* from its transitive to its apparent intransitive sense to constitute "an important change in mentality."[10] In 1978, with an allusion to Nancy and Lacoue-Labarthe's study, Barthes understands this change of mentality to have taken place at the time of the Early German Romantics when the question of intransitive writing emerged (see *PN*, 143–4). Here Barthes implicitly revises a claim from his early work from 1953, *Writing Degree Zero*, in which he conceptualized the 1850s as the modern moment when literature emerges as an object of knowledge.[11]

My concern here is not to resolve the question whether intransitive writing in fact exists in itself. Rather, my aim has been to trace how the paradigm of writerly necessity conditions this thought of intransitive writing. On the one hand, it is visible how the literary absolute constitutes a writer who must write since his very being is conditioned by literature. On the other hand, we can see how the literary absolute produces itself as an intransitive act of pure a priori writing. The subject who is constituted by the literary absolute is the writer who must write intransitively. This link between the necessity to write and the intransitive work indicates the reason for Barthes's inability to confirm intransitive writing: The intransitive work, which is supposed to *be* without work, is in fact intrinsically linked to the thinking of the absolute work as the writer's condition. Both the necessity to write and the thinking of the intransitive work emerge when Barthes transposes the concept of the literary absolute into being the condition of the writer. However, in the lectures, Barthes is not only concerned with this current position of the writer as someone who must write literature. Rather, he proposes that the literary work of the future "should cease to be, or be only discretely, a *discourse of the work about the work*" (*PN*, 300). The work of the future should not be absolutely marked by intransitivity so as to produce the subject who says, "I can't write a work, there's no longer any work to be written, the only thing left for me to write is that there's nothing to write (*PN*, 300)." Barthes fantasized moment of temporalization is "a time when you'll stop writing, when you'll finally take a break, less from writing than from the perpetual reactivation of the desire" (*PN*, 149). This is a fantasy in which there is an interruption of the desire of writing. Here the desire *as* desire is put into question, which opens up the possibility of interrupting the desire of the subject who *must* desire to write. But this interruption of desire should not necessarily be a break from writing; rather, the question is whether it is possible to enact a practice of writing in which the will-to-write, the desire of writing, is suspended. Since for Barthes the necessity to write is intrinsically linked to the impossibility of finishing an actual work, it is an illusion that there could ever be an absolute work: "You labor on the work like a maniac, *in order to finish it*—but as soon as it's finished, you start another one, under the same illusory conditions" (*PN*, 148). For

Barthes, the writer is situated in the position of the will-to-write between the desire for a work and the impossibility of any intransitive work. In order to resists this suspended position, Barthes is thus constantly approaching the limit of this will-to-write. With reference to Heidegger, Barthes says,

> You remember the citation from Heidegger: in Nature, each thing remains within the allotted sphere of the Possible; only 'will' takes us outside of the Possible. I said that Writing, as Will, was an Impossible (which I was opposing to *Idleness*, as Nature).—We can now say: even within the will to write, that is, within its Impossible, the task of Talent is to remain within its Possible: to precisely delineate the Nature within this Non-Nature that is Writing. (*PN*, 198)

Since the will-to-write is a necessity to write the impossible intransitive work, the task of the writer must be to position himself at the site in which writing becomes possible as a form of idle nonwriting or inoperativity. But it is significant that Barthes rejects both the Hegelian and the Blanchotian project. Barthes explication of the writer who can only write that there is nothing to write is manifest in both Hegel and Blanchot even if their evaluations differ. For Hegel, this subject is the romantic-ironic writer who is nothing but a self-nihilating form without content. For Blanchot, the subject is the writer who writes the absence of work that interrupts thetic Being.

Barthes' conceptualization of the interruption of the desire of writing is neither identical to Hegel's understanding of the form without content nor to Blanchot's insistence on intransitive writing. Barthes thus says that Blanchot "sticks too rigidly to the opposition personal / impersonal" (*PN*, 167). The worry is here that the impersonal demand that demands nothing but itself *as* demand emerges as an inessential necessity that utterly destroys the writer as an individual. Barthes instead proposes that there is "a dialectic inherent to literature (with, I think, future potential) that makes it possible for the subject himself to be presented as a work of art" (*PN*, 167). If art produces the subject as a work of art, there would be "less of a conflict between the man and the work" (*PN*, 167). It is possible to reduce Barthes proposal of the subject as a work of art to a form of writerly necessity in which there would be no distinction between the producer and the production. But such a reduction would neglect that Barthes's concern for a new thinking of the subject as a work of art is precisely an attempt to think beyond the possibilities of the paradigm of writerly necessity.

Barthes current writerly position is thus precisely the position of the critic who coincides with the writer who cannot not-write intransitively. Insofar as the will-to-write is Rilke's necessity to write in which the verb to write appears to be intransitive, the question for Barthes is how to interrupt this necessity to write so as to delimit a new inoperative practice of writing. But this question of how to interrupt the desire of writing thus concerns not only Barthes own position as a writer but also the very question of literature. An example here is Gérard Genette who in "The Obverse of Signs," with reference to the critic Barthes as a "writer postponed," proposes that literature should be understood as the incessant postponement of the work:

> Literature is for the semiologist (the critic) a permanent temptation, an endless vocation postponed until later, experienced only this dilatory mode ... but the postponement is only apparent, for this intention to write, this "Moses-like gaze" on the work to come is already Literature.[12]

The fact that this subject *must* write does not mean that he *can* write; rather, the writer-critic is precisely situated in the suspension between a necessity to write (without object) and the impossibility of writing (an object). Unless literary thought aims to stay within a thinking of the absolute, the question on the level of the act of writing is how it is possible to interrupt this necessity to write intransitively.

The Amateur

How are we to think beyond the paradigm of writerly necessity? How can we think a future of literature? I will argue that the verb *to write* as *either* transitive *or* intransitive must be rethought. The question of literature emerges as the question of intransitivity. On the one hand, this question excludes the actual (transitive) work as the literary truth in order to propose a pure writing a priori. On the other hand, the question becomes whether intransitivity indicates the abstract form without content that lacks the actuality of the work or the affirmative absence of work that interrupts the Subject. But, insofar as this thought of intransitivity emerges as the paradigm of writerly necessity, the act of writing is always already linked to the essence of the "born poet" who cannot not-write literature. Within this paradigm it is never possible to decide whether intransitivity is the interruption as the negativity of the Subject or the interruption of the Subject. Rather, this *suspension* of an answer to the question of intransitivity, which coincides with the very posing of the question of literature, arises as the truth of literature.

I will suggest that it is necessary to render inoperative this question of literature in order to think *désœuvrement* anew. The new inoperative practice of writing must be the "enactment" of the verb *to write* as neither transitive nor intransitive but as *in-transitive* in which the hyphen indicates a possibility of suspending the paradigm of writerly necessity. The hyphen thus indicates a suspension of the suspended position of incessantly posing the question of literature. Insofar as this question emerges within the paradigm of writerly necessity (and thus within the horizon of the literary absolute), the question of literature can never escape the thinking of the Subject.

It is however possible to see the contours of an inoperative position in Barthes's works when he addresses the figure of the *Amateur*. In one of the sessions, Barthes says that the lecture course "comes out of a general interest ... in the *Amateur*, in the practices and values of the Amateur. Amateur = someone who *simulates* the Artist (on occasion, the artist would do well to simulate the Amateur)" (*PN*, 168). The question is how the figure of the amateur emerges within the paradigm of writerly necessity and to what extent this figure makes it possible to conceptualize a position that eludes this paradigm.

In *Roland Barthes by Roland Barthes* (*Roland Barthes par Roland Barthes*, 1975), there is a fragment entitled "The Amateur" [*L'amateur*]. Barthes suggests that the amateur "establishes himself *graciously* (for nothing) in the signifier ... he is—he will be perhaps—the counter-bourgeois artist."[13] Following Barthes in his "Inaugural Lecture" (1977), the fabric of signifiers can support an ethical practice of trickery and displacement. "The forces of freedom," Barthes says, depend "on the labor of displacement he [the writer] brings to bear upon the language."[14] The amateur embodies a form of outplaying of the limits of discourse.[15] The amateur's mode of Being is the movement of the signifier, which exceeds the bounds of propriety: The signifier is out of place, a non-place, an *atopia*.[16] Atopic as a mode of Being, the signifier is a "drifting habitation [*l'habitacle en dérive*]."[17] The amateur thus appears to occupy a spatiotemporal gap that is not actuality but an interruption that is irreducible to the thinking of the Subject.

From this perspective, the amateur could be an effective figure by which it is possible to think the writer outside the paradigm of writerly necessity. But is this in fact the case? The subject who cannot not-write literature is not simply characterized by a certain impotence; rather, this subject's very life depends on this inability to not-write. It is only because the paradigm of writerly necessity produces the writer that this subject must write intransitively and that literature *as* literature (poetry a priori) is possible. According to Barthes, the amateur is somebody who engages in art "without the spirit of mastery or competition ... he is anything but a hero (of creation, of performance)."[18] The amateur is here the opposite figure of the subject who cannot not-write: the writer as the sovereign creator. The amateur is without the spirit of mastery and thus has no reason to try to master writing. Indeed, there is no reason why the amateur should write at all. The amateur does not lack the ability to not-write; however, the ability to not-write constitutes this subject's very lack of necessity. The amateur is not in a position to emerge as a writer since this subject lacks the very mode of emergence that is the *literary* subject's condition of possibility. The amateur cannot exceed the paradigm of writerly necessity insofar as this subject is always already excluded from the paradigm.

The amateur is somebody whose mode of Being is a suspension between an ability to not-write and the lack of ability to write, a position between a writerly contingency and a writerly impossibility. Insofar as the amateur is a writer, this subject lacks the constitution of his own subjectivity, since the writer is a subject whose "essence" is writerly necessity. Within the paradigm of writerly necessity, the amateur can neither be a true or false writer since this subject is not a writer at all. The amateur constitutes a point of nonsense of writing that cannot be integrated into the paradigm of writerly necessity. But the figure of the amateur is thus also the possibility of thinking literature outside this paradigm insofar as this figure is not perceived simply as the (non) writer, in opposition to the subject who cannot not-write literature. Barthes indicates an etymological possibility of the *amator*: "The Amateur renews his pleasure (*amator*: one who loves and loves again) [amator: *qui aime et aime encore*]."[19] In this "etymological" possibility, it is not a question of the true origin of the word but of the possibility of displacement. Barthes writes, "In etymology it is not the truth or the origin of the word which pleases him but rather the *effect of overdetermination* which it authorizes: the word is seen as a palimpsest: it then seems to me that I have ideas *on the level of language*—which is quite simply: to write (I am speaking here of a praxis, not of a value)."[20] The figure of the amateur constitutes itself as a palimpsest, but this constitution is a subject position whose very mode of emergence is contingent. The amateur writer is itself the writing material that is altered but still bears visible traces of another writing. The amateur is the one who loves and loves *again*, which means that the effect of overdetermination is inscribed into his very mode of Being. The amateur is *atopical*, contingent, impossible to classify, or to give a definitive name. The amateur is the dispersion of the Subject, an interruption, which cannot be imprisoned by any stereotype, but marks an indecisive stammering. The amateur is neither a loving subject nor a loved subject but the very relation as the undoing of that relation. The amateur does not try to express his love. The subject does not say: "I shall produce an immortal work by writing my passion."[21] The amateur does not try to write love; rather, this being's very Being "is" love of writing. Instead of writing with the ability to not-write, or writing with the ability to write, the amateur is somebody who writes with an ability to love. In a fragment, Barthes describes a potential evolution that could prove as decisive as any anthropological change encountered in any natural history of man:

According to the Leroi-Gourhan hypothesis, it was when he could free his upper limbs from the task of locomotion and, in consequence, his mouth from predation, that man could speak. I would add: *and embrace*. For the phonatory system is also the osculatory system. Shifting to upright posture, man found himself free to invent language and love: this is perhaps the anthropological birth of a concomitant double perversion: speech and kissing. By this accounting, the freer men have been (with their mouths), the more they have spoken and embraced; and logically, when progress will rid men of every manual task, they will then do nothing but discourse and make love! [*ils ne feront plus que discourir et s'embrasser!*][22]

The future is the future of writing and kissing. Barthes imagines man's dual function as a simultaneous process: "to kiss while embracing, to embrace while speaking."[23] This manner would be "the function *which is disturbed*: in a word: *the stammered body*."[24] It is perhaps possible to think this stammered body, the body that writes and kisses, as the amateur's body. This writer would then not be the subject who writes intransitively because he is constituted with the inability to not-write; rather, this writer would write with his ability to not-write because she or he loves writing. But how are we to think this ability to not-write as an act of affirmation that interrupts the dialectic of the paradigm of writerly necessity?

The Pure Potentiality of Writing

My concern has been to make the paradigm of writerly necessity transparent so as to indicate the contingency of the literary absolute and show how the necessity to write is linked to the emergence of literature as the question of intransitivity. For the literary subject, contingency manifests the capacity both to write and to not-write. Agamben writes, "Contingency is not one modality among others, alongside possibility, impossibility, and necessity: it is the actual giving of a possibility, the way in which a potentiality exists as such. It is an event (*contingit*) of a potentiality as the giving of a caesura between a capacity to be and a capacity not to be."[25] For the literary subject, contingency is the manifestation of the aporia of the paradigm of writerly necessity, which is also the exposition of the contingency of the necessity to write.

In "On Potentiality," Agamben notes that contingency is the giving of a pure potentiality insofar as the potentiality to not-be "*preserves itself* as such in actuality."[26] To understand pure potentiality to preserve itself in actuality is to conceive a potentiality *as* potentiality. This possibility is unthinkable from Hegel's perspective. Kojève notes that Hegel allows for contingency insofar as Hegel's method is not an a priori deduction since "the 'deduction' is possible only after the fact or *a posteriori*, as we say. To say that the Spirit's becoming is 'contingent and free' is to say that, starting with spirit which is the end or result of becoming, one can reconstruct the path of the becoming, but one can neither foresee its path from its beginning, nor deduce the Sprit from it."[27] But for Hegel, the absolute is always already conceived from the perspective of mediation insofar as the self-relating movement has always already begun: "Hegel *starts* with Spirit, which he says is a 'result.' "[28]

Dieter Henrich shows that Hegel acknowledges contingency since Hegel does not pretend to "deduce" every contingency in the system; however, Hegel still proposes that there is a necessity of the whole or the totality of beings.[29] For Hegel, it is contingent whether "A" or "not-A" happens, but it is then necessary that either "A" or "not-A" happens, which means that any possibility can only be an actuality that is not yet actualized. Stephen Houlgate writes, "Hegel claims that contingent events are *groundless* insofar as they simply occur or could just as well not occur. But, he claims that they also have a *ground* insofar as they are contingent *upon* one possibility or another being actualized."[30] Hegel's necessity concerns not whether this or that occurs but the this-or-that-occurs as a whole. One alternative must occur, but which one that occurs is contingent. But, as the system actualizes itself, necessity is the impossibility of there being a possibility that is not actualized. Houlgate writes, "Necessity is generated by the self-*negation* or self-*Aufhebung* of possibility itself. ... He [Hegel] is simply pointing out that possibility *cannot not* be actual and so *must* be present as actual possibility or contingency."[31] Insofar as the question of literature concerns a pure potentiality, a potentiality that can *also* not actualize itself, literature is the question of the interruption of the dialectic.

The question of literature is the question of whether it is possible to expose the contingency of absolute positing. If it is possible to think the writer who writes with his or her ability to love, it is as the experience of pure potentiality that would be a non-dialectical experience. This writer would preserve the ability to not-write without losing the ability to write. This would be a writerly life in which the possibility for a non-dialectical experience manifests itself: an interruption that is not dialectical negation but the withdrawal of thetic Being.

Threshold

In the paradigm of writerly necessity, the writer and the critic, literature and criticism coincide. The journal of the Romantics, the *Athenaeum*, embodies the inauguration of the concept of literature. Criticism is the very self-consciousness of the literary work but also marks the absence of work. In order to produce an overview of the meaning of this absence of work, I will retrace the last part of this archaeology of literary theory.

1. *In the paradigm of writerly necessity, both the true literary writer and the true literary critic are subjects who cannot not-write intransitively*. It is not possible to distinguish between literature and criticism, the writer and the critic, the subject and the work. The reflection of reflection immanent to the literary work constitutes the auto-production of the work as its critical consciousness.

2. *The age of criticism is the death of art.* The age of criticism signifies that art is a thing of the past since it is not anymore the self-presentation of the absolute. Romanticism signifies a form without content. The literary Subject is a subject who cannot not-write intransitively, which means that this writer is unable to produce a Work in which form and content coincide as absolute presence.

3. *The age of criticism is the birth of art.* The age of criticism signifies the end of art, but criticism also inaugurates the possibility of the future of literature. This future is the absence of work as the space of inoperativity, which cannot be sublated into the dialectical operation of the self-relating negativity of the Work. The literary writer is the subject who cannot not-write intransitively, which means that this writer is able to produce the absence of work in which absolute presence withdraws as nothing but a pure interruption.

4. *The amateur is the critic-writer who can not-write in-transitively.* If the amateur is not simply the opposite of the writer who cannot not-write, but a writer who loves writing, the amateur "is" in-transitively in which the work is rendered inoperative. It is possible to conceive Barthes's lectures as an experiment into such an inoperative writerly life: a writerly practice of thought that retains its possibility of contingency.

What remains to be thought in literary criticism is the aporia of positing, the two lacks of the paradigm of writerly necessity, which disclose the contingency of this paradigm. This unthought is unworking or inoperativity (*désœuvrement*). The question is how we are to think this inoperative space.

Afterthought on Literary Inoperativity

Insofar as "literature" is a metaphysical practice, a thinking of *parousia*, the question of literature is a philosophical question. It is a "solution" to the metaphysical question of how to present philosophy: the question of a pure writing a priori. But "literature" also puts in question the presence of metaphysics itself. In "The Fable" ("La Fable (philosophie et littérature)," 1969), Lacoue-Labarthe asks whether literature exists "for anything but metaphysics" (*SP*, 2), or whether literature can mean "the letter (*gramma*, trace, mark, inscription … writing)" (*SP*, 2). On the one hand, the pure absolute writing appears to be nothing but the metaphysical will that desires its own unity. On the other hand, the pure intransitive writing appears as the contingency of a supplement. For Lacoue-Labarthe, the question of literature is first of all a question of *writing*, of an *experience* of writing, which is "certainly an *experience*, no matter how dubious the connotative power of this word" (*SP*, 12). But, writing is then the experience as "the very failure [*défaut*] of experience" (*SP*, 12/26). Lacoue-Labarthe writes, "Writing is first of all that reflection of experience wherein reflection (and hence experience) is constantly undone" (*SP*, 12). Writing is the undoing of dialectical experience, of absolute presence, of the Work. But how are we to understand this undoing?

Is it the interruption as the supplement of writing? In *Of Grammatology*, Derrida calls the supplement of writing (*grammata*) an "absolute contingency."[1] The supplement is that which might always already *not* have taken place when it takes place and that which has never taken place even when it apparently takes place: "It is the strange essence of the supplement not to have essentiality: it may always not have taken place. Moreover, literally, it has never taken place: it is never present, here and now. If it were, it would not be what it is, a supplement, taking and keeping the place of the other."[2] Since the supplement is not an origin, not a presence, the supplement has not taken place. But, insofar as the supplement adds itself to absolute presence, it takes place *as* what is removed so that this absolute can take place and this removal indicates the *contingent* trace of the taking place of the absolute.

How are we to think such contingency? How are we to think literary inoperativity? The literary absolute is the operation of the *opus*, of the Work, of the Subject. On the one hand, there can be no question of isolating an origin, the poet's birth, as the "essence" of the subject who cannot not-write. On the other hand, there can also be no question of isolating language insofar as intransitivity is the self-reference of thetic Being. In order to approach literary inoperativity, it is necessary to interrupt the relation between the Subject and language that manifests itself as the paradigm of writerly necessity. The archaeology of writerly necessity exposes this paradigm as precisely the relation of a Subject to its own (linguistic) death. For the subject who cannot not-write intransitively, interruption is always already inscribed as the contingent essence of the act of writing absolutely.

When literary thought approaches the truth of literature as the absolute presence, this thought only finds that signification is always already lacking. When literary thought aims to think the truth of literature in the linguistic interruption of the Subject, this thought only finds the self-referential absence of the Subject that is only the confirmation of the Subject's death. For the subject who aims to write the absolute Work, signification never emerges as the full presence. For the subject who aims to write the absence of work that does not signify anything, literature emerges as a necessity to write that commands to write nothing. In either case, the paradigm of writerly necessity is the imperative to write absence, an empty imperative that commands nothing, wills nothing, signifies nothing but its own will to signify. It is the imperative of thetic Being as the will to will.

The archaeology of writerly necessity manifests the contingency of this imperative of writing. The question of literary inoperativity is the question of how to think the contingency of this necessity of writing: to think the contingency of writerly necessity. This involves thinking the aporia of positing by which the paradigm of writerly necessity constitutes itself. A double lack constitutes the paradigm of writerly necessity: The subject cannot not-write the absence of work. On the one hand, the literary writer can never reach his own negativity, the lack, which constitutes this writer as a subject who must write absence. The subject who always already must write can never expose the contingency of the "cannot not-write." On the other hand, the literary work is that which is impossible to write since it is nothing but the absence of work. Insofar as the absence of work constitutes the truth of literature, it is never possible to write a true literary work. In order to think the contingency of the truth of literature as intransitivity, the contingency of the "cannot write" must be exposed as the possibility to write the absence of work rather than as the impossibility to write a work. The truth of the paradigm of writerly necessity is thus the truth of the criterion of intransitivity. The truth of this criterion is its own history, the history of literary truth, which is exposed in the archaeology of writerly necessity. The truth is the contingency of any literary truth. To begin to think literary inoperativity is to begin to think such contingency.

In "Pardes: The Writing of Potentiality" ("Pardes: la scrittura della potenza," 1990), Agamben approaches the deconstructive trace as a thinking of contingency.[3] Agamben suggests that the "aporias of self-reference" can be "transformed into *euporias*."[4] The negativity of the dialectical Subject can be transformed into a pure affirmation. Agamben writes,

> The name can be named and language can be brought to speech, because self-reference is displaced onto the level of potentiality; what is intended is neither the word as object nor the word insofar as it *actually* denotes a thing but, rather, a pure potentiality to signify (and not to signify), the writing tablet on which nothing is written. But this is no longer meaning's self-reference, a sign's signification of itself; instead, it is the materialization of a potentiality, the materialization of its own possibility.[5]

The loving act of writing is not the pure imperative to write, the will to signify, the empty necessity to write the absence of work. Rather, such an act of writing is potentiality to write or not-write that is materialized as possibility. In this place, here and now, the amateur can begin writing or not begin writing and always stop writing at the very moment she or he writes. The subject who cannot not-write the absence of work emerges as the amateur who *can* not-write. But it is thus possible that the writer does not write, that the writer does not *want* to write. When the writer suddenly can write, when the writer does not have to write, it is possible that this subject has no desire to write. It is possible that no one will write. But, for the amateur, for the writer who loves writing, this possibility is then the possibility of writing: to write, to be, for the first time, without *not* being able *not* to write. Where there is somebody who loves writing, there can never be a will to write. Only when there is no will to write is it possible for the writer to love writing.

Conclusion

My archaeology of literary theory has been concerned with literature as absolute. I have aimed to show how the literary absolute emerges as the paradigm of writerly necessity, which constitutes the "truth" of literature. In post-Kantian thought, literature emerges as the fictional possibility of a pure intransitive work. The paradigm of writerly necessity emerges as *the subject who cannot not-write intransitively*. This paradigm becomes the condition of possibility for the emergence of "sincerity" and "intransitively" as criteria of literary criticism in the nineteenth and twentieth century. In literary criticism, the central question becomes how to determine the relation between producer and product, life and work, writer and literature, and Subject and language. Moreover, literature itself emerges as a form of criticism. Within the paradigm of writerly necessity, it becomes impossible to distinguish between literature and criticism, between the true literary writer and the true literary critic. The question becomes whether criticism is the end of literature or the future of literature.

Literature emerges as the question of literature: Does literature manifest the dialectic or the interruption of the dialectic? It is the paradigm of writerly necessity that constitutes the horizon for understanding this question of literature. This paradigm delimits a space between the Subject and intransitive language. This space is a space of dispersion in which the contingency of the Subject manifests itself. Since the literary Subject cannot not-write, this necessity to write appears as the "essence" of the literary existence. But insofar as the Subject must write the absence of work, the Subject must die in order to write literature. In this "death" emerges the question of literature as the question of intransitivity: Does intransitivity indicate the self-reference of an act of writing or the interruption of the act of writing? Does intransitivity indicate the empty necessity to write the absence of work, or is literature the contingency of this necessity to write?

With respect to the work, the question of literature emerges as the question whether this absence of work is the abstract form without content or the possibility of the interruption of the absolute Work. Insofar as the paradigm of writerly necessity exposes its contingency, it is possible to think a future of literature as the interruption of the absolute. But within the paradigm of writerly necessity, the literary absolute has arisen as nothing but the incessant necessity to write intransitively in which the "truth" of literary criticism remains suspended. The aim of my archaeology of literary theory has been to expose the contingency of this necessity to write intransitively.

NOTES

Introduction: Writerly Necessity

1 Rainer Maria Rilke, *Letters to a Young Poet & the Letter from the Young Worker*, trans. Charlie Louth (London: Penguin, 2011), 7.

2 Rilke, *Letters*, 7–8; Rainer Maria Rilke, *Briefe an einen jungen Dichter* (Leipzig: Insel Verlag, 1929), 10.

3 Rilke, *Letters*, 6.

4 Ibid., 9.

5 The necessity to write thus constitutes a "monopoly of literary legitimacy," that is, "the monopoly of the *power of consecration* of producers and products" (Pierre Bourdieu, *The Rules of Art: Genesis and Structure of the Literary Field*, trans. Susan Emanuel [Stanford, CA: Stanford University Press, 1996], 224). Regarding the expression "not-write," see note 20.

6 Rilke, *Letters*, 10.

7 I. A. Richards, *Practical Criticism: A Study of Literary Judgment* (London: Routledge & Kegan Paul, 1929), 3.

8 Ibid., 4.

9 Ibid., 69.

10 Ibid., 300.

11 Paul de Man, *Allegories of Reading: Figural Language in Rousseau, Nietzsche, Rilke, and Proust* (New Haven, CT: Yale University Press, 1979), 48.

12 W. K. Wimsatt, *The Verbal Icon: Studies in the Meaning of Poetry* (Lexington: University of Kentucky Press, 1954), 222.

13 Ibid., 231.

14 Friedrich Schlegel, *Friedrich Schlegel's Lucinde and the Fragments*, trans. Peter Firchow (Minneapolis: University of Minnesota Press, 1971), 157.

15 Friedrich Schlegel, "On Goethe's Meister," in *Classic and Romantic German Aesthetics*, ed. J. M. Bernstein (Cambridge: Cambridge University Press, 2003), 269–86 (281); Friedrich Schlegel, "Über Goethes Meister," in *Kritische Friedrich-Schlegel-Ausgabe. Bd. 2. Charakteristiken und Kritiken 1 (1796–1801)*, ed. Hans Eichner (Paderborn: Verlag Ferdinand Schöningh, 1967), 126–46 (140).

16 See René Wellek, *Discriminations: Further Concepts of Criticism* (New Haven, CT: Yale University Press, 1970), 4–9; *Wörterbuch der Literaturwissenschaft*, ed. Claus Träger (Leipzig: Veb Bibliographisches Institut, 1986), 299–303; *Encyclopedia of Contemporary Literary Theory: Approaches, Scholars, Terms*, ed. Irena R. Makaryk (Toronto: University of Toronto Press, 1993), 581–2; *Reallexikon der deutschen Literaturwissenschaft*, ed. Harald Fricke (Berlin: Walter de Gruyter, 2000), 444–5; *Dictionnaire des littératures de langue française*, ed. Jean-Pierre de Beaumarchais, Daniel Couty, and Alain Rey (Paris: Bordas, 1998), 1405–10. As a translation of the Greek *grammatiké* (from *gramma*, "letter"), the Latin *litteratura* (from *littera*, "letter") means knowledge of writing and reading (i.e., literacy). According to Klaus Weimar (*Reallexicon*), the decisive shift of meaning happened in the sixteenth century when *literatura* was separated from *littera* so as to emerge as *literatus* (i.e., man of learning or man of letters). From around the 1750s, literature is given its present sense as "the entirety of literary texts" (*Gesamtheit der literarischen Texte*), but this usage is first generally established in Germany, France, and England in the nineteenth century. Derrida argues that there is an irreducible link between writing and literature (see Jacques Derrida, *Of Grammatology*, trans. Gayatri Chakravorty Spivak, Corrected Edition [Baltimore, MD: Johns Hopkins University Press, 1997], 59).

17 In this study, I focus on literary theory; however, with reference to the metaphysics of will, the paradigm of writerly necessity could be related to other fields of knowledge (e.g., Giorgio Agamben, *The Kingdom and the Glory: For a Theological Genealogy of Economy and Government*, trans. Lorenzo Chiesa [Stanford, CA: Stanford University Press, 2011], 56–7; Giorgio Agamben, *Opus Dei: An Archaeology of Duty*, trans. Adam Kotsko [Stanford, CA: Stanford University Press, 2013], 126–9).

18 Michel Foucault, *The Archaeology of Knowledge and the Discourse on Language*, trans. A. M. Sheridan Smith (New York: Vintage, 2010), 95.

19 I use the negative form *cannot not-write* in order to underline that the necessity to write entails an essential lack, which means that an inability to not-write constitutes this subject; however, I will also be using the verbs *must write* synonymously with this form (*cannot not-write*). I use the hyphen (*not-write*) in order to avoid any ambiguity with respect to the modalities of literary writing between necessity (*cannot not-write*), contingency (*can not-write*), possibility (*can write*), and impossibility (*cannot write*). Even if this ambiguity arises only with respect to the relation between the modalities of contingency (*can not write*) and impossibility (*can not write*), I have decided to consistently use the form *not-write* in relation to both of the modalities of necessity and contingency.

20 The term "writerly" is a translation of Barthes's neologism *scriptible* (see Roland Barthes, *S/Z*, trans Richard Miller [Oxford: Blackwell, 1990]; Roland Barthes, *S/Z* [Paris: Seuil, 1970]). However, I use the word "writerly" with no reference to Barthes's conceptualization of this term. In my archaeology, "writerly necessity" refers to nothing but the paradigm, which produces a subject who cannot not-write intransitively. But it is visible how "writerly

necessity" instantiates itself in Barthes's conceptualization of the "writerly" as "production without product" (Barthes, *S/Z*, 5) and in the notion that "the writerly text is *ourselves writing* [*le texte scriptible, c'est* nous en train d'écrire]" (Barthes, *S/Z*, 5/11).

21 The history of "veridictions" is the history of "truth-saying." "Veridical" comes from the Latin *verus* ("true") and *dicere* ("say"). For a sustained analysis of the difference between the "acceptability" and the "predication" of truth in Foucault's archaeology, see Béatrice Han, *Foucault's Critical Project: Between the Transcendental and the Historical*, trans. Edward Pile (Stanford, CA: Stanford University Press, 2002), 79–92.

22 Giorgio Agamben, *The Signature of All Things: On Method*, trans. Luca D'Isanto and Kevin Attell (New York: Zone, 2009), 94. In *The Archaeology of Knowledge*, Foucault writes that the historical a priori is "the group of rules that characterize a discursive practice: but these rules are not imposed from the outside on the elements that they relate together; they are caught up in the very things that they connect" (Foucault, *Archaeology of Knowledge*, 127).

23 Cf. Agamben, *Signature of All Things*, 19.

24 Cf. Claude Romano, *Event and World*, trans. Shane Mackinlay (New York: Fordham University Press, 2009), 39–45.

25 In *Event and World*, Claude Romano addresses the temporality of an event that determines how any understanding of the event takes place. If we replace the concept of the event with the concept of the paradigm, we can transpose Romano's analysis of temporality to the method of archaeological investigation. Romano writes, "Understanding is retrospective precisely to the extent that the event itself is *prospective*, precedes itself, and is accessible solely from its future" (Romano, *Event and World*, 64). In Romano's terms, this retroactive understanding turns the event into an "*un-condition*: a 'condition' that is conditioned in turn, and more originally, by what it conditions" (Romano, *Event and World*, 72).

26 In *Foucault's Critical Project*, Béatrice Han conceives this aporia of the historical a priori as a defect inherent to the method of archaeology since it is not possible to distinguish between the transcendental and the empirical. This critique is a development of Dreyfus and Rabinow's claim that archaeology "still suffers from a version of the transcendental/empirical" double, which Foucault ascribes to the human sciences in *The Order of Things* (Hubert L. Dreyfus and Paul Rabinow, *Michel Foucault: Beyond Structuralism and Hermeneutics* [New York: Harvester Wheatsheaf, 1982], 92). The problem of the historical a priori is that this a priori must appear within experience in order to take place, but experience itself presupposes the condition a priori, which means that it is never possible to ascribe priority to a "foundation" (see Han, *Foucault's Critical Project*, 38–69). Han is indeed right that the historical a priori displays an aporia; however, I argue that this aporia is the very concern of philosophical archaeology insofar as the aporia exposes the contingency of every positing of a subject in relation to an object.

27 For a sustained analysis of this aporia of positing, see Werner Hamacher, "Premises," in *Premises: Essays on Philosophy and Literature from Kant to*

Celan, trans. Peter Fenves (Stanford, CA: Stanford University Press, 1999), 1–43. Regarding the temporality of philosophical archaeology, see also Agamben, *Signature of All Things*, 105–7.

28 Blanchot's essay "La Littérature et le droit à la mort" was first published in *Critique*, no. 20 (January 1948), 30–47.

29 Roland Barthes, "To Write: An Intransitive Verb?" in *The Structuralist Controversy: The Languages of Criticism and the Sciences of Man*, ed. Richard Macksey and Eugenio Donato (Baltimore, MD: Johns Hopkins University Press, 2007), 134–45 (142). Regarding this conference at the Johns Hopkins University, see Chapter 8.

30 Jean-Paul Sartre, *"What Is Literature?" and Other Essays*, trans. Steven Ungar (Cambridge, MA: Harvard University Press, 1988), 140.

31 Ibid., 135.

32 Ibid., 140.

33 Ibid., 138. Sartre's exposition of the dialectic of literature is a transposition of Hegelian classicism. Regarding this classicism, see Chapter 10.

34 Sartre, *"What Is Literature?"*, 103.

35 Ibid., 111.

36 Ibid., 100.

37 Ibid., 105.

38 Ibid., 111.

39 See Roland Barthes, *Writing Degree Zero*, trans. Annette Lavers and Colin Smith (New York: Hill and Wang, 2012), 3. For readings of Barthes's *Writing Degree Zero*, see Mary Bittner Wiseman, *The Ecstasies of Roland Barthes* (London: Routledge, 1989), 15–37; George R. Wasserman, *Roland Barthes* (Boston, MA: Twayne, 1981), 23–46.

40 Barthes, *Writing Degree Zero*, 61.

41 Ibid., 38.

42 Ibid., 2–3.

43 Ibid., 60.

44 Ibid., 61.

45 Ibid., 87–8.

46 Ibid., 38.

47 Roland Barthes, *Roland Barthes by Roland Barthes*, trans. Richard Howard (New York: Hill and Wang, 2010), 87.

48 Ibid., 87.

49 Jacques Rancière, *The Politics of Aesthetics: The Distribution of the Sensible*, trans. Gabriel Rockhill (London: Bloomsbury, 2013), 8.

50 Jacques Rancière, *Mute Speech: Literature, Critical Theory, and Politics*, trans. James Swenson (New York: Columbia University Press, 2011), 32.

51 Ibid., 81.

52 Ibid., 83.

53 Ibid., 50.

54 Bourdieu, *Rules of Art*, 58.

55 Ibid., xvi.

56 Ibid., 236.

57 Ibid., 333.

58 Ibid., 184.

59 The word "Being" is here capitalized in order to mark its difference from "being" understood as an "entity," that is, as an "object" that can be said to be *something*. Regarding this question of the distinction between "Being" and "beings," I refer to Heidegger's analysis of the ontological difference (see Martin Heidegger, *The Basic Problems of Phenomenology*, Revised Edition, trans. Albert Hofstadter [Bloomington: Indiana University Press, 1988], 318–30).

60 Agamben, *Signature of All Things*, 89. For a study of Agamben's method, see William Watkin, *Agamben and Indifference: A Critical Overview* (London: Rowman & Littlefield, 2014), 3–48.

Chapter 1

1 For a good analysis of Nancy's reading of Kant, see Ian James, *The Fragmentary Demand: An Introduction to the Philosophy of Jean-Luc Nancy* (Stanford, CA: Stanford University Press, 2006), 26–48.

2 Regarding the concept of *Darstellung*, see Martha B. Helfer, *The Retreat of Representation: The Concept of* Darstellung *in German Critical Discourse* (Albany: State University of New York Press, 1996).

3 Regarding this lecture course, see Martin Heidegger, *Phenomenological Interpretation of Kant's Critique of Pure Reason*, trans. Parvis Emad and Kenneth Maly (Bloomington: Indiana University Press, 1997).

4 Friedrich Schlegel, *Dialogue on Poetry and Literary Aphorisms*, trans. Ernst Behler and Roman Struc (London: Pennsylvania State University Press, 1968), 116; Friedrich Schlegel, "Gespräch über die Poesie," Kritische Friedrich-Schlegel-Ausgabe. Bd. 2., 284–362 (350).

5 Cf. the Kantian question in the first *Critique*: "How are synthetic judgments *a priori* possible?" (*CR*, B19).

6 Johann Gottlieb Fichte, "Foundations of the Entire Science of Knowledge," in *The Science of Knowledge*, ed. Peter Lauchlan Heath and John Lachs (Cambridge: Cambridge University Press, 1982), 97; Johann Gottlieb Fichte, "Grundlage der gesammten Wissenschaftslehre," in *Fichtes Werke*, ed. Immanuel Hermann Fichte (Berlin: Walter de Gruyter, 1971), vol. I, 83–328 (I: 96).

7 Fichte, "Foundations of the Entire Science of Knowledge," 97; Fichte, "Grundlage der gesammten Wissenschaftslehre," 96. See also Werner Hamacher's study on the foundation of Romanticism in Fichte's ontology in "Position Exposed: Friedrich Schlegel's Poetological Transposition of Fichte's Absolute Proposition," in *Premises*, 222–60. Here Hamacher conceives Fichte's absolute self-active Subject (I = I) as "the site of Being" (Hamacher, *Premises*, 231), that is to say, as a certain understanding of *Sein* as pure positing.

8 Georg Wilhelm Friedrich Hegel, *Hegel's Science of Logic*, trans. Arnold V. Miller (New York: Humanities Press, 1976), 536. Regarding the Absolute as the self-manifestation of actuality, see Robert Pippin, *Hegel's Idealism: The Satisfactions of Self-Consciousness* (Cambridge: Cambridge University Press, 1989), 224; Markus Gabriel, *Transcendental Ontology: Essays in German Idealism* (New York: Continuum, 2011), 112.

9 Heidegger lectured on Hegel in the winter semester 1930–1 at the University of Freiburg. This lecture course was first published in German in 1980 whereas Nancy's *The Speculative Remark* was published in French in 1973. However, Heidegger's reading of Hegel was already available in the essay "Hegel's Concept of Experience" ("Hegels Begriff der Erfahrung," 1942–3), which was published in German in *Holzwege* in 1950 (see Martin Heidegger, "Hegel's Concept of Experience," in *Off the Beaten Track*, trans. Julian Young and Kenneth Haynes [Cambridge: Cambridge University Press, 2002], 86–156; Martin Heidegger, "Hegels Begriff der Erfahrung," in *Holzwege* [Frankfurt am Main: Vittorio Klostermann, 1980], 111–204).

10 See also Heidegger, "Hegel's Concept of Experience," 102.

11 Regarding examinations of Hegel's speculative proposition, see *SR*, 7–19; Werner Hamacher, *Pleroma: Reading in Hegel*, trans. Nicholas Walker and Simon Jarvis (London: Athlone Press, 1998), 5–7; Catherine Malabou, *The Future of Hegel: Plasticity, Temporality and Dialectic*, trans. Lisabeth During (London: Routledge, 2005), 8–13; Daniel J. Cook, *Language in the Philosophy of Hegel* (The Hague: Mouton, 1973), 142–8; Günter Wohlfart, *Der Spekulative Satz: Bemerkungen zum Begriff der Spekulation bei Hegel* (Berlin: Walter de Gruyter, 1981). Wohlfart notes, "The problem of the speculative proposition is the problem of the linguistic presentation [*Darstellung*] of the speculative" (Wohlfart, v; my translation).

12 Nancy's reading of Hegel is linked to Derrida's deconstructive gesture. In the essay "The Pit and the Pyramid: Introduction to Hegel's Semiology," Derrida considers the possibility of a negativity that would not be "to sublate" (*aufheben, relever*) but that would work as "pure loss" (Jacques Derrida, "The Pit and the Pyramid: Introduction to Hegel's Semiology," in *Margins of Philosophy*, trans. Alan Bass [Brighton: Harvester Press, 1982], 69–108 [107]). In "From Restricted to General Economy," Derrida addresses a written (or supplementary) suspension of sense, an *epochē* of meaning, which cannot be thought in Hegel's *Phenomenology* (Jacques Derrida, "From Restricted to General Economy: A Hegelianism without reserve," in *Writing and Difference*, ed. Alan Bass [London: Routledge, 2001], 317–50 [339]). The question of literature is the question of what it means to think such an *epochē*.

Chapter 2

1   See Daniel J. Hoolsema, "The Echo of an Impossible Future in 'The Literary
    Absolute,'" *MLN*, vol. 119, no. 4 (2004), 845–68. Hoolsema writes, "*The
    Literary Absolute* has presented its readers with something of a conundrum.
    Proof of its resistance to interpretation appears in the mutually exclusive
    messages it has generated. On the one hand, authors Lacoue-Labarthe and
    Nancy state explicitly that their book's aim is to help usher us beyond the era
    of the subject of metaphysics. On the other hand, the authors' critics have
    consistently argued that, because their study of early German Romanticism is
    finally uncritical, it only ends up endorsing the Romantics' effort to establish
    the subject in its autarky" (Hoolsema, "Echo of an Impossible Future," 845).
    In order to examine the equivocal statements on the question of the Subject
    in *The Literary Absolute*, Hoolsema's aim is "to offer a clear reading of *The
    Literary Absolute*. It is time simply to understand the book on its own terms.
    In order to do so, we will need to ground our reading of it appropriately,
    which is to say, in philosophy" (Hoolsema, "Echo of an Impossible Future,"
    848). But Hoolsema's investigation turns out to be a reading of *The Literary
    Absolute* from the perspective of Nancy's later works. Hoolsema touches
    on the problem of Kantian *Darstellung*, but without any reference to Nancy
    and Lacoue-Labarthe's earlier works, and Heidegger's early readings of
    Kant and German Idealism that are presupposed in *The Literary Absolute*.
    Despite this lacuna, Hoolsema perceives that the fundamental question in *The
    Literary Absolute* is whether Romanticism only presents a thinking within
    the metaphysics of the Subject or indicates a form of interruption "that takes
    place by withdrawing itself from presence, by absenting itself from any will
    to presence or system" (Hoolsema, "Echo of an Impossible Future," 853).
    Hoolsema refers to this interruption as Blanchot's "unworking of the work
    of the will to system" (Hoolsema, "Echo of an Impossible Future," 854).
    He also recognizes that Nancy and Lacoue-Labarthe conceive that "the
    Romantics themselves never successfully grasped the essence of the event
    they inaugurated" (Hoolsema, "Echo of an Impossible Future," 858), which
    is unworking as the essence of literature. But for Hoolsema, "by introducing
    Blanchot's concept of *désœuvrement* that will emerge as the center of their
    book, Lacoue-Labarthe and Nancy court disaster and imperil their entire
    program of writing" (Hoolsema, "Echo of an Impossible Future," 848). The
    reason for this is that, according to Hoolsema, unworking "reveals only an
    interruption that never succeeds in becoming a new beginning" (Hoolsema,
    "Echo of an Impossible Future," 867). But the question is then whether the
    possibility of a new "writing" in fact does lie in a "new beginning" (or in a
    new political "myth") or in the *epochē*, the "interruption" itself.

2   For studies on the philosophy of the Romantics, see especially Frederick C.
    Beiser, *The Romantic Imperative: The Concept of Early German Romanticism*
    (Cambridge, MA: Harvard University Press, 2003); Manfred Frank,
    Einführung in die frühromantische Ästhetik: Vorlesungen (Frankfurt am
    Main: Suhrkamp, 1989). Beiser aims "to introduce the *philosophy* behind early
    German romanticism" (Beiser, *Romantic Imperative*, ix). His focus is on moral

and political issues, which he claims have been neglected in the reception of the concept of *romantische Poesie*. Beiser's reading opposes so-called postmodern interpretations, which for Beiser includes Frank, Nancy, and Lacoue-Labarthe. For Beiser, these "postmodernists" are "anachronistic" since they impose "contemporary concerns upon" Romanticism (Beiser, *Romantic Imperative*, x). Since the explicit focus of *The Literary Absolute* is not the philosophy of the Romantics but the "question of literature," this critique appears to be based on a misunderstanding of Nancy and Lacoue-Labarthe's study. *The Literary Absolute* does not attribute a literary philosophy to the Romantics that was never there; rather, the focus on the "question of literature" implies that the question is not only how the *Athenaeum* inaugurates the literary absolute but also how the present receives and understands the Early German Romantics. Beiser in fact also admits that he has not understood the sense of the literary absolute: "They [Lacoue-Labarthe and Nancy] virtually define romanticism in terms of its absolutization of literature. The object of their study, they explicitly insist, is 'the question of literature.' Although they also insist that romanticism is not just literature but also theory of literature (p. 12), they still see it essentially as 'this absolute literary operation' (whatever that is). This is a step backward in the study of *Frühromantik*" (Beiser, *Romantic Imperative*, 194, note 7). Manfred Frank's study of *Frühromantik* situates the Romantics in relation to Kant and post-Kantian German Idealism but also explicitly claims that the romantic absolute (*das romantische Absolute*) is a ground that precedes the thinking (*unvordenklicher Grund*) of the (idealist) Subject. For Frank, the romantic absolute is thus not the empowerment of Subjectivity (*Selbstmächtigung von Subjektivität*); rather, it is the showing of the concealed ground of Being (*Seinsgrund*) (see Frank, Einführung in die frühromantische Ästhetik, 127–8).

3   In his dissertation, Walter Benjamin understands "reflection" as the key to understanding the Romantics (see *SW*, 120–48; see also my analysis of Benjamin's dissertation later in this chapter). In "L'Absolu littéraire: Friedrich Schlegel and the Myth of Irony," Kevin Newmark suggests that the interruption of philosophy also names the "irony within romanticism" (Kevin Newmark, "L'Absolu littéraire: Friedrich Schlegel and the Myth of Irony," *MLN*, vol. 107, no. 5 (1992), 905–30 [907]). But, according to Newmark, this irony is never "tackled directly" in *The Literary Absolute* (Newmark, "L'Absolu littéraire," 908). For Newmark, this irony is the "self-resisting … truth about the literary structure of all philosophical meaning" (Newmark, "L'Absolu littéraire," 925). This irony is that which "forever disrupts the mythological unity of literature and philosophy" (Newmark, "L'Absolu littéraire," 927). For Newmark, irony thus appears to occupy the position of interruption, which is reserved for the concept of unworking (or writing) in *The Literary Absolute* (see Newmark, "L'Absolu littéraire," 927, note 6). Newmark moreover pays attention to the political stakes in Romanticism and the question of a new political "mythology," which is addressed in Nancy and Lacoue-Labarthe's later work. Regarding this "politics," see especially Jean-Luc Nancy, *The Inoperative Community*, ed. Peter Connor (Minneapolis: University of Minnesota Press, 1991), 43–70; Philippe Lacoue-Labarthe, *Heidegger, Art and Politics: The*

Fiction of the Political, trans. Chris Turner (Oxford: Basil Blackwell, 1990); Philippe Lacoue-Labarthe and Jean-Luc Nancy, *Retreating the Political*, ed. Simon Sparks (London: Routledge, 1997).

4 In "Re-Re-Re-Reading Jena" (*MLN*, vol. 110, no. 4 [1995], 834–55), Susan Bernstein understands Nancy and Lacoue-Labarthe's analysis in *The Literary Absolute* to be a form of Heideggerian "repetition" (*Wiederholung*) by which a tradition is appropriated in order to engage "in the suspended moments— that is, the *possibilities*—made available by the past" (Bernstein, "Re-Re-Re-Reading Jena," 842). Bernstein is thus very much concerned with how to read *The Literary Absolute* and also underlines the necessity of rereading; however, the question of literature as a problem of *Darstellung* is not examined in detail and Bernstein never addresses the dialectic that takes place within the text of *The Literary Absolute*. Christopher A. Strathman does also not interrogate the question of *Darstellung* but rather relies on Hoolsema's reading of *The Literary Absolute* (cf. Christopher A. Strathman, *Romantic Poetry and the Fragmentary Imperative: Schlegel, Byron, Joyce, Blanchot* [Albany: State University of New York Press, 2006], 179, note 5).

5 Simon Critchley, *Very Little … Almost Nothing: Death, Philosophy, Literature*, 2nd ed. (London: Routledge, 2004), 136. This fluidity of concepts is without a doubt a deconstructive strategy. Derrida writes regarding the problem of definitive concepts: "If words and concepts receive meaning only in sequences of differences, one can justify one's language, and one's choice of terms, only within a topic [an orientation in space] and an historical strategy. The justification can therefore never be absolute and definitive" (Jacques Derrida, Of Grammatology, trans. Gayatri Chakravorty Spivak, Corrected Edition [Baltimore, MD: Johns Hopkins University Press, 1997], 70). For Critchley's reading of Derrida from the perspective of Levinas's ethics, see Simon Critchley, *The Ethics of Deconstruction: Derrida and Levinas*, 3rd ed. (Edinburgh: Edinburgh University Press, 2014).

6 The Hegelian *Aufhebung* marks the Subject's return (*retour, Wiederkehr*) to itself by becoming other than itself. In *The Speculative Remark*, Nancy also uses the word *retour* to describe the work of sublation: "The 'return' [*Wiederkehr*] of the *aufheben* is always the return of a past, or the return to the past, unless it be the return of a still-to-come [*Le 'retour' [Wiederkehr] de l'*aufheben *est toujours le retour d'un passé, ou le retour au passé, à moins qu'il ne soit le retour d'un encore-à-venir*]" (*SR*, 30/45).

7 Derrida, *Of Grammatology*, 314.

8 Ibid., 303–4.

9 Ibid., 163.

10 Ibid., 159.

11 Ibid., 144.

12 Ibid., 26; see *SR*, 164–5, note 17.

13 Derrida, *Of Grammatology*, 26.

14 Friedrich Schlegel, *Friedrich Schlegel's Lucinde and the Fragments*, trans. Peter Firchow (Minneapolis: University of Minnesota Press, 1971),175.

15 Derrida, *Of Grammatology*, 158.

16 Schlegel, *Friedrich Schlegel's Lucinde and the Fragments*, 175.

17 Giorgio Agamben, *Opus Dei: An Archaeology of Duty*, trans. Adam Kotsko (Stanford, CA: Stanford University Press, 2013), 41.

18 Ibid., 63–4. Agamben here reworks Heidegger's analysis of the history of metaphysics in which Being emerges as constant presence as that which endures (*ousia*). According to Heidegger, Aristotle's *ergon* ("work") is not a work in the modern sense as the actuality of an effect; rather, Aristotle understands the *ergon* as "what is completely at rest in presencing in unconcealment" (*EP*, 5). It is *energeia*, presence-as-work, in which presence is understood verbally. In *The Essence of Human Freedom*, Heidegger says, "The Greeks, and above all Aristotle, see the workhood of work not in terms of its origin, nor in terms of the person who sets the work into motion, but in the moment of being finished and ready" (Martin Heidegger, *The Essence of Human Freedom: An Introduction to Philosophy*, trans. Ted Sadler [London: Continuum, 2005], 48). According to Heidegger, with the later translation of the Greek *energeia* into the Roman Latin *actualitas*, the word Being is displaced. An entire transposition of thought thus takes place: "The *ergon* is no longer what is freed in the openness of presencing [as in Aristotle], but rather what is effected in working, what is accomplished in action" (*EP*, 12). Heidegger notes, "The essential determination of Being as *actualitas* underlies all history in advance" (*EP*, 13).

19 Agamben, *Opus Dei*, 129.

20 Derrida, *Of Grammatology*, 7.

21 Friedrich Schlegel, *Kritische Friedrich-Schlegel-Ausgabe. Bd. 2. Charakteristiken und Kritiken 1 (1796–1801)*, ed. Hans Eichner (Paderborn: Verlag Ferdinand Schöningh, 1967), 239.

22 Schlegel, *Friedrich Schlegel's Lucinde and the Fragments*, 144; Schlegel, *Kritische Friedrich-Schlegel-Ausgabe. Bd. 2*, 148.

23 See Georg Wilhelm Friedrich Hegel, *Hegel's Science of Logic* trans. Arnold V. Miller (New York: Humanities Press, 1976), 106–8. Hegel writes, "'*To sublate*' [Aufheben] has a twofold meaning in the language: on the one hand it means to preserve, to maintain, and equally it also means to cause to cease, to put an end to. … The double meaning of the Latin *tollere* (which has become famous through the Ciceronian pun [*Witz*]: *tollendum est Octavium*) does not go so far; its affirmative determination signifies only a lifting up" (Hegel, *Hegel's Science of Logic*, 107; Georg Wilhelm Friedrich Hegel, *Wissenschaft der Logik*, I–II, Werke 5–6, ed. Eva Moldenhauer and Karl Markus Michel (Frankfurt am Main: Suhrkamp, 1969), vol. 1, 114). See also *SR*, 24.

24 Philippe Büttgen, *Dictionary of Untranslatables: A Philosophical Lexicon*, ed. Barbara Cassin (Princeton, NJ: Princeton University Press, 2014), 74.

25 Jean-Luc Nancy, "Menstruum Universale," in *The Birth to Presence*, trans. Brian Holmes and others (Stanford, CA: Stanford University Press, 1993), 248–65 (265).

26 Vincent Descombes, *Modern French Philosophy*, trans. L. Scott-Fox and J.
    M. Harding (Cambridge: Cambridge University Press, 1980), 10. Regarding
    the reception of Hegel in modern France, see also Michael S.
    Roth, *Knowing
    and History: Appropriations of Hegel in Twentieth-Century France* (Ithaca,
    NY: Cornell University Press, 1988); Judith Butler, *Subjects of Desire: Hegelian
    Reflections in Twentieth-Century France* (New York: Columbia University
    Press, 1987); Bruce Baugh, *French Hegel: From Surrealism to Postmodernism*
    (New York: Routledge, 2003).

27 For a critical exposition of Benjamin's dissertation on the Romantic theory
    of reflection, see Winfried Menninghaus, "Walter Benjamin's Exposition of
    the Romantic Theory of Reflection," in *Walter Benjamin and Romanticism*,
    ed. Beatrice Hanssen and Andrew Benjamin (London: Continuum, 2002),
    19–50. Menninghaus shows how "selectively" (Menninghaus, "Walter
    Benjamin's Exposition," 27) Benjamin uses source material but nevertheless
    assesses Benjamin's investigation as "a largely valid 'derivation' of the
    cardinal concepts of Romantic poetology from the theory of reflection as
    their centre" (Menninghaus, "Walter Benjamin's Exposition," 50). The reason
    for this might be that, as Menninghaus argues, "Benjamin's approach to the
    Romantic theory of reflection have to a great extent been prepared already in
    his theory of language, which is likewise a Romantic theory" (Menninghaus,
    "Walter Benjamin's Exposition," 28). In "The Sober Absolute," Rodolphe
    Gasché acknowledges Menninghaus's critique of Benjamin's exposition but
    also attempts to show how Benjamin's own critical thinking differs from the
    romantic theory (see Rodolphe Gasché, "The Sober Absolute: On Benjamin
    and the Early Romantics," in *Walter Benjamin and Romanticism*, ed. Beatrice
    Hanssen and Andrew Benjamin [London: Continuum, 2002], 51–68).

28 See Marc Redfield, "Romanticism, Bildung, and the Literary Absolute," in
    Lessons of Romanticism: A Critical Companion, ed. Thomas Pfau and Robert
    F. Gleckner (Durham: Duke University Press, 1998), 41–54. Marc Redfield
    criticizes that Nancy and Lacoue-Labarthe's study "tends to underplay or
    forget the most incisive gesture in Walter Benjamin's thesis: his contention
    that Romantic criticism understands 'reflection in the absolute of art' to be in
    the strictest sense *nonsubjective*" (Redfield, "Romanticism, Bildung, and the
    Literary Absolute," 47–8).

29 In his dissertation on Romanticism, Benjamin understands not only the
    Romantics but also Hölderlin to propose the absolute of art as the medium
    of reflection (see *SW*, 175). But Benjamin also indicates that there is a
    difference between the Romantics and Hölderlin (see *SW*, 198, note 287).
    Regarding Benjamin's reading of Hölderlin, see Chapter 9. For studies on
    the question regarding Benjamin's understanding of the romantic absolute,
    focusing in general on the question of interruption, see Samuel Weber,
    "Criticism Underway: Walter Benjamin's *Romantic Concept of Criticism*,"
    in *Romantic Revolutions: Criticism and Theory*, ed. Kenneth R. Johnston
    and others (Bloomington: Indiana University Press, 1990), 302–19; Rebecca
    Comay, "Benjamin and the Ambiguities of Romanticism," in *The Cambridge
    Companion to Walter Benjamin*, ed. David S. Ferris (Cambridge: Cambridge
    University Press, 2004), 134–51; Kevin McLaughlin, "Benjamin

Now: Afterthoughts on the Arcades Project," *Boundary 2*, vol. 30, no. 1 (2003), 191–7; Thomas Pfau, "Thinking before Totality: Kritik, Übersetzung, and the Language of Interpretation in the Early Walter Benjamin," *MLN*, vol. 103, no. 5 (1988), 1072–97.

30   The later Heidegger's history of Being consists in the *destruktion*, or deconstruction (*ab-bau*), of the history of "the metaphysics of the will." Heidegger traces the beginning of this history to the initial distinction between whatness ("what a being is") and thatness ("that a being is"), which in later scholastic language will emerge as the division of Being between *essentia* and *existentia*. This division grounds metaphysics but is also a division that metaphysics cannot think, since the origin of the division conceals itself in the very emergence of this division of Being. The division of Being is thus the oblivion of Being itself, "the self-concealing of the origin of Being divided into whatness and thatness in favor of Being which opens out beings as beings and remains unquestioned *as Being*" (*EP*, 3–4). The history of metaphysics is the history of (the concealment) of Being, which is our very possibility of history, but also a history that has become nontransparent. This is the reason why Heidegger undertakes this destruction, which is to make history transparent to itself. Regarding the development of the concept of "will" in Heidegger's works, see Bret W. Davis, *Heidegger and the Will: On the Way to* Gelassenheit (Evanston, IL: Northwestern University Press, 2007).

31   I will come back in Chapter 3 to the question of the Kantian transcendental Subject and the Hegelian dialectical Subject as certain understandings of Being.

32   Lacoue-Labarthe and Nancy, *L'Absolu littéraire: théorie de la littérature du romantisme allemand* (Paris: Seuil, 1978), 47.

33   Martin Heidegger, Schellings Abhandlung *über das Wesen der menschlichen Freiheit (1809)*, ed. Hildegard Feick (Tübingen: Max Niemeyer Verlag, 1995), 29.

34   Ibid., 234.

35   For Nancy and Lacoue-Labarthe's own analysis of the "will to system," see *LA*, 33.

36   *IC*, 79; Maurice Blanchot, "L'Interruption," *La Nouvelle Revue Française*, no. 137 (1964), 869–81 (874); my translation. A part of this essay reappears in *L'Entretien infini* (see *IC*, 75–9/106–12). With reference to Blanchot's distinction between two forms of interruption, Leslie Hill notes that from "the mid-1950s onwards, all Blanchot's texts, in one way or another, would participate explicitly in the fragmentary" (Leslie Hill, *Maurice Blanchot and Fragmentary Writing: A Change of Epoch* [London: Continuum, 2012], 68).

37   Maurice Blanchot, "L'Athenaeum," *La Nouvelle Revue Française*, no. 140 (1964), 301–13 (312). This essay was republished in *L'Entretien infini* (see *IC*, 351–9/515–27).

38   Jean-Luc Nancy and Philippe Lacoue-Labarthe, "Noli Me Frangere," in Nancy, *The Birth to Presence*, 266–78 (266).

39   Regarding Blanchot's relation to Romanticism, see the essays collected in Hannes Opelz and John McKeane, eds., Blanchot Romantique: *A Collection of Essays* (Bern: Peter Lang, 2011).

40   Novalis, *Monologue*, in *Philosophical Writings*, trans. Margaret Mahony Stoljar (Albany: State University of New York Press, 1997), 84; Novalis, *Monolog*, in *Novalis Schriften: Die Werke Friedrich von Hardenbergs II*, ed. Paul Kluckhohn and Richard Herbert Samuel (Stuttgart: W. Kohlhammer Verlag, 1960), 672–3 (672).

41   Novalis, *Monologue*, 84.

42   Ibid., 83.

43   See also Heidegger's analysis of Hegel's Absolute as "subjectity" in "Hegel's Concept of Experience." Heidegger writes, "As the subjectity (*Subjektität*) of the subject, unconditional self-knowing is the absoluteness of the absolute. Philosophy is absolute knowledge. Philosophy is science because it wills the will of the absolute, i.e., the absolute in its absoluteness" (Martin Heidegger, "Hegel's Concept of Experience," in *Off the Beaten Track*, trans. Julian Young and Kenneth Haynes [Cambridge: Cambridge University Press, 2002], 100; Martin Heidegger, "Hegels Begriff der Erfahrung," in *Holzwege* (Frankfurt am Main: Vittorio Klostermann, 1980), 129.

44   Jacques Derrida, *Dissemination*, trans. Barbara Johnson (Chicago, IL: University of Chicago Press, 1981), 7.

45   "The Oldest Programme for a System of German Idealism," in Friedrich Hölderlin, *Essays and Letters*, ed. Jeremy D. Adler and Charlie Louth (London: Penguin, 2009), 341–2; "Das älteste Systemprogramm des deutschen Idealismus," in Georg Wilhelm Friedrich Hegel, *Frühe Schriften*, Werke 1, ed. Eva Moldenhauer and Karl Markus Michel (Frankfurt am Main: Suhrkamp 1979), 234–6.

46   For a survey of the reception of the "System-Programme" and of the question of authorship, see Frank-Peter Hansen, *"Das älteste Systemprogramm des deutschen Idealismus": Rezeptionsgeschichte und Interpretation* (Berlin: Walter de Gruyter, 1989).

47   See Dieter Henrich, "Hegel und Hölderlin," in *Hegel im Kontext*, Vierte, veränderte Auflage (Frankfurt am Main: Suhrkamp, 1971), 9–40; translated as "Hegel and Hölderlin," in Dieter Henrich, *The Course of Remembrance and Other Essays on Hölderlin*, ed. Eckart Förster (Stanford, CA: Stanford University Press, 1997), 119–40.

48   See *EL*, 62–3; Schlegel, *Friedrich Schlegel's Lucinde and the Fragments*, 240; *LA*, 48.

49   Martin Heidegger, *Elucidations of Hölderlin's Poetry*, trans. Keith Hoeller (Amherst, NY: Humanity, 2000), 52; Martin Heidegger, *Erläuterungen zu Hölderlins Dichtung* (Frankfurt am Main: Vittorio Klostermann, 2012), 34.

50   Heidegger, *Elucidations*, 52; Heidegger, *Erläuterungen*, 33.

51   Heidegger, *Elucidations*, 64–5; Heidegger, *Erläuterungen*, 47.

52 Martin Heidegger, *Identity and Difference*, trans. Joan Stambaugh (Chicago, IL: University of Chicago Press, 2002), 47.

53 Ibid., 72, 141.

54 Ibid., 51.

55 Heidegger, *Elucidations*, 64; Heidegger, *Erläuterungen*, 47. Regarding Heidegger's relation to the Early German Romantic tradition, see Lacoue-Labarthe's *Heidegger, Art and Politics*.

56 Regarding the question of the caesura, see Hölderlin's "Remarks on 'Oedipus' " in which he introduces the caesura in relation to the issue that "poetry is in need of especially certain and characteristic principles and limits" (*ET*, 101). For Hölderlin, the tragic "*caesura*, the pure word, the counter-rhythmic rupture" is that which in the poetic meter manifests not "the change of representation but the representation itself [*nicht mehr der Wechsel der Vorstellung, sondern die Vorstellung selber erscheint*]" (*ET*, 102; *SA* 5, 196). In a chapter on the caesura from *Heidegger, Art and Politics*, Lacoue-Labarthe shows how the caesura is the pure interruption of thetic Being in which any speculative form of the proposition is suspended: "an empty or null event, in which is revealed—without revealing itself—a withdrawal or the nothing-ness' (Lacoue-Labarthe, *Heidegger, Art and Politics*, 45).

Chapter 3

1 Friedrich Hölderlin, "The Ground for Empedocles" in *ET*, 50–61. I here retain the English titles given to Hölderlin's texts by Thomas Pfau in his translations from the *Grosse Stuttgarter Ausgabe*. But, it should be noted that not all these titles were given by Hölderlin himself (cf. *FA*). The title in the *Grosse Stuttgarter Ausgabe* is "Grund zum Empedokles" (*SA* 4:1, 149–62). The title in the *Frankfurter Ausgabe* is "Die tragische Ode ..., Allgemeiner Grund, Grund zum Empedokles, Plan zum dritten Entwurf" (*FA* 13 II, 839–82).

2 Friedrich Hölderlin, "Remarks on 'Oedipus,' " in *ET*, 101–8; Friedrich Hölderlin, "Anmerkungen zum Oedipus," in *SA* 5, 193–202; Friedrich Hölderlin, "Anmerkungen zum Oedipus," in *FA* 16, 247–58.

3 Friedrich Hölderlin, "On the Operations of the Poetic Spirit," in *ET*, 62–82; Friedrich Hölderlin, "Über die Verfahrungsweise des poëtischen Geistes," in *SA* 4:1, 241–65; Friedrich Hölderlin, "Wenn der Dichter einmal des Geistes mächtig ...," in *FA* 14, 179–322.

4 For a detailed investigation into the question of unity and difference (*Einheit und Differenz*) in Hölderlin's theoretical texts from the perspective of the German reception of Hölderlin (but also with a basis in Lacoue-Labarthe's focus on the relation between the idealistic and nonidealistic in Hölderlin), see Marion Hiller, *Harmonisch Entgegengesetzt: Zur Darstellung und Darstellbarkeit in Hölderlins Poetik um 1800* (Tübingen: Max Niemeyer Verlag, 2008). For other detailed explorations of Hölderlin's theoretical texts, see also Dieter Henrich, *Der Grund im Bewußtsein: Untersuchungen*

zu Hölderlins Denken (1794–1795) (Stuttgart: Klett-Cotta, 1992); Johann Kreuzer, *Erinnerung: Zum Zusammenhang von Hölderlins Theoretischen Fragmenten "Das untergehende Vaterland ..." und "Wenn der Dichter einmal des Geistes mächtig ist..."* (Königstein: Verlag Anton Hain, 1985); Fred Lönker, *Welt in der Welt: Eine Untersuchung zu Hölderlins "Verfahrungsweise des poetischen Geistes"* (Göttingen: Vandenhoeck & Ruprecht, 1989); Lawrence J. Ryan, *Hölderlins Lehre vom Wechsel der Töne* (Stuttgart: W. Kohlhammer, 1960).

5 For a study on the essay "The Caesura of the Speculative" analyzed from the perspective of Lacoue-Labarthe's general project, see John Martis's *Philippe Lacoue-Labarthe: Representation and the Law of the Subject* (New York: Fordham University Press, 2005), 95–127.

6 Blanchot here implicitly opposes Sartre's investigation of literature undertaken in the work entitled *What Is Literature?* (*Qu'est-ce la littérature?*, 1948). Regarding Sartre's investigation of literature, see my Introduction.

7 Martin Heidegger, *The Essence of Human Freedom: An Introduction to Philosophy*, trans. Ted Sadler (London: Continuum, 2005), 28.

8 See Heidegger, *Essence of Human Freedom*, 24. Aristotle writes in Book VII of the *Metaphysics*: "The essence of a thing is what the thing is said to be in its own right" (Aristotle, *Selections*, ed. Terence Irwin and Gail Fine [Indianapolis, IN: Hackett, 1995], 1029b14–15). The essence is *to ti esti*, literally "the what it is," which is linked to the notion of "definition" (*horismos*): "Hence the things that have an essence are those whose account is a definition" (Aristotle, *Selections*, 1030a6–7).

9 Heidegger, *Essence of Human Freedom*, 43.

10 Ibid., 46. Aristotle writes in the *Metaphysics*, "Indeed, the old question—always pursued from long ago till now, and always raising puzzles—'What is being?' is just the question 'What is substance?' " (Aristotle, *Selections*, 1028b4–5). Moreover, whatness is said to indicate substance: "The primary being is the what-it-is, which signifies substance" (1028a14–15). In the *Categories*, Aristotle defines "substance" as that which endures through change and as the subject in which everything inheres: "All the other things are either said of the primary substances as subjects or in them as subjects. If, then, the primary substances did not exist, neither could any of the other things exist" (2b4–6). For an analysis of Aristotle's notion of substance, see S. Marc Cohen's "Substances," in *A Companion to Aristotle*, ed. Georgios Anagnostopoulos (Chichester: Wiley-Blackwell, 2009), 197–212.

11 For a study of Derrida's understanding of literature, see Timothy Clark, *Derrida, Heidegger, Blanchot: Sources of Derrida's Notion and Practice of Literature* (Cambridge: Cambridge University Press, 1992). In *Dissemination*, Derrida writes, "If, as we have precisely been tempted to think, literature is born/dead of a relatively recent break, it is nonetheless true that the whole history of the interpretations of the arts of letters has moved and been transformed within the diverse logical possibilities opened up by the concept of *mimēsis*" (Jacques Derrida, *Dissemination*, trans. Barbara Johnson [Chicago, IL: University of Chicago Press, 1981], 187). For Derrida, *mimēsis*

indicates not solely "imitation" as an adequate relation between two terms but also "the presentation of the thing itself," unconcealedness, "*alētheia*" (Derrida, *Dissemination*, 193). As Timothy Clark writes, this "presentation" is the withdrawal of Being: "Being, as the *appearing* (as distinct from the entity which becomes so apparent), necessarily disappears in the very unveiling of that which it makes present. Being *withdraws*, never becoming present, through the very structure of presentness-at-hand which it effects" (Clark, *Derrida, Heidegger, Blanchot*, 33). Clark investigates the relation of Derrida's notion of literature to Heidegger's history of Being and Blanchot's experience of literature. He shows how Derrida's notion of literature distinguishes itself from a form of "deconstructive" literary criticism insofar as this latter criticism is understood as "the negation of positivism and its derivative notions of representation" (Clark, *Derrida, Heidegger, Blanchot*, 5). For Derrida, literature is thus not the negative self-reference of a "thesis" but a possibility of the interruption of positing. Clark writes, "The consideration that this absence-of-any-entity may never become the *object* of any representation renders the literary a peculiar structure of *appearance as withdrawal*" (Clark, *Derrida, Heidegger, Blanchot*, 108). In my archaeology, I show how the paradigm of writerly necessity constitutes this emergence of "literature" as the withdrawal of thetic Being.

12 Derrida, "This Strange Institution Called Literature: An Interview with Jacques Derrida," in *Acts of Literature*, ed. Derek Attridge (New York: Routledge, 1992), 46.

13 In "Music and Letters," Mallarmé poses this question that relates to what he names the "ideal crisis": "With such benevolence as an invitation to speak about what I love; and also the considerable apprehension of a foreign audience, brings back an old wish, many times denied by solitude, to account deeply and completely for the ideal crisis, which, as much as the other, social, roils many: or, right away, despite what might be abrupt about such a question in front of an audience to scriptural elegance, ask: Does something like Letters exist?" (Stéphane Mallarmé, *Divagations*, trans. Barbara Johnson [Cambridge, MA: Belknap Press of Harvard University Press, 2007], 185).

14 See also Kant's pre-critical "The Only Possible Argument in Support of a Demonstration of the Existence of God" (1763), in *Theoretical Philosophy, 1755–1770*, trans. David Walford and Ralf Meerbote (Cambridge: Cambridge University Press, 1992), 107–201. Kant writes here: "The concept of positing or setting [*Position oder Setzung*] is perfectly simple: it is identical with the concept of being in general [*Sein überhaupt*]" (119). Regarding Kant's understanding of Being, see also Howard Caygill, *A Kant Dictionary* (Oxford: Blackwell, 1995), 93–5.

15 Martin Heidegger, "Kant's Thesis about Being," in *Pathmarks*, ed. William McNeill (Cambridge: Cambridge University Press, 1998), 337–63; Martin Heidegger, "Kants These über das Sein," in *Wegmarken* (Frankfurt am Main: Vittorio Klostermann, 1967), 273–307.

16 Georg Wilhelm Friedrich Hegel, *Hegel's Science of Logic*, trans. Arnold V. Miller (New York: Humanities Press, 1976), 843.

17 Ibid., 824; Georg Wilhelm Friedrich Hegel, *Wissenschaft der Logik*, ed. Eva
Moldenhauer and Karl Markus Michel (Frankfurt am Main: Suhrkamp,
1969), vol. 2, 549.

18 Hegel, *Hegel's Science of Logic*, 843; Hegel, *Wissenschaft der Logik*, vol. 2,
573; translation modified.

19 Cf. Werner Hamacher's "Premises," in *Premises: Essays on Philosophy and
Literature from Kant to Celan*, trans. Peter Fenves (Stanford, CA: Stanford
University Press, 1999), 1–43. For Hamacher, this constitutes a fundamental
aporia of positing: "A positing that is supposed to be unconditioned must be a
positing without presupposition and thus a subjectless positing. It must purely
posit itself; but by positing itself, *it* already posits *itself*, and so the positing
that it is first supposed to perform must already *allow* itself to be presupposed.
But such an allowance, admission, or concession of a presupposition can no
longer be thought according to the logic of positing. ... And it means that
positing affected by something other than Being understood as position, never
is—never 'is' according to its own sense of 'is', according to the sense of thetic
Being" (Hamacher, *Premises*, 13–14). Hamacher moreover notes that this
"aporia, as a displacement of every positing, *is* not – and therefore cannot
be a theme for understanding" (Hamacher, *Premises*, 14). This suspension
of understanding pertains to literature "understood" as unworking. Hans-
Jost Frey is aware of this question when he understands Blanchot's texts to
"continuously suspend, more than others, the possibility of understanding
... Reading happens through the suspension of understanding" ("The Last
Man and the Reader," in *The Place of Maurice Blanchot*, ed. Thomas Pepper
[New Haven, CT: Yale University Press, 1998], 252–79 [269]). The question
of literature is thus a question not only of the impossibility of writing but
also of reading. In its emergence as "the question of literature," literature thus
also questions the very possibility of archaeological understanding; however,
precisely this interruption of understanding also exposes the contingency,
which is the concern of the archaeology of writerly necessity. Since
archaeology, like literature, exposes the positing of the subject–object relation,
it is also a form of thought that exposes the very aporia of understanding.

20 This is also the reason why it is questionable whether there can be any science
of literature (*Literaturwissenschaft*) that would conceive literature as an object
of study for a knowing subject (see Hamacher, "Lectio: de Man's Imperative,"
in *Premises*, 181–221).

21 Derrida, "This Strange Institution Called Literature," 47.

22 Derrida himself admits to having this "romantic" dream: "Still now, and
more desperately than ever, I dream of a writing that would be neither
philosophy nor literature, nor even contaminated by one or the other, while
still keeping—I have no desire to abandon this—the memory of literature
and philosophy. ... You will say, and quite rightly, that this is the dream of
every literary work" (Derrida, "This Strange Institution Called Literature,"
73). In postwar France, there is in general a focus on literature as the question
of the interruption of the Hegelian dialectic. For an intellectual history of
this French milieu, see Patrick ffrench, *The Time of Theory: A History* of *Tel*

Quel (1960–1983) (Oxford: Clarendon Press, 1995). ffrench focuses on the history of the review *Tel Quel* and the development of a theory of literature in this review, which manifests "the drama of the possibility of getting beyond Hegel" (ffrench, *Time of Theory*, 27). Literature emerges as the question of the loss of sense that cannot be posited in any dialectic: "Literature is not communication, neither does it have a social function. It is fundamentally a *dépense*, a radical loss, and it cuts across any posited economy" (ffrench, *Time of Theory*, 111).

23   See Jean-Luc Nancy, "The Calculation of the Poet," in *The Solid Letter: Readings of Friedrich Hölderlin*, ed. Aris Fioretos (Stanford, CA: Stanford University Press, 1999), 44–73 (48); Jean-Luc Nancy, *The Sense of the World*, trans. Jeffrey S. Librett (Minneapolis: University of Minnesota Press, 1997), 123–39; Jean-Luc Nancy, "Hyperion's Joy," in *The Birth to Presence*, 58–81 (76). For studies on Nancy's later works, see Ian James, *The Fragmentary Demand: An Introduction to the Philosophy of Jean-Luc Nancy* (Stanford, CA: Stanford University Press, 2006); Daniele Rugo, *Jean-Luc Nancy and the Thinking of Otherness: Philosophy and Powers of Existence* (London: Bloomsbury, 2013); B. C. Hutchens, *Jean-Luc Nancy and the Future of Philosophy* (Chesham: Acumen, 2005). See also the collection of essays on Nancy in Darren Sheppard, Simon Sparks and Colin Thomas, eds., *On Jean-Luc Nancy: The Sense of Philosophy* (London: Routledge, 1997).

24   Maurice Blanchot, *The Book to Come*, trans. Charlotte Mandell (Stanford, CA: Stanford University Press, 2003), 195.

Chapter 4

1   See Michel Foucault, *Folie et déraison. Histoire de la folie à l'âge classique* (Paris: Plon, 1961); Michel Foucault, *Histoire de la folie à l'âge classique* (Paris: Gallimard, 1972).

2   Michel Foucault, *History of Madness*, ed. Jean Khalfa, trans. Jonathan Murphy and Jean Khalfa (London: Routledge, 2009), xxxiii. In his critique of Foucault's *History of Madness*, Derrida addresses this "purity," which means that the "attempt to write the history of the decision, division, difference runs the risk of construing the division as an event or a structure subsequent to the unity of an original presence, thereby confirming metaphysics in its fundamental operation" (Jacques Derrida, "Cogito and the History of Madness," in *Writing and Difference*, ed. Alan Bass [London: Routledge, 2001], 36–76 [48]).

3   Regarding the question of the purity of madness and the different editions, see Ian Hacking's foreword in *History of Madness*, ix–xii.

4   Foucault, *History of Madness*, 351.

5   Foucault's review "Le 'Non' du père" first appeared in *Critique*, no. 178 (1962), 195–209; for an English translation, see "The Father's 'No,' " in *AM*, 6–20. Regarding Jean Laplanche's *Hölderlin and the Question of the Father*, see my

analysis of Hölderlin as a desiring writer in Chapter 6. Following Agamben's definition of a paradigm, Foucault can be said to understand Hölderlin's position as precisely a *paradigmatic* position (at once singular and exemplary). Agamben writes, "The paradigmatic case becomes such by suspending and, at the same time, exposing its belonging to the group, so that it is never possible to separate its exemplarity from its singularity" (Giorgio Agamben, *The Signature of All Things: On Method*, Luca D'Isanto and Kevin Attell [New York: Zone, 2009], 31). There is thus no contradiction between the "unique" and the "exemplary" in Foucault's statement. Derrida is also aware of this possibility: "It could be thought that, by definition, the unique cannot be an example or case of a universal figure. But it can. Exemplarity only apparently contradicts unicity" (Jacques Derrida, "La Parole soufflée," in *Writing and Difference*, ed. Alan Bass [London: Routledge, 2001], 212–45 [218]).

6 The fundamental finitude in which Man (the Subject) arises is a mode of Being in which the absence of gods is a fundamental experience (see *OT*, 344–5). Foucault says that it is time, "the time that he [Man] himself is" (*OT*, 365), which, on the one hand, divides Man from his own origin and, on the other, makes Man a figure of anticipation, divided from "that other dawn promised him as still to come" (*OT*, 365). Man's mode of Being is a hiatus of no-longer and not-yet. The fundamental finitude divides Man so that he is always already too late and too early. For studies on *The Order of Things* and the theme of the "finitude of man" in Foucault, see Béatrice Han, "The Analytic of Finitude and the History of Subjectivity," in *The Cambridge Companion to Foucault*, ed. Gary Gutting, 2nd ed. (Cambridge: Cambridge University Press, 2005), 176–209; Hubert L. Dreyfus and Paul Rabinow, *Michel Foucault: Beyond Structuralism and Hermeneutics*, 2nd ed. (New York: Harvester Wheatsheaf, 1982), 16–43; Gary Gutting, *Michel Foucault's Archaeology of Scientific Reason* (Cambridge: Cambridge University Press, 1989), 139–226; Patrice Maniglier, "*The Order of Things*," in *A Companion to Foucault*, ed. Christopher Falzon, Timothy O'Leary, and Jana Sawicki (Chichester: Wiley-Blackwell, 2013), 104–21.

7 Michel Foucault, "The Subject and Power," in *Power: Essential Works of Foucault, 1954–1984, Volume 3*, ed. James Faubion (London: Penguin, 2002), 326–48 (326).

8 For a study on the role of literature in Foucault, see especially Simon During, *Foucault and Literature: Towards a Genealogy of Writing* (London: Routledge, 1992). Even if During rejects the possibility of writing an archaeology of literary theory today, he poses the question: "What would an archaeology of literary studies look like? It is strange that one does not actually exist" (During, *Foucault and Literature*, 116). Regarding the role of literature in Foucault, see also, Gutting, *Michel Foucault's Archaeology of Scientific Reason*, 196–8; John Rajchman, *Michel Foucault: The Freedom of Philosophy* (New York: Columbia University Press, 1985). Specifically regarding the thought of the outside, see Kas Saghafi, "The 'Passion for the Outside': Foucault, Blanchot, and Exteriority," *International Studies in Philosophy*, vol. 28, no. 4 (1996), 79–92; Gilles Deleuze, *Foucault*, trans. Seán Hand (London: Athlone Press, 1988). Deleuze notes that the "space of the

Outside" is precisely the space of "a 'non-relation', the place of a 'non-place' "
(Deleuze, *Foucault*, 87). For a study on Foucault's thought of the "outside"
from the perspective of the philosophy of Gilles Deleuze, see also Keith A.
Robinson, *Michel Foucault and the Freedom of Thought* (Lewiston: Edwin
Mellen Press, 2001).

9 Michel Foucault, *The Archaeology of Knowledge and the Discourse on
Language*, trans. A. M. Sheridan Smith (New York: Vintage, 2010), 203.

10 Ibid., 12.

11 Foucault's essay on Blanchot first appeared as "La Pensée du dehors," in
Critique, no. 229 (1966), 523–46; for an English translation, see "The
Thought of the Outside," in *AM*, 147–69. For studies on Foucault's method
of archaeology, see Christopher Falzon, "Making History," in *A Companion
to Foucault*, ed. Christopher Falzon, Timothy O'Leary, and Jana Sawicki
(Chichester: Wiley-Blackwell, 2013), 282–98; Michael Donnelly, "Foucault's
Genealogy of the Human Sciences," in *Towards a Critique of Foucault*, ed.
Mike Gane (London: Routledge & Kegan Paul, 1986), 15–32. For studies on
the relation between Foucault's archaeology and the methodological concerns
of the *Annales* school of historiography (Lucien Febvre and Marc Bloch), and
the historical epistemologies of Gaston Bachelard and Georges Canguilhem,
see Martin Kusch, *Foucault's Strata and Fields: An Investigation into
Archaeological and Genealogical Science Studies* (Dordrecht: Kluwer, 1991);
Gutting, *Michel Foucault's Archaeology of Scientific Reason*, 9–54.

12 Foucault's concern for the (interrupting) exteriorization in opposition to
the (self-relating) interiorization has not protected him from being read in a
Hegelian mode as an ironic thinker of "spiritual" self-interiorization. See, for
example, Carl Rapp, "Hegel's Concept of the Dissolution of Art," in *Hegel
and Aesthetics*, ed. William Maker (Albany: State University of New York
Press, 2000), 13–30. Hegel's thinking is the dialectic of internalization, of
Er-innerung, as the self's return to itself (see *PS*, 492–3). Paul de Man noted in
1982 that this internalization organizes the "ideology of the symbol" that is
"very familiar to us in the common-places of our own historical discourse on
literature" (Paul de Man, "Sign and Symbol in Hegel's 'Aesthetics,' " *Critical
Inquiry*, vol. 8, no. 4 [1982], 761–75 [771]).

13 Regarding the relation of Kant's understanding of the finitude of the Subject to
Foucault's understanding of the historical contingency of rationality, see Marc
Djaballah, *Kant, Foucault, and Forms of Experience* (New York: Routledge,
2008), 184–200. Djaballah writes regarding Foucault's archaeology, "His
[Foucault's] criticism does not imply that reason is contingent within a
form of experience, but rather that in history there have been many forms
of experience; Foucault's historical analysis allows one to appreciate that
rationality, in its varying arrangements, generates *a priori* cognition in each
case. The contingency that Foucault unmasks is not of rational cognition, but
of the rational itself" (Djaballah, *Kant, Foucault, and Forms of Experience*,
197). Djaballah also analyzes Foucault's understanding of "literature" as a
discursive form that can think its own disappearance (see Djaballah, *Kant,
Foucault, and Forms of Experience*, 249–88): "The Kantian way of thinking

about the interplay between what is possible within an experience and the regulating factors (laws, concepts, rules, orders, types, etc.) that form it buoys the space of what Foucault considers to be the distinctive feature of the capacity of literature, considered as a receptive discursive form: namely, a thought's *contestation* of its own form, the possibility of *transgressing* its own rules" (Djaballah, *Kant, Foucault, and Forms of Experience*, 274).

14 Literature emerges in Modernity as a counter-discourse of Modernity. Literature indicates the disappearance of Modernity, but it is itself a part of the modern age. It is possible that the very method of archaeology occupies a similar discursive position. Foucault indeed confirms that archaeology could itself be nothing but a conjecture in the modern age. He states this explicitly in *The Archaeology of Knowledge*: "It may turn out that archaeology is the name given to a part of our contemporary theoretical conjuncture. … I am in no position at the moment to decide" (Foucault, *Archaeology of Knowledge*, 208). Insofar as archaeology, like literature, is a discourse of contingency this discourse can be designated as a counter-discourse of Modernity, since it manifests the possible disappearance of the contemporary historical a priori.

15 Friedrich Nietzsche, *The Will to Power*, ed. Walter Kaufmann, trans. Walter Kaufmann and R. J. Hollingdale (New York: Vintage, 1968), 157.

16 Such a "distance" should be understood as a "non-place," that is to say, as nothing but the contingent site of emergence of the modern subject position (cf. Foucault's "Nietzsche, Genealogy, History," in *AM*, 369–91 [377]).

17 *OT*, xxvi. Foucault writes, "The history of the order imposed on things would be the history of the Same—of that which, for a given culture, is both dispersed and related, therefore to be distinguished by kinds and to be collected into identities."

18 For a overview of Foucault's *History of Madness*, see Colin Gordon, "History of Madness," in *A Companion to Foucault*, ed. Christopher Falzon, Timothy O'Leary, and Jana Sawicki (Chichester: Wiley-Blackwell, 2013), 84–103. Regarding the *History of Madness*, see also especially Gutting's *Michel Foucault's Archaeology of Scientific Reason*, 55–110; and Georges Canguilhem, "The Death of Man, or Exhaustion of the Cogito?" in *The Cambridge Companion to Foucault*, ed. Gary Gutting, 2nd ed. (Cambridge: Cambridge University Press, 2005), 74–94. For a critical bibliography of secondary texts on Foucault's *History of Madness*, see Foucault, *History of Madness*, 677–93.

19 Foucault, *History of Madness*, 47.

20 Ibid., 86.

21 Ibid., 82.

22 Ibid., 140.

23 Ibid., xxix.

24 Ibid., 548.

25 Ibid., xxxiii.

26 Ibid., 352.

27   Ibid., 351.

28   Ibid., 528–9.

29   Ibid., 537.

30   Foucault is not consistent as to the "time" for the emergence of literature. In the appendix to *The History of Madness*, Foucault comprehends the moment of Mallarmé (the end of the nineteenth century) as the time of literature understood as an intransitive gesture of writing: "Before Mallarmé, [literary] writing was a matter of establishing one's speech inside a given language, so that a work made of language was of the same nature as any other language, but for the signs (and they were majestic) of Rhetoric, the Subject, of Images. At the close of the nineteenth century … it [the work] suspended the reign of language in the present of a gesture of writing" (Foucault, *History of Madness*, 547–8). It is possible that the reason for this ambiguity with respect to the time of the emergence of literature is, on the one hand, that the paradigm of writerly necessity is not visible for Foucault. Even if Foucault recognizes literature as a "gesture of writing," this gesture never becomes visible as the gesture of a subject who cannot not-write intransitively. But, on the other hand, insofar as literature is the withdrawal of Being, there is also no "objective" *date* for the emergence of literature. In the later essay "Lives of Infamous Men" ("La Vie des hommes infâmes," 1977), Foucault will consider a radically different time of emergence for literature. This essay was first published in *Les Cahiers du Chemin* (no. 29 [1977], 12–29) as an introduction to an anthology concerning the prison archives of the Hôpital général and the Bastille. In this essay, Foucault traces the "conditions of existence" of literature, which he understands to arise out of an "ethic" that is characterized by "the duty of saying what is most resistant to being said—the worst, the most secret, the most insufferable, the shameless" (Foucault, "Lives of Infamous Men," 157–75 [174]). Foucault here dates the moment of emergence of literature to the turn of the seventeenth and eighteenth century, that is, approximately a century before the Early German Romantics.

31   For Blanchot's review of the *History of Madness*, see Maurice Blanchot, "L'Oubli, la déraison," *La Nouvelle Revue Française*, no. 106 (1961), 676–86; republished and translated in *IC*, 194–201/289–99). For Blanchot's reading of Hölderlin in relation to the question of madness, see Maurice Blanchot, "La Folie par excellence," *Critique*, no. 45 (1951), 99–118; translated as "Madness *par excellence*," in Maurice Blanchot, *The Blanchot Reader*, ed. Michael Holland (Oxford: Blackwell, 1995), 110–28. For the publication history of Foucault's review "The Father's 'No' " and "The Thought of the Outside," see, respectively, note 5 and note 11 in this chapter. Regarding Laplanche's work and Blanchot's thoughts on Hölderlin's "madness," see Chapter 6.

Chapter 5

1   Michel Foucault, *The Archaeology of Knowledge and the Discourse on Language*, trans. A. M. Sheridan Smith (New York: Vintage, 2010), 54.

2   See Leslie Hill, *Blanchot: Extreme Contemporary* (London: Routledge, 1997), 14.

3   Paul Davies notes in an article on Blanchot that Romanticism makes possible Blanchot's thinking of the absence of the work: "More than anything else it is romanticism that turns the theoretical instability of the work into the artistic quest for the work. Romantic writing on the work will henceforth also be a writing on the absence of the work" (Paul Davies, "The Work and the Absence of the Work," in *Maurice Blanchot: The Demand of Writing*, ed. Carolyn Bailey Gill [London: Routledge, 1996], 91–107 [101]). Opelz and Mckeane write that Blanchot's primary Romanticism is the thought of the *Athenaeum*: "Blanchot's reading of Romanticism, particularly from the 1960s onwards, does privilege, as suggested earlier, a place (Jena) and a period (1798–1800)" (Hannes Opelz and John Mckeane, "Introduction: The Absolute, the Fragmentary," in *Blanchot Romantique: A Collection of Essays* [Bern: Peter Lang, 2011], 1–54 [14]). But the question is thus what the conditions are for this "romantic writing."

4   Regarding a necessity or imperative of writing, see also Jeff Fort's *The Imperative to Write* (New York: Fordham University Press, 2014), in which he traces how a Kantian categorical imperative, linked to a thought of the sublime, emerges in Kafka, Blanchot, and Beckett.

5   For studies on Blanchot's thinking of unworking in relation to Hegel's dialectic, see especially Rodolphe Gasché's "The Felicities of Paradox: Blanchot on the Null-Space of Literature," in *Maurice Blanchot: The Demand of Writing*, ed. Carolyn Bailey Gill (London: Routledge, 1996), 34–69; Andrzej Warminski, "Dreadful Reading: Blanchot on Hegel," *Yale French Studies*, no. 69 (1985), 267–75. Gasché understands the question of literature to arise as an act of writing: "The becoming question of literature occurs in the act of writing in which the writer's pen, without asking why it writes, will always have passively performed that question" (Gasché, "Felicities of Paradox," 35–6). Furthermore, Gasché recognizes Blanchot's understanding of negativity (death) as the possibility of contingency: "Death is thus first and foremost this minimal ambiguity of an always other possibility" (Gasché, "Felicities of Paradox," 66). But the question is then how literature takes place as an act of writing. My aim here is to make visible how this act of writing is produced by the paradigm of writerly necessity.

6   Simon Critchley, *Very Little … Almost Nothing: Death, Philosophy, Literature*, 2nd ed. (London: Routledge, 2004), 35–97 (74); see also Simon Critchley's "*Il y a*—Holding Levinas's Hand to Blanchot's Fire," in *Maurice Blanchot: The Demand of Writing*, ed. Carolyn Bailey Gill (London: Routledge, 1996), 108–22 (111). See furthermore: Ullrich Haase and William Large, *Maurice Blanchot* (London: Routledge, 2001), 67–84; Christopher Fynsk: "Crossing the Threshold: On 'Literature and the Right to Death,'" in *Maurice Blanchot: The Demand of Writing*, ed. Carolyn Bailey Gill (London: Routledge, 1996), 70–90 (76); Lars Iyer, *Blanchot's Vigilance: Literature, Phenomenology, and the Ethical* (New York: Palgrave Macmillan, 2005), 17–22; Hill, *Blanchot*, 62–3; Alain Toumayan, "Blanchot, Reader of Baudelaire: 'Baudelaire's failure,' " in *After Blanchot: Literature,*

Criticism, Philosophy, ed. Leslie Hill, Brian Nelson, and Dimitris Vardoulakis (Newark: University of Delaware Press, 2005), 137–48 (138–9). Regarding the theme of the "primal scene" in Blanchot, see Maurice Blanchot, *The Writing of the Disaster*, trans. Ann Smock (Lincoln: University of Nebraska Press, 1995), 72, 125–8; Philippe Lacoue-Labarthe, *Ending and Unending Agony: On Maurice Blanchot*, trans. Hannes Opelz (New York: Fordham University Press, 2015); Michael Newman: "The Trace of Trauma: Blindness, Testimony and the Gaze in Blanchot and Derrida," in *Maurice Blanchot: The Demand of Writing*, ed. Carolyn Bailey Gill (London: Routledge, 1996), 153–73; Kevin Hart, *The Dark Gaze: Maurice Blanchot and the Sacred* (Chicago, IL: University of Chicago Press, 2004), 50–75.

7   See Chapter 2.

8   Regarding Hegel's aesthetics, and the general relation between the paradigm of writerly necessity and the aesthetic experience of the work of art, see Part 4. Heinrich Gustav Hotho, one of Hegel's students, edited the first editions of Hegel's lectures on aesthetics based on Hegel's lecture notes, which are now lost, and student notes and transcripts (first edition, 1835; second edition, 1842). Hegel lectured on aesthetics in Heidelberg (1818) and in Berlin (1820–1, 1823, 1826, and 1828–9) (see T. M. Knox, "Translator's Preface," in *A*, v–xvi; Allen Speight, "Hegel and the 'Historical Deduction' of the Concept of Art," in *A Companion to Hegel*, ed. Stephen Houlgate and Michael Baur [Oxford: Wiley-Blackwell, 2011], 353–68 [365, note 1 and 366, note 7]). For a critical evaluation of Hotho's edition, see Annemarie Gethmann-Siefert's *Einführung in Hegels Ästhetik* (München: Wilhelm Fink Verlag, 2005). Gethmann-Siefert claims that Hotho's editions are unreliable. Notably is the famous (Hegelian) definition of beauty (art) as "the sensible presentation of the idea [*das sinnliche* Scheinen *der Idee*]" (*A*, 111, translation modified; Georg Wilhelm Friedrich Hegel, *Vorlesungen über die Ästhetik I–II*, Werke 13–14, ed. Eva Moldenhauer and Karl Markus Michel [Frankfurt am Main: Suhrkamp, 1986], I, 151) contested since it appears nowhere else than in Hotho's edition (see Gethmann-Siefert, *Einführung in Hegels Ästhetik*, 241–4). However, Pippin remarks that this is the only "serious issue" with respect to the question of the reliability of Hotho's version. The question whether this formulation can be attributed to Hegel is furthermore an issue that appears "unresolvable" (see Robert Pippin, "The Absence of Aesthetics in Hegel's Aesthetics," in *The Cambridge Companion to Hegel and Nineteenth-Century Philosophy*, ed. Frederick C. Beiser [Cambridge: Cambridge University Press, 2008], 394–418 [394–5, note 3; 396, note 7]).

9   Foucault notes that literature takes place in this *recurrent* affirmation of its disappearance. Literature is thus an interruption that incessantly (re)constitutes itself (the *dying* of the Subject). On this issue, see Chapter 8.

10 See also Blanchot's *The Book to Come* in which he writes, "'Where is literature going?' … literature is going toward itself, toward its essence, which is disappearance" (Maurice Blanchot, *The Book to Come*, trans. Charlotte Mandell [Stanford, CA: Stanford University Press, 2003], 195). Thomas Carl Wall also identifies Blanchot's experience of literature as the experience of the

instability of thetic Being: "The 'experience' Blanchot refers to must be prior to Kantian experience and would refer to the *pure position of the subject*. To experience the event as an image, then, is not to experience an object (since the object disappears into itself), but to experience the self *as* the pure passivity of position, or, 'thereness.' … It is the passivity of *absolute* instability. That is to say, this experience closes in on itself and leaves no trace because it is never even opened" (Thomas Carl Wall, *Radical Passivity: Levinas, Blanchot, and Agamben* [Albany: State University of New York Press, 1999], 111).

11   In *Blanchot: Extreme Contemporary*, Leslie Hill notes how certain concepts are displaced in Blanchot's different works throughout his oeuvre (see especially Hill, *Blanchot: Extreme Contemporary*, 127–42). Hill argues that "in the mid- to late 1960s, Blanchot embarked on a major reformulation of his critical and philosophical position" (Hill, *Blanchot*, 135); however, Hill also recognizes that "what continues to count in Blanchot's text are not individual words or concepts, but, more profoundly, the very texture of his writing in the way it inscribes concepts only to displace and transform them" (Hill, *Blanchot*, 135). Nevertheless, Hill claims that in *The Infinite Conversation* "even 'désœuvrement'—suspected perhaps of being too easy a hostage to dialectical negativity—is deleted and re-inscribed as the phrase: 'absence d'œuvre' ('absence of work')" (Hill, *Blanchot*, 135). But, Blanchot nevertheless appears to use these terms interchangeably in *The Infinite Conversation*. For example, in this sequence, "To write is to produce the absence of the work (worklessness, unworking [*le désœuvrement*]). Or again: writing is the absence of the work [*l'absence d'œuvre*] as it *produces itself* through the work, traversing it throughout. Writing as unworking (in the active sense of the word) is the insane game, the indeterminacy that lies between reason and unreason" (*IC*, 424/622–3). Christopher Bident argues that a thought of the "neuter" (*le neutre*) manifests itself throughout Blanchot's work (see Christopher Bident, "The Movements of the Neuter," in *After Blanchot: Literature, Criticism, Philosophy*, ed. Leslie Hill, Brian Nelson, and Dimitris Vardoulakis [Newark: University of Delaware Press, 2005], 13–34). This tendency of the "neuter" is indeed visible in Blanchot's works. In *The Infinite Conversation*, Blanchot writes that the "exigency of the neutral tends to suspend the attributive structure of language: the relation to being [*l'être*], implicit or explicit, that is immediately posited [*posé*] in language as soon as something is said" (*IC*, 386/567; translation modified). The neutral tendency is thus the suspension of positing, of thetic Being, which is visible in both of the terms "unworking" and "the absence of work." I understand both these terms to concern the conceptualization of literature as a non-dialectical experience of the interruption of thetic Being.

Chapter 6

1   Slavoj Žižek, *Less Than Nothing: Hegel and the Shadow of Dialectical Materialism* (London: Verso, 2012), 750.

2   Regarding the status of Lacan's Subject, see Philippe Lacoue-Labarthe and Jean-Luc Nancy, *The Title of the Letter: A Reading of Lacan*, trans. François Raffoul and David Pettigrew (Albany: State University of New York Press, 1992), 98. Nancy and Laocue-Labarthe's *The Title of the Letter* is a seminal work of the "deconstructive" approach to Lacan and was first presented at Jacques Derrida's seminar in 1972 at the École Normale Supérieure before being published in 1973 as *Le Titre de la lettre: une lecture de Lacan* (Paris: Galilée). See also Bruce Fink, *The Lacanian Subject: Between Language and Jouissance* (Princeton, NJ: Princeton University Press, 1995).

3   Regarding this event, see Chapter 3.

4   Lacan compares the signifier to such an act of enunciation, to the "shifter" as the very taking place of language, in opposition to the statement as signification, as the meaning of that which is said: "In a concern for method, we can try to begin here with the strictly linguistic definition of *I* as signifier, where it is nothing but the shifter or indicative that, qua grammatical subject of the statement, designates the subject insofar as he is currently speaking. That is to say, it designates the enunciating subject, but does not signify him" (*E*, 677). For linguistic studies on the form of this act of enunciation as the "shifter" (Jakobson) and the "indicator of utterance" (Benveniste), see Roman Jakobson, "Shifters, Verbal Categories, and the Russian Verb," in *Russian and Slavic Grammar: Studies 1931–1981*, ed. Linda R. Waugh and Morris Halle (Berlin: Mouton, 1984), 41–58; Émile Benveniste, *Problems in General Linguistics*, trans. Mary Elizabeth Meek (Coral Gables: University of Miami Press, 1971), 223–30. For Agamben's thorough analysis of this act of enunciation as the indication of the very taking place of language, which corresponds to thetic Being in Western metaphysics, see *LD*, 23–6.

5   Jacques Lacan, *The Four Fundamental Concepts of Psychoanalysis. The Seminar of Jacques Lacan. Book XI*, ed. Jacques-Alain Miller, trans. Alan Sheridan (London: W. W. Norton, 1981), 168.

6   Cf. Žižek, *Less Than Nothing*, 665.

7   This relation constitutes Lacan's formula for fantasy $\$<>a$ (the split subject desires object *a*); see *E*, 653.

8   Žižek, *Less Than Nothing*, 664.

9   According to Lacan, "The unconscious is structured as a function of the symbolic" (Jacques Lacan, *The Ethics of Psychoanalysis 1959–1960. The Seminar of Jacques Lacan. Book VII*, ed. Jacques-Alain Miller, trans. Dennis Porter [London: Routledge, 1992], 12). The unconscious, as a symbolic function, is to be understood as a twofold movement that occurs in the subject. Lacan writes, "The symbolic function presents itself as a twofold movement in the subject: man makes his own action into an object, but only to return its foundational place to it in due time" (*E*, 236). Žižek comments on these two phases of the symbolic function: "One does something, one counts oneself as (declares oneself) the one who did it, and, on the base of this declaration, one does something new—the proper moment of subjective transformation occurs at the moment of declaration, not at the moment of the act" (Slavoj Žižek, *How to Read Lacan* [New York: W. W. Norton, 2007], 16). The transformation

of the subject happens by means of a declaration, that is, at the time the subject identifies himself in a symbolic structure. It is possible to exemplify this twofold movement in relation to literature. In the first phase, a subject who writes literature considers himself to be a literary writer. In the second phase, since the subject *is* a literary writer, the subject begins to structure his or her life in accordance with this "literary" being. This twofold movement of the symbolic function is visible in John Keats's letters. In a letter to J. H. Reynolds, Keats writes (April 17/18, 1817), "I find that I cannot exist without poetry—without eternal poetry—half the day will not do—the whole of it—I began with a little, but habit has made me a Leviathan—I had become all in a Tremble from not having written any thing of late" (John Keats, *The Letters of John Keats, Volume I, 1814–1821,* ed. Hyder Edward Rollins [Cambridge: Cambridge University Press, 1958], 133). The poet says that habit, the regular practice of writing, has made him dependent on poetry. Keats writes that he must write so as to live. He has physical reactions when he has not written anything for some time. Keats has made it a habit to write poetry, and this habit has made Keats identify his whole existence with poetry. Insofar as the poet says that he cannot live without poetry, poetry (the symbolic) structures his life.

10 Cf. Žižek, *Less Than Nothing,* 664–6. Žižek writes, "The fact that the assertion of the existence of a particular element goes against the universal notion supposed to cover or contain this element should not be dismissed as a case of the wealth of particular content overwhelming abstract notional frameworks. The empirical excess should rather be read as an indication of the inherent inconsistency or failure of the universal notion itself" (665). In terms of the paradigm of writerly necessity, we should understand the historicity of the a priori condition as the inherent contingency of the condition itself. See my sections on the temporality of the "historical a priori" in the Introduction.

11 See Lacan, *Four Fundamental Concepts of Psychoanalysis,* 154, 183–6. I will come back to the concept of *jouissance* later, but here it can be identified with an impossible "pain/enjoyment" that transgresses the pleasure principle.

12 Lacan, *Four Fundamental Concepts of Psychoanalysis,* 103.

13 See Slavoj Žižek, *The Sublime Object of Ideology* (London: Verso, 1989), 44–5.

14 Ibid., 118.

15 Lacan, *Ethics of Psychoanalysis,* 119.

16 Sigmund Freud, "Mourning and Melancholia," in *The Standard Edition of the Complete Psychological Works of Sigmund Freud. Volume 14 (1914–1916). On the History of the Psycho-Analytic Movement. Papers on Metapsychology and Other Works,* ed. James Strachey (London: Hogarth Press and the Institute of Psycho-Analysis, 1957), 243–58 (245).

17 In *The Psychic Life of Power,* Judith Butler is concerned with such a melancholic "loss" that "forms the condition of possibility for the subject" (Judith Butler, *The Psychic Life of Power: Theories in Subjection* [Stanford, CA: Stanford University Press, 1997], 24). Butler writes, "This is a loss not merely of the object or some set of objects, but of love's own possibility: the

loss of the ability to love, the unfinishable grieving for that which founds the subject" (Butler, *Psychic Life of Power*, 24). For the subject who cannot not-write, the love for literature precisely constitutes the loss of the very ability to love (an object) since literature is the very interruption of thetic Being.

18 Lacan understands the law to be fundamentally the law of the signifier: "This law, then, reveals itself clearly enough as identical to a language order" (*E*, 229).

19 Jacques Lacan, *Freud's Papers on Technique 1953–1954. The Seminar of Jacques Lacan. Book I*, ed. Jacques-Alain Miller, trans. John Forrester (New York: W. W. Norton, 1991), 102.

20 Ibid.

21 Freud, "Mourning and Melancholia," 249.

22 See also Freud, "Mourning and Melancholia," 251.

23 Ibid., 252.

24 Ibid., 253–5.

25 From a Lacanian perspective, melancholia indicates the writer's ambivalent relation to literature as an ego with its primary narcissism. The drama of the mirror stage repeats itself in the poet's process of writing. On the one hand, the poet experiences temporary instances of jubilation in which he feels that he masters art. On the other hand, these instances of limited duration then make visible his lack of mastery, which produces a growing aggression and feeling of alienation in the ego (see Jacques Lacan, "The Mirror Stage as Formative of the *I* Function as Revealed in Psychoanalytic Experience," in *E*, 75–81).

26 Cf. Lacan: "The dialectical relationship between desire and the Law causes our desire to flare up only in relation to the Law, through which it becomes the desire for death" (Lacan, *Ethics of Psychoanalysis*, 83–4).

27 Lacan, *Ethics of Psychoanalysis*, 184.

28 See Dieter Henrich, *The Course of Remembrance and Other Essays on Hölderlin*, ed. Eckart Förster (Stanford, CA: Stanford University Press, 1997), 179

29 Cf. my analysis of Agamben's concept of the author as gesture in Chapter 8.

30 I am here amalgamating Lacan's propositions on the *phallus* and *jouissance*. In *The Four Fundamental Concepts of Psychoanalysis*, Lacan writes that the *objet a* functions as a symbol of "the phallus, not as such, but in so far as it is lacking" (Lacan, *Four Fundamental Concepts of Psychoanalysis*, 103). *Objet a* is thus the symbol of the lack itself. In "The Subversion of the Subject and the Dialectic of Desire in the Freudian Unconscious," Lacan speaks of Alcibiades as "a man who pursues [the path of] jouissance as far as possible" (*E*, 671–702 [700]).

31 In his reading of Hölderlin's theoretical writings, Žižek understands Hölderlin to present a failed dialectic: "Hölderlin's starting point is the same as Hegel's: the gap between (the impossible return to) traditional organic unity and the modern reflective freedom—how are we to overcome it?" (Slavoj Žižek, "Burned by the Sun," in *Lacan: The Silent Partners*, ed.

Slavoj Žižek [London: Verso, 2006], 217–30 [227]). Žižek thus identifies Hölderlin's problem as the question of how to produce the pure (unity) in the impure (reflection). In *Less than Nothing*, Žižek specifies that what Hegel "adds to Hölderlin is a purely formal shift of transposing the tragic gap that separates the reflecting subject from pre-reflexive Being into this Being itself. Once we do this, the problem becomes its own solution: it is our very division from absolute Being which unites us with it, since this division is immanent to Being" (Žižek, *Less Than Nothing*, 15). According to Žižek, what for Hölderlin is an impasse is for Hegel the possibility for understanding negativity itself as the actual auto-production of dialectical Being. But, for Žižek, Hegel's dialectic is in fact not the system of necessity but necessity as a self-sublated contingency: "The 'eternal essence' (or, rather, concept) of a thing is not given in advance, it emerges, forms itself in an open contingent process—the eternally past essence is a *retroactive* result of the dialectical process" (Žižek, *Less Than Nothing*, 468). Žižek thus understands the Hegelian dialectic as itself a contingent process; however, insofar as this Hegelian contingency is the work of *Aufhebung*, of thetic Being, Hegelian contingency can never "be" the very interruption of the dialectic itself (unworking). Žižek himself in fact recognizes that Hegel does not consider such contingency: "He [Hegel] never considers a constellation in which a new spiritual principle continues to coexist with the old one in an inconsistent totality" (Žižek, *Less Than Nothing*, 487).

32 See Henning Bothe, "*Ein Zeichen sind wir, deutungslos*": *Die Rezeption Hölderlins von ihren Anfängen bis zu Stefan George* (Stuttgart: Metzler, 1992), 21.

33 Ibid., 27; my translation.

34 Ibid., 13; my translation.

35 Wilhelm Lange, *Hölderlin: Eine Pathographie* (Stuttgart: Ferdinand Enke, 1909). The psychiatric diagnosis is schizophrenia: *Dementia praecox catatonica* or *vorzeitiger Blödsinn* (Lange, *Hölderlin*, 71). For Lange, there is no relation between Hölderlin's "genius" and his "madness" (*Wahnsinn*); rather, Hölderlin sickness (*Geisteskrankheit*) destroys his productivity and the literary quality of his works (see Lange, *Hölderlin*, 216–17). Lange thus confirms Möbius categorization of Hölderlin's poetry as a form of *Lazarethpoesie* (quoted in Lange, *Hölderlin*, 169; see also Lange, *Hölderlin*, 170).

36 Pierre Bertaux, *Friedrich Hölderlin* (Frankfurt am Main: Suhrkamp, 1978), 12.

37 For Lange, Hölderlin's mental illness begins to appear around 1800, manifests itself clearly in 1802 before Hölderlin's stay in Bordeaux, and sets decisively in around 1806 (Lange, *Hölderlin*, 214–17; see also Jean Laplanche, *Hölderlin and the Question of the Father*, trans. Luke Carson [Victoria: ELS Editions, 2007], 8). In his study on Hölderlin's madness, Karl Jaspers relies on this chronology established by Lange (see Karl Jaspers, *Karl Jaspers' Strindberg and Van Gogh: An Attempt at a Pathographic Analysis with Reference to Parallel Cases of Swedenborg and Hölderlin*, trans. Oskar Grunow and David Woloshin [Tucson: University of Arizona Press, 1977], 146).

38 Laplanche, *Hölderlin and the Question of the Father*, 14. For a sympathetic
    but also critical reading of Laplanche's work on Hölderlin, see Foucault's essay
    "The Father's 'No'" in *AM*, 5–20.

39 Laplanche, *Hölderlin and the Question of the Father*, 7.

40 Ibid., 15.

41 Ibid.

42 Ibid., 22.

43 Ibid., 40. As Fink notes, Lacan's concept of the Name-of-the-Father is not
    tied to any actual father but only indicates the splitting of "an initial child-
    mother unity (as a logical, i.e., structural, moment, if not a temporal one"
    (Fink, *Lacanian Subject*, 55) by which "a child can attempt to mediate the
    Other's desire, keeping it at bay and symbolizing it ever more completely"
    (Fink, *Lacanian Subject*, 58). Psychosis emerges precisely when a child fails "to
    assimilate a 'primordial' signifier which would otherwise structure the child's
    symbolic universe" (Fink, *Lacanian Subject*, 55).

44 Laplanche, *Hölderlin and the Question of the Father*, 40.

45 Ibid., 39.

46 Ibid., 38.

47 Ibid., 49.

48 Ibid., 75–6.

49 Ibid., 111.

50 Maurice Blanchot, "Madness *par excellence*," in *Maurice Blanchot, The
    Blanchot Reader*, ed. Michael Holland (Oxford: Blackwell, 1995), 121; see
    Laplanche, *Hölderlin and the Question of the Father*, 11–14.

51 Blanchot, "Madness *par excellence*," 120.

52 Ibid., 124.

53 Friedrich Hölderlin, *Hyperion and Selected Poems*, ed. Eric L. Santner
    (New York: Continuum, 1990), 273; *SA* 2:1, 195.

54 Ibid., 157; *SA* 2:1, 48.

55 See also Blanchot's reading of this poem in *SL*, 269–76.

Chapter 7

1 M. H. Abrams's *The Mirror and the Lamp: Romantic Theory and the Critical
   Tradition* (London: Oxford University Press, 1971), 57.

2 I. A. Richards, *Practical Criticism: A Study of Literary Judgment*
   (London: Routledge & Kegan Paul, 1929), 289.

3 Ibid., 318; see also 317–20. For a good survey of the emergence of the
   concept of "sincerity" in the literary criticism of the nineteenth century and
   its disappearance in the twentieth century, see Patricia M. Ball, "Sincerity: The
   Rise and Fall of a Critical Term," *Modern Language Review*, vol. 59, no. 1

(1964), 1–11. Ball identifies the beginning of the nineteenth century as the point of emergence of the literary criterion of sincerity: "Thus in Romantic theory the poet 'means what he says' in this psychological sense, and the idea of sincerity becomes influential in nineteenth-century criticism, not primarily because of its traditional moral implications but because of this extended implication, dependent on these poets' belief in poetry produced by a movement of the inner being: the artist attuned to himself in order to create authentically" (Ball, "Sincerity," 2). Ball also notes, "Until the nineteenth century the implications of sincerity were predominantly religious" (Ball, "Sincerity," 1). This is congruent with other studies on the literary criterion of "sincerity," which understands this criterion to emerge around 1800. Henri Peyre writes, "The claim is put forward by several romantics that their greater sincerity endows them with a peculiar merit and makes them more vulnerable to the scoffings and the scorn of the world. Sincerity also becomes a critical criterion, and in it lies the higher value of some works" (Henri Peyre, *Literature and Sincerity* [New Haven, CT: Yale University Press, 1963], 132). David Perkins writes, "During the later part of the eighteenth century in England, poets and readers began to be influenced by a relatively novel assumption: that poetry should be written with a personal sincerity" (David Perkins, *Wordsworth and the Poetry of Sincerity* [Cambridge, MA: Belknap Press of Harvard University Press, 1964], vii). Leon Guilhamet notes that there "are few explicit statements regarding sincerity in the formal criticism of the eighteenth century" (Leon Guilhamet, *The Sincere Ideal: Studies on Sincerity in Eighteenth-Century English Literature* [Montreal McGill-Queen's University Press, 1974], 283). But he also claims, "Sincerity in poetry is not a new phenomenon, but critical concern with it is" (Guilhamet, *Sincere Ideal*, 27). This claim does, however, not refrain him from proposing (so late as the year 1974): "Wordsworth enables himself to write the first truly 'sincere' poetry. In this lies the great originality of his achievement" (Guilhamet, *Sincere Ideal*, 277).

4   Abrams, *Mirror and the Lamp*, 23.

5   Ibid., 100.

6   Ibid., 102.

7   Ibid., 101.

8   Ibid., 23–6.

9   John Stuart Mill, "What Is Poetry?" in *Essays on Poetry*, ed. F. Parvin Sharpless (Columbia: University of South Carolina Press, 1976), 3–22 (4–5).

10   Ibid., 5.

11   Ibid.

12   Ibid.

13   Ibid., 8.

14   Ibid., 13.

15   Ibid., 10.

16   John Stuart Mill, "The Two Kinds of Poetry," in *Essays on Poetry*, ed. F. Parvin Sharpless (Columbia: University of South Carolina Press, 1976), 28–43 (31).

17 Ibid., 31.

18 Ibid., 32.

19 Ibid., 34.

20 Ibid., 35.

21 Ibid. Abrams notes the irony in Mill's decision to make Wordsworth
    his example of the insincere poet: "Shelley represents the poet born and
    Wordsworth the poet made; and with unconscious irony Mill turns
    Wordsworth's own criterion, 'the spontaneous overflow of feeling,' against
    its sponsor" (Abrams, *Mirror and the Lamp*, 24). For Abrams, Wordsworth's
    preface to *Lyrical Ballads* (1800/2) is the exemplary mark of "the displacement
    of the mimetic and pragmatic by the expressive view of art in English
    criticism" (Abrams, *Mirror and the Lamp*, 22; see William Wordsworth,
    "Preface and Appendix to *Lyrical Ballads*," in *Wordsworth's Literary
    Criticism*, ed. W. J. B. Owen [London: Routledge and Kegan Paul, 1974],
    68–95). In the later "Essay upon Epitaphs" (1810), Wordsworth emphatically
    aims "to establish a criterion of sincerity, by which a Writer may be judged"
    (William Wordsworth, "Essays upon Epitaphs," in *Wordsworth's Literary
    Criticism*, ed. W. J. B. Owen [London: Routledge & Kegan Paul, 1974],
    120–69 [141]). Moreover, Wordsworth later notes that a poetic reason for
    writing is the inability to not-write: "It [the poem] was written for one of the
    best reasons which in a poetical case can be given, viz. that the author could
    not help writing it" (William Wordsworth, *The Poetical Works of William
    Wordsworth*, ed. E. de Selincourt and Helen Darbishire [Oxford: Clarendon
    Press, 1947], vol. IV, 427); also quoted in Perkins (*Wordsworth and the Poetry
    of Sincerity*, 72). Already for Wordsworth, the sincere writer is the subject who
    cannot not-write.

22 W. K. Wimsatt and M. C. Beardsley, "The Intentional Fallacy," *Sewanee
    Review*, vol. 54, no. 3 (1946), 468–88 (468).

23 W. K. Wimsatt and M. C. Beardsley, "The Affective Fallacy," *Sewanee Review*,
    vol. 57, no. 1 (1949), 31–55 (31).

24 Wimsatt and Beardsley, "Intentional Fallacy," 470.

25 Wimsatt and Beardsley, "Affective Fallacy," 41.

26 Wimsatt and Beardsley, "Intentional Fallacy," 469.

27 Ibid.

28 W. K. Wimsatt, *The Verbal Icon: Studies in the Meaning of Poetry*
    (Kentucky: University of Kentucky Press, 1954), 232.

29 Ibid., 222.

30 Ibid., 231.

31 Wimsatt and Beardsley, "Intentional Fallacy," 476.

32 Ibid.

33 John Paul Russo notes the apparent irony in the fact that Richard's *Practical
    Criticism* is understood as the foundation of New Criticism (formalism) when
    Richard's work at the same time retains the criterion of sincerity: "Sincerity

is the moral climax of *Practical Criticism* (ironically, a book recalled as the foundation of modern formalism)" (John Paul Russo, "Belief and Sincerity in I. A. Richards," *Modern Language Quarterly*, vol. 47, no. 2 [1986], 154–91 [155]). But, as Paul H. Fry writes, "The theoretical aspects of the Richards legacy have been passed along—with some alteration—through the writings of the American New Critics" (Paul H. Fry, "I. A. Richards," in *The Cambridge History of Literary Criticism. Volume 7. Modernism and the New Criticism*, ed. A. Walton Litz, Louis Menand, and Lawrence Rainey [Cambridge: Cambridge University Press, 2000], 181–99 [181]). Fry also notes, "Richards is an affective critic who differs most sharply from his successors among the New Critics—as John Crowe Ransom, Allen Tate, Cleanth Brooks, and W. K. Wimsatt themselves proclaimed in chorus—in displacing the desiderata of order and unity from the poem itself, considered as an iconic object, to the mental experience of the poet (at times) and, preeminently, of the reader" (Fry, "I. A. Richards," 196).

34 Richards, *Practical Criticism*, 300.

35 Ibid., 282–3.

36 Ibid., 280.

37 Ibid., 288.

38 See Wimsatt and Beardsley, "Affective Fallacy," 46–7.

39 Cleanth Brooks, *Modern Poetry and the Tradition* (Chapel Hill: University of North Carolina Press, 1939), 22.

40 Brooks, *Modern Poetry and the Tradition*, 37.

41 Wimsatt and Beardsley, "Intentional Fallacy," 488, note 15.

42 T. S. Eliot, "Tradition and the Individual Talent," *Perspecta*, vol. 19 (1982), 36–42 (41).

43 Ibid., 42.

44 Ibid., 40.

45 See also Austin Warren and Rene Wellek's *Theory of Literature*, in which the authors decisively dismiss the criterion of the author's sincerity as "meaningless" only to allow the concept to be understood as the expression of the literary work itself: "As for 'sincerity' in a poem: the term seems almost meaningless. A sincere expression of what? Of the supposed emotional state out of which it came? Or of the state in which the poem was written? Or a sincere expression of the poem, i.e. the linguistic construct shaping in the author's mind as he writes? Surely it will have to be the last: the poem is a sincere expression of the poem" (René Wellek and Austin Warren, *Theory of Literature*, 3rd ed. [London: Jonathan Cape, 1966], 208). But Wellek and Warren's exposition of literary theory also points negatively to literature as a nonobject. Timothy Clark writes, "Wellek concludes that a text is only a matter of 'norms' which serve as 'a potential cause of experiences' ... This, however, is less an answer to the question than an acknowledgement of the empty space left by the various failures of the positivist approach" (Timothy

Clark, *Derrida, Heidegger, Blanchot: Sources of Derrida's Notion and Practice of Literature* [Cambridge: Cambridge University Press, 1992], 1–2).

46 Cleanth Brooks, *The Well Wrought Urn: Studies in The Structure of Poetry* (London: Dennis Dobson, 1968), 159. In the essay "The Formalist Critics," Brooks writes that one of the "articles of faith" he could subscribe to is the following: "That the primary concern of criticism is with the problem of unity—the kind of whole which the literary work forms or fails to form, and the relation of the various parts to each other in building up this whole" (Cleanth Brooks, "The Formalist Critics," *Kenyon Review*, vol. 13, no. 1 [1951], 72–81 [72]). For Brooks, this is a principle that defines "the area relevant to literary criticism" without constituting "a method for carrying out the criticism" (Brooks, "Formalist Critics," 72). For Brooks, the unity of the work is thus the "truth" of literature that delimits the space for criticism and constitutes the criterion of literature without determining the critical "method."

47 Brooks, *Well Wrought Urn*, 164.

48 Ibid., 168.

49 Ibid., 164.

Chapter 8

1 François Cusset, *French Theory: How Foucault, Derrida, Deleuze, & Co. Transformed the Intellectual Life of the United States*, trans. Jeff Fort (Minneapolis: University of Minnesota Press, 2008), 30. For Derrida's paper, see "Structure, Sign, and Play in the Discourse of the Human Sciences," in *The Structuralist Controversy: The Languages of Criticism and the Sciences of Man*, ed. Richard Macksey and Eugenio Donato (Baltimore, MD: Johns Hopkins University Press, 2007), 247–72.

2 Claude Lévi-Strauss, *The Savage Mind* (London: Weidenfeld and Nicolson, 1966); Jacques Ehrmann, ed., *Yale French Studies: Structuralism*, nos 36–7 (1966).

3 Derrida, "Structure, Sign, and Play," 268.

4 See Cusset, *French Theory*, 28–30.

5 Roland Barthes, "The Death of the Author," in Roland Barthes, *Image, Music, Text*, trans. Stephen Heath (London: Fontana Press, 1977), 142–8 (147).

6 Ibid., 146.

7 Roman Jakobson, "Shifters, Verbal Categories, and the Russian Verb," in *Russian and Slavic Grammar: Studies 1931–1981*, ed. Linda R. Waugh and Morris Halle (Berlin: Mouton, 1984), 43.

8 Benveniste, *Problems in General Linguistics*, trans. Mary Elizabeth Meek (Coral Gables, FL: University of Miami Press, 1971), 230.

9 Barthes, "Death of the Author," 145.

10 Ibid.

11 Roland Barthes, "Écrivains et écrivants," in *Essais Critiques*, ed. Philippe Sollers (Paris: Éditions du Seuil, 1964), 147–54.

12 Roland Barthes, "Authors and Writers," in *A Barthes Reader*, ed. Susan Sontag (London: Jonathan Cape, 1982), 185–93 (185).

13 Ibid., 188.

14 Ibid., 187; Barthes, "Écrivains et écrivants," 149.

15 Barthes, "Authors and Writers," 189.

16 In "Linguistics and Poetics," Jakobson writes that the "poetic function is not the sole function of verbal art but only its dominant, determining function" and that this function is characterized by the "focus on the message for its own sake" (Roman Jakobson, "Linguistics and Poetics," in *Language in Literature*, ed. Krystyna Pomorska and Stephen Rudy [Cambridge, MA: Belknap Press of Harvard University Press, 1987], 62–94 [69]). In "What Is Poetry," Jakobson writes, "Poeticity is present when the word is felt as a word and not a mere representation of the object being named or an outburst of emotion" (Roman Jakobson, "What Is Poetry?" in *Language in Literature*, ed. Krystyna Pomorska and Stephen Rudy [Cambridge, MA: Belknap Press of Harvard University Press, 1987], 368–78 [378]). For Jakobson, the truth of literature is the intransitive self-reference of language itself that cannot be reduced to the actual work-object or to the author's sincere expression.

17 The paradigm of writerly necessity also emerges in the criterion for the evaluation of Rilke's poetry in Paul de Man's *Allegories of* Reading (1979). For de Man, "Rilke's most advanced poetic achievement" is the pure poems that are "by necessity brief and enigmatic, often consisting of one single sentence" (Paul de Man, *Allegories of Reading: Figural Language in Rousseau, Nietzsche, Rilke, and Proust* [New Haven, CT: Yale University Press, 1979], 48). Rilke's "pure poetry" indicates literature as an intransitive event of constitution without anything constituted: "In those poems, an emblematic object is revealed to be a figure without the need of any discourse, by the very structure of its constitution" (de Man, *Allegories of Reading*, 48). De Man notes the ambivalence of such pure poetry in which the play of the signifier is a liberation since the poet is not restrained by any referential meaning but in which this liberation is also a negation that "implies a complete drying up of thematic possibilities" (de Man, *Allegories of Reading*, 48). This ambivalence manifest the question of intransitivity as the problem of how to think the *inability* to write a *transitive* work as the *ability* to write *intransitively*.

18 See *Bulletin de la Société Française de Philosophie*, 63ᵉ année, no. 3 (1969), 73–104. For an investigation of the differences between Foucault's essay and Barthes's essay on the author, see Adrian Wilson, "Foucault on the 'Question of the Author': A Critical Exegesis," *Modern Language Review*, vol. 99, no. 2 (2004), 339–63.

19 Seán Burke, *The Death and Return of the Author: Criticism and Subjectivity in Barthes, Foucault and Derrida*, 3rd ed. (Edinburgh: Edinburgh University Press, 2008), 41. Jason Holt writes, "None of the interpretations to which

a text is open is de facto privileged, much less canonical, and so there is no
such thing as *the* meaning of a text. As a result, textual meaning can, and
furthermore should, proliferate" (Jason Holt, "The Marginal Life of the
Author," in *The Death and Resurrection of the Author?*, ed. William Irwin
[Westport, CT: Greenwood Press, 2002], 65–78 [66]). Alexander Nehamas
writes, "The author, for Foucault, prevents us from thinking of criticism as an
extension and elaboration of literature, as an activity essentially continuous
with its object, aiming to produce new meanings and not to describe old
ones" (Alexander Nehamas, "Writer, Text, Work, Author," in *The Death and
Resurrection of the Author?*, ed. William Irwin [Westport, CT: Greenwood
Press, 2002], 95–115 [98–9]). Peter Lamarque writes, "An underlying
assumption in both Barthes and Foucault is that there is intrinsic merit in
what Foucault calls the 'proliferation of meaning' " (Peter Lamarque, "The
Death of the Author: An Analytical Autopsy," in *The Death and Resurrection
of the Author?*, ed. William Irwin [Westport, CT: Greenwood Press, 2002],
79–91 [91]).

20   Barthes, "Death of the Author," 147.

21   Ibid.

22   Giorgio Agamben, "The Author as Gesture," in *Profanations*, trans. Jeff Fort
(New York: Zone, 2007), 61–72 (64–5).

23   Ibid., 65.

24   Ibid., 66.

25   Giorgio Agamben, *Means without End: Notes on Politics*, trans. Vincenzo
Binetti and Cesare Casarino (Minneapolis: University of Minnesota Press,
2000), 59.

26   Ibid., 80.

27   Ibid.

28   Agamben, "Author as Gesture," 71.

29   Ibid.

30   Regarding Agamben's concept of gesture, see William Watkin, *The Literary
Agamben: Adventures in Logopoiesis* (London: Continuum, 2010), 41–68.
Regarding the concept of gesture, see also Werner Hamacher, "The Gesture in
the Name: On Benjamin and Kafka" in *Premises: Essays on Philosophy and
Literature from Kant to Celan*, trans. Peter Fenves (Stanford, CA: Stanford
University Press, 1999), 294–336. In his reading of Benjamin's reading of
Kafka, Hamacher understands the gesture as the exposure of thetic Being. The
gesture is the caesura that interrupts the linguistic proposition (S is P): "The
decision—as a pure caesura in the language of predication, as an exposure
of that which says without saying something—lies in what Benjamin calls
gesture" (Hamacher, *Premises*, 332).

31   For general introductions to Agamben's analysis in *Language and Death*,
see William Watkin, *Agamben and Indifference: A Critical Overview*
(London: Rowman & Littlefield, 2014), 49–64; Alex Murray, *Giorgio
Agamben* (London: Routledge, 2010), 11–21; Catherine Mills, *The Philosophy*

of *Agamben* (Stocksfield: Acumen, 2008), 9–22; Sergei Prozorov, *Agamben and Politics: A Critical Introduction* (Edinburgh: Edinburgh University Press, 2014), 64–74. Specifically regarding the role of the "shifter" in Agamben's work, see Justin Clemens, "The Role of the Shifter and the Problem of Reference in Giorgio Agamben," in *The Work of Giorgio Agamben: Law, Literature, Life*, ed. Justin Clemens, Nicholas Heron, and Alex Murray (Edinburgh: Edinburgh University Press, 2008), 43–65. For an immanent critique of Agamben's project, which focuses on the "taking place" (*aver luogo*) of language in *Language and Death*, see Jenny Doussan, *Time, Language, and Visuality in Agamben's Philosophy* (Basingstoke: Palgrave Macmillan, 2013), 6–22.

32 For a comparative analysis of Blanchot and Agamben, see Thomas Carl Wall's *Radical Passivity: Levinas, Blanchot, and Agamben* (Albany: State University of New York Press, 1999). Wall writes, "The region of Agamben's politics is the region of Blanchot's 'Essential Solitude'—emptied of subject and object and radically impersonal" (Wall, *Radical Passivity*, 161). In his analysis, Wall identifies Blanchot's writer as the subject who cannot not-write and shows how Agamben's always-already removed "voice" compares to the locus of Blanchot's thinking of literature as a non-dialectical experience of withdrawal: "In Agamben's terms, the Blanchotian writer would be someone who cannot not speak and who has become capable of this impotence. ... Blanchot (or 'Blanchot') is completely absorbed in language, is an image of himself, but as he is completely absorbed in language, he is outside himself and is thus an image of no one. 'Blanchot' is the name of an infinite dispersion: language itself as a pure *potentia*, or as the emptiness or pure exteriority that is not a 'beyond' but instead an eternal return to a never-having-been or an extreme youth" (Wall, *Radical Passivity*, 6). For the subject who cannot not-write, to be capable of one's impotence (necessity to write) is precisely to be able to not not-write.

Chapter 9

1 The conception of literature as a linguistic "entity" separated from life emerges in deconstructive readings when "life" is conceived as an extralinguistic actuality. Paul de Man's *Allegories of Reading* is an example of such an understanding of the relation between life and literature. De Man argues that Rilke's pure poetry reveals "an emblematic object" that is "a figure without the need of any discourse" (Paul de Man, *Allegories of Reading: Figural Language in Rousseau, Nietzsche, Rilke, and Proust* [New Haven, CT: Yale University Press, 1979], 48). De Man can therefore say that this figure of Rilke's poetry is inaccessible through any reference to the "meaning" of life: "The figure stripped of any seduction besides that of its rhetorical elasticity can form, together with other figures, constellations of figures that are inaccessible to meaning and to the senses, located far beyond any concern for life or for death in the hollow space of an unreal sky" (de Man, *Allegories of Reading*, 48).

2   In *The End of the Poem*, Agamben proposes a form of literary criticism
    in which literature and life are conceived as indistinct in the "medium of
    language" (Giorgio Agamben,*The End of the Poem: Studies in Poetics*, trans.
    Daniel Heller-Roazen [Stanford, CA: Stanford University Press, 1999], 93).
    Within this medium, there is "on the one hand, appropriation and habit; on
    the other, expropriation and nonidentity" (Agamben, *End of the Poem*, 98).
    This medium is the "ethos" (habit) of the being-in-language in which the
    contingency of the dialectical identity of identity and nonidentity becomes
    visible.

3   Regarding the sense of the Kantian term "limit concept," see *CR*, A255/
    B310–11. Peter Fenves writes, "To say of the poetized that it is a limit
    concept means, in Kantian terms, that no intuition corresponds to it—but
    it is not therefore empty. Rather, it functions as a methodological principle
    that guides the investigation in which it is generated" (Peter Fenves, *The
    Messianic Reduction: Walter Benjamin and the Shape of Time* [Stanford,
    CA: Stanford University Press, 2011], 25). As a limit concept, the critical
    concept of the poetized does not corresponds to any sensible intuition;
    however, it guides Benjamin's investigation of the truth of literature as poetry
    a priori. Fenves (*Messianic Reduction*, 18–43) convincingly shows to what
    extent the terminology of Benjamin's essay on Hölderlin has its sources in
    the phenomenologist Edmund Husserl and in the work of the neo-Kantian
    writers Hermann Cohen and Ernst Cassirer (both associated with the Marburg
    School of Kantian thought). But Fenves's focus on Kantian terminology also
    means that he does not address Benjamin's understanding of *Aufhebung* and
    its relation to the Hegelian conceptualization of this word. Accordingly, Fenves
    regards the concept of plasticity as "a technical term of his [Benjamin's] own"
    (Fenves, *Messianic Reduction*, 29).

4   In the essay "Goethe's Elective Affinities," Benjamin understands poetry to
    produce Goethe's life insofar as "Goethe bent his life to the hierarchies that
    made it the occasion of his poetry" (*SW*, 297–360 [328]). Benjamin here also
    reiterates that Hölderlin's "Timidity" is a testimony to how poetry is not the
    expression of experience of life; rather, for the poet who must write, life is
    "full of themes and opportunities for 'the poet' " (*SW*, 328).

5   In the first *Critique*, Kant writes, "Every cognition is called *pure* [rein],
    however, that is not mixed with anything foreign to it. But a cognition is called
    absolutely pure, in particular, in which no experience or sensation at all is
    mixed in it, and that is thus fully a priori" (*CR*, A11). The pure poetry a priori
    can therefore not be drawn from experience.

6   *Halten Sie es etwa für unmöglich, zukünftige Gedichte a priori zu
    konstruieren?* (Friedrich Schlegel, *Kritische Friedrich-Schlegel-Ausgabe.
    Bd. 2. Charakteristiken und Kritiken 1 (1796–1801)*, ed. Hans Eichner
    [Paderborn: Verlag Ferdinand Schöningh, 1967], p. 350).

7   Walter Benjamin, *The Correspondence of Walter Benjamin, 1910–1940*, ed.
    Theodor W. Adorno and Gershom Scholem, trans. Manfred R. Jacobson and
    Evelyn M. Jacobson (Chicago, IL: University of Chicago Press, 1994), 81;
    Walter Benjamin, *Gesammelte Briefe*, ed. Christoph Gödde and Henri Lonitz

(Frankfurt am Main: Suhrkamp, 1995), vol. I, 327; translation modified. Benjamin notes in the letter that this view on "sober" writing corresponds to the aims of the essay "The Life of Students" (1914–15), which was written at the same time as the essay on Hölderlin (see *SW*, 46): "Intrinsically, my essay in *Das Ziel* [i.e. 'The Life of Students'] was entirely in keeping with the sense of what I have said above, but that was very hard to tell since it appeared in what was a most inappropriate outlet" (Benjamin, *The Correspondence*, 81). As we shall see, this is also the case for the essay on Hölderlin in which the artistic task of a priori poetry coincides with the political task of sober (intransitive) writing.

8 Benjamin, *The Correspondence*, 80; Benjamin, *Gesammelte Briefe* I, 326. Translation modified.

9 Benjamin, *The Correspondence*, 80.

10 Ibid.; Benjamin, *Gesammelte Briefe* I, 326–7. Translation modified.

11 In his introduction to Benjamin's dissertation on Romanticism, Philippe Lacoue-Labarthe reads Benjamin's letter to Buber and also identifies the "pure language" that underlies Benjamin's "own practice of writing" as a "purely intransitive language" (Philippe Lacoue-Labarthe, "Introduction to Walter Benjamin's 'The Concept of Art Criticism in German Romanticism,'" *Studies in Romanticism*, vol. 31, no. 4 [1992], 421–32 [424]). In the essay "Afformative, Strike," Hamacher shows how "Benjamin's sketch of a politics of pure means is a theory not of positing, producing and presenting, not of forming and transforming action, but a theory of the *abstention* from action" (Werner Hamacher, "Afformative, Strike: Benjamin's 'Critique of Violence,'" in *Walter Benjamin's Philosophy: Destruction and Experience*, ed. Andrew Benjamin and Peter Osborne [London: Routledge, 1994], 110–38 [126]). In the essay "Parataxis: On Hölderlin's Late Poetry" (1963), Theodor W. Adorno transposes Benjamin's concept of *das Gedichtete* (the poetized) into his own analysis of Hölderlin in which he identifies Benjamin's conception of pure passivity as the manifestation of the "paratactic" character of Hölderlin's poetry (see Theodor W. Adorno, "Parataxis: On Hölderlin's Late Poetry," in *Notes to Literature, Volume Two*, ed. Rolf Tiedemann, trans. Shierry Weber Nicholsen [New York: Columbia University Press, 1992], 109–49 [135]). Adorno recognizes the intransitive character of the concept of the poetized: "What has been composed could not exist without the content falling silent, any more than it could without what it falls silent about" (Adorno, "Parataxis," 112). But Adorno nevertheless understands Hölderlin's "experience" as a dialectical experience in which the "paratactic revolt against synthesis attains its limit in the synthetic function of language as such" (Adorno, "Parataxis," 136). For Adorno, the poetized can thus never be the interruption of thetic Being. Regarding the question of positing, see also Beatrice Hanssen, "'Dichtermut' and 'Blödigkeit': Two Poems by Friedrich Hölderlin, Interpreted by Walter Benjamin," in *Walter Benjamin and Romanticism*, ed. Beatrice Hanssen and Andrew Benjamin (London: Continuum, 2002), 139–62 (156).

12 Howard Caygill is correct in his characterization of *das Gedichtete* as a
    non-Hegelian "speculative concept" (Howard Caygill, *Walter Benjamin: The
    Colour of Experience* [London: Routledge, 1998], 36). Caygill writes, "The
    speculative force of [Benjamin's] immanent critique arises from this distinction
    between the poem as a singular actualised configuration and the 'Poetic'
    [i.e. the poetized] as its speculative principle which can assume a number
    of possible configurations" (Caygill, *Walter Benjamin*, 37). Caygill thus
    recognizes the speculative character of Benjamin's literary criticism. Caygill
    writes, "In the criticism of Hölderlin's poems Benjamin discovered a method
    of immanent critique which he refined but did not fundamentally change in
    his subsequent writings" (Caygill, *Walter Benjamin*, 39). Samuel Weber writes,
    "The ability to be determined—the 'greater determinability' of the poetized—
    depends directly on the ability to indetermine: to avert one's view from what
    cannot be taken in. Looking at and looking away are not mutually exclusive,
    but rather inseparable" (Samuel Weber, *Benjamin's -abilities* [Cambridge,
    MA: Harvard University Press, 2008], 18). Weber also notes the awkwardness
    of Benjamin's formulation in which it seems that the last two words *und
    anderer* are "appended, *angehängt*, at the end of the sentence as a kind of
    afterthought" (Weber, *Benjamin's -abilities*, 18). Weber writes, "The poetized
    cannot limit itself simply to the determinations *actually present* in the poem: it
    must also take into account '*anderer*' " (Weber, *Benjamin's -abilities*, 18). My
    concern in this chapter is the question regarding the *conditions* of Benjamin's
    literary criticism in which the "truth" of literature emerges as a priori poetry.

13 Walter Benjamin, *Selected Writings: Volume 4, 1938–1940*, ed. Michael
    W. Jennings (Cambridge, MA: Belknap Press of Harvard University Press,
    2006), 391.

14 Benjamin, *Selected Writings: Volume 4*, 392.

15 Ibid., 390.

16 Ibid., 389.

17 For an examination of Benjamin's concept of history, see Werner Hamacher,
    " 'Now': Walter Benjamin on Historical Time," in *The Moment: Time and
    Rupture in Modern Thought*, ed. Heidrun Friese (Liverpool: Liverpool
    University Press, 2001), 161–96.

18 For an examination of Benjamin's possible integration and transposition
    of Hölderlin's theoretical reflections into the essay on Hölderlin, see Tom
    McCall, "Plastic Time and Poetic Middles: Benjamin's Hölderlin," *Studies in
    Romanticism*, vol. 31, no. 4 (1992), 481–99. Regarding Hölderlin's possible
    "influence" on Benjamin's "theory of criticism," see Michael W. Jennings,
    "Benjamin as a Reader of Hölderlin: The Origins of Benjamin's Theory of
    Literary Criticism," *German Quarterly*, vol. 56, no. 4 (1983), 544–62.

Chapter 10

1 For Hegel, the end of art signifies that art is no longer the medium of the
   absolute in which the truth of the human condition manifests itself. The

question is not so much whether artistic activity will cease but whether art will cease to be the true substance of society. For an overview of the debate between the commentators on this Hegelian question, see Benjamin Rutter, *Hegel on the Modern Arts* (Cambridge: Cambridge University Press, 2010), 6–14.

2   Hegel writes, "Thereby it [art] has lost for us genuine truth and life [*echte Wahrheit und Lebendigkeit*], and has rather been transferred into our *ideas* [Vorstellung] instead of maintaining its earlier necessity in reality and occupying its higher place. What is now aroused in us by works of art is not just immediate enjoyment [*unmittelbaren Genuß*] but our judgement [*Urteil*] also, since we subject to our intellectual consideration (i) the content [*Inhalt*] of art, and (ii) the work of art's means of presentation [*Darstellungsmittel des Kunstwerks*], and the appropriateness or unappropriateness of both to one another. The *philosophy* of art [*Die* Wissenschaft *der Kunst*] is therefore a greater need in our day than it was in days when art by itself as art yielded full satisfaction. Art invites us to intellectual consideration, and that not for the purpose of creating art again, but for knowing philosophically [*wissenschaftlich*] what art is" (*A*, 11/I, 25–26).

3   Regarding the editorial history of Hegel's lectures on aesthetics, see Chapter 5, note 8.

4   My archaeology of writerly necessity concerns not all the arts but only writerly art (literature). However, as Nancy notes, since the time of Kant there is "a dominant tendency" in aesthetics to conceptualize "poetry" (written art) as the essence of art as such (Jean-Luc Nancy, *The Muses*, trans. Peggy Kamuf [Stanford, CA: Stanford University Press, 1996], 4). Benjamin notes that when Friedrich Schlegel "speaks of art, he thinks above all of literature" (*SW*, 118). Hegel says in his lectures, "Poetry is the universal art of the spirit which has become free in itself and which is not tied down for its realization to external sensuous material …. Yet, precisely, at this highest stage, art now transcends itself, … and passes over from the poetry of the imagination to the prose of thought. This we may take to be the articulated totality of the particular arts: the external art of architecture, the objective art of sculpture, and the subject art of painting, music, and poetry" (*A*, 89). For Hegel, poetry is the self-transcendence of art as such. Paul Oskar Kristeller shows how the constellation of the five arts of painting, sculpture, architecture, music, and poetry only emerge in the eighteenth century as a systematic framework of Art (see Paul Oskar Kristeller, "The Modern System of the Arts: A Study in the History of Aesthetics Part I," *Journal of the History of Ideas*, vol. 12, no. 4 [1951], 496–527; Paul Oskar Kristeller, "The Modern System of the Arts: A Study in the History of Aesthetics (II)," *Journal of the History of Ideas*, vol. 13, no. 1 [1952], 17–46). Nancy writes, "We have been saying 'art' in the singular and without any other specification only recently, only since the romantic period" (Nancy, *The Muses*, 4). When Hegel addresses romantic art as the end of art, this question thus concerns *literature* ("poetry" understood as the form without content).

5   On the relation between these three forms of art, see Peter Szondi, *Poetik und Geschichtsphilosophie I: Antike und Moderne in der Ästhetik der Goethezeit. Hegels Lehre von der Dichtung*, ed. Senta Metz and Hans-Hagen Hildebrandt

(Frankfurt am Main: Suhrkamp, 1974); William Desmond, "Art and the Absolute Revisited: The Neglect of Hegel's Aesthetics," in *Hegel and Aesthetics*, ed. William Maker (Albany: State University of New York Press, 2000), 1–12 (6–7); William Desmond, *Art and the Absolute: A Study of Hegel's Aesthetics* (Albany: State University of New York Press, 1986), 40–9; Stephen Houlgate, *An Introduction to Hegel's Philosophy: Freedom, Truth and History*, 2nd ed. (Oxford: Blackwell, 2005), 211–41; Robert Wicks, "Hegel's Aesthetics: An Overview," in *The Cambridge Companion to Hegel*, ed. Frederick C. Beiser (Cambridge: Cambridge University Press, 1993), 348–77; Stephen Bungay, *Beauty and Truth: A Study of Hegel's Aesthetics* (Oxford: Oxford University Press, 1987), 56–9. For an alternative account of Hegel's understanding of aesthetics, see David James, *Art, Myth and Society in Hegel's Aesthetics* (London: Continuum, 2009). James bases his reading of Hegel's aesthetics solely on the student transcripts of the lectures (and not on Hotho's edition), which leads him to claim that "Hegel provides an historically oriented theory of art that can be isolated from his speculative logic or any claims concerning a metaphysical entity called the Absolute" (James, *Art, Myth and Society*, 4).

6   Szondi, *Poetik und Geschichtsphilosophie I*, 428–9.

7   Ibid., 430.

8   Ibid., 405.

9   For Hegel, art "must disclose to us the higher interests of our spirit and will, what is in itself human and powerful, the true depths of the heart" (*A*, 279), and this task of art concerns the spirit of a people as a whole since "art does not exist for a small enclosed circle of a few eminent *savants* but for the nation at large and as a whole" (*A*, 273).

10   See *A*, 518ff; Szondi, *Poetik und Geschichtsphilosophie I*, 311, 427.

11   For an overview and examination of Hegel's understanding of romantic irony as a Subject without substance (a form without content), see Otto Pöggeler, *Hegels Kritik der Romantik* (München: Wilhelm Fink Verlag, 1998). Szondi understands Schlegel's romantic irony to be the attempt to reconcile the oppositions of the subject and the object, the ideal and the actual. In contradistinction to romantic irony, Hegel's system is not the attempt to reconcile oppositions; rather, the system is this actual unity itself (see Szondi, *Poetik und Geschichtsphilosophie I*, 295, 331–2). In opposition to such an understanding of Romanticism, Hamacher argues that irony is not the "synthesis" of thesis and antithesis; rather, the romantic task is "literally to analyze both, thesis and antithesis—to dissolve them, set them apart" (Werner Hamacher, *Premises: Essays on Philosophy and Literature from Kant to Celan*, trans. Peter Fenves (Stanford, CA: Stanford University Press, 1999), 246). Moreover, Hamacher proposes in the essay ("The End of Art with the Mask") that what is problematic for Hegel with respect to Schlegel's romantic irony is not the infinitization of a false dialectic, but that the romantic end of art undermines Hegel's own conceptualization of the end of art: "What Hegel may have found unbearable in Schlegel was not only the sustained mobility of the negative force of the dialectical as infinite paradox and 'permanent parabasis' instead of their being bound in the unity of subject and substance, but also that

his end, his *own* end, the end *itself* was thereby contested" (Werner Hamacher, "The End of Art with the Mask," in *Hegel after Derrida*, ed. Stuart Barnett [London: Routledge, 1998], 105–30 [124]; regarding the romantic "parabasis," see Hamacher's "Position Exposed: Friedrich Schlegel's Poetological Transposition of Fichte's Absolute Proposition," in *Premises*, 222–60).

12 Friedrich Schlegel, *Friedrich Schlegel's Lucinde and the Fragments*, trans. Peter Firchow (Minneapolis: University of Minnesota Press, 1971), 151; Friedrich Schlegel, *Kritische Friedrich-Schlegel-Ausgabe. Bd. 2. Charakteristiken und Kritiken 1 (1796–1801)*, ed. Hans Eichner (Paderborn: Verlag Ferdinand Schöningh, 1967), 155; translation modified.

13 Schlegel, *Friedrich Schlegel's Lucinde and the Fragments*, 151.

14 Ibid.

15 Schlegel, *Kritische Friedrich-Schlegel-Ausgabe. Bd. 2*, 155; my translation.

16 Schlegel, *Friedrich Schlegel's Lucinde and the Fragments*, 151.

17 Schlegel writes, "Geist *wohl eigent[lich] das absolute Vermögen*" (Friedrich Schlegel, *Kritische Friedrich-Schlegel-Ausgabe. Bd. 18. Philosophische Lehrjahre (1796–1806)*, ed. Ernst Behler [Paderborn: Verlag Ferdinand Schöningh, 1963], 113).

18 Schlegel writes, "Eigent[lich] ist doch alles was *Werk* an einem Werke ist, Poesie; der Buchstabe, d[er] Geist ist φσ [Philosophie]" (Schlegel, *Kritische Friedrich-Schlegel-Ausgabe. Bd. 18*, 91).

Chapter 11

1 Heidegger addresses this destruction of metaphysics in §6 of *Being and Time*. For Heidegger, the destruction of metaphysics is possible only within the horizon of the question of Being. The aim of the destruction is to disclose that which is concealed in the tradition of metaphysics in order to make the "transmission" of tradition transparent (see Martin Heidegger, *Being and Time*, trans. Joan Stambaugh [Albany: State University of New York Press, 1996], 17–23).

2 See Martin Heidegger, *Introduction to Metaphysics*, trans. Gregory Fried and Richard Polt (New Haven, CT: Yale University Press, 2000), 140.

3 Martin Heidegger, "The Origin of the Work of Art," in *Basic Writings*, ed. David Farrell Krell, Revised and Expanded Edition (New York: Harper Perennial, 2008), 139–212 (205).

4 Heidegger, "Origin of the Work of Art," 204.

5 Ibid.; Martin Heidegger, "Der Ursprung des Kunstwerkes," in *Holzwege* (Frankfurt am Main: Vittoria Klostermann, 1980), 1–72 (65).

6 Heidegger, "Origin of the Work of Art," 153; Heidegger, "Der Ursprung des Kunstwerkes," 11.

7 Agamben's interpretation of rhythm as *epochē* has its basis in a short statement by Hölderlin and a short lecture by Heidegger. On the one hand,

Agamben reads a proposition that Bettina von Arnim ascribes to Hölderlin in which the work of art is understood as a heavenly rhythm. Hölderlin did not write it down; rather, Arnim who visited Hölderlin in his tower in Tübingen during the poet's years of "madness" transcribes the formula in *Die Günderode*: "Everything is rhythm, the entire destiny of man [*Schicksal des Menschen*] is one heavenly rhythm, just as every work of art is one rhythm, and everything swings from the poetizing lips of the god [*Dichterlippen des Gottes*]" (quoted in *MC*, 94; cf. Bettina von Arnim, *Die Günderode* [Frankfurt am Main: Insel Verlag, 1982], 294). On the other hand, Agamben understands *epochē* as the showing of interruption, the withdrawal of thetic Being, which we can lead back to Heidegger's attempt in the lecture "Time and Being" ("Zeit und Sein," 1962) "to think Being without beings [*Sein ohne das Seiende zu denken*]" (Martin Heidegger, *On Time and Being*, trans. Joan Stambaugh [Chicago, IL: University of Chicago Press, 2002], 2; Martin Heidegger, *Zur Sache des Denkens* [Tübingen: Max Niemeyer Verlag, 1969], 2). Heidegger here understands *epochē* as Being's (*Sein*) holding back of itself. For Heidegger, Being not only grounds beings but also vanishes in the event of appropriation (*Sein verschwindet im Ereignis*; Heidegger, *Zur Sache Des Denkens*, 22). Heidegger understands the withdrawal (*Entzug*) of Being as itself a part of the constitution of beings. In the *Ereignis*, the event of expropriation and appropriation, Being both grounds beings and withdraws itself as ground: "Expropriation belongs to Appropriation as such. By this expropriation, Appropriation does not abandon itself—rather, it preserves what is its own" [*Zum Ereignis als solchem gehört die Enteignis. Durch sie gibt das Ereignis sich nicht auf, sondern bewahrt sein Eigentum*] (Heidegger, *On Time and Being*, 23; Heidegger, *Zur Sache Des Denkens*, 23).

8   See Agamben's "On Potentiality" in Giorgio Agamben, *Potentialities: Collected Essays in Philosophy*, trans. Daniel Heller-Roazen (Stanford, CA: Stanford University Press, 1999), 177–84; Giorgio Agamben, "Bartleby, or On Contingency," in *Potentialities: Collected Essays in Philosophy*, trans. Daniel Heller-Roazen (Stanford, CA: Stanford University Press, 1999), 243–71. Alex Murray, Leland de la Durantaye, and Claire Colebrook all identify the thought of potentiality in Agamben's *The Man without Content*. Murray writes, "We see the emergence of what will later be reformulated as inoperativity" (Alex Murray, *Giorgio Agamben* [London: Routledge, 2010], 84). Durantaye writes, "What interests Agamben in art is the potential it has lost, or that has gone unrecognized in it, which he works to reveal" (Leland de la Durantaye, *Giorgio Agamben: A Critical Introduction* [Stanford, CA: Stanford University Press, 2009], 51). Colebrook writes, "Art is open relationality, a relation or potential *to*, where the infinitive is not governed by anything that already *is*" (Claire Colebrook, "Agamben: Aesthetics, Potentiality, and Life," *South Atlantic Quarterly*, vol. 107, no. 1 [2008], 107–20 [112]).

9   Regarding Agamben's thinking of literature and art, see Watkin's *The Literary Agamben*. Watkin notes that this "rhythm" is "the basis for Agamben's later construction of messianic time, as well as providing an early prototype for the Idea of Prose and its subsequent reformulation as potential" (Watkin, *The Literary Agamben: Adventures in Logopoiesis* (London: Continuum, 2010),

191). In *The Man without Content*, this rhythmic interruption is the "truth of art," which in modern aesthetics has been forgotten in the thinking of the Author's operative praxis (see *MC*, 70; Watkin, *Literary Agamben*, 71–114).

10   Agamben never addresses the paradigm of writerly necessity directly, but he identifies the artist as the subject whose very life depends on the work. For Agamben, Hölderlin is here exemplary: "To prove how little this idea [that the author's life is at stake in artistic production] is merely one metaphor among those forming the 'properties' of the 'literary histrio,' it suffices to quote what Hölderlin wrote on the brink of madness: 'I fear that I might end like the old Tantalus who received more from the Gods than he could take, and 'I may say that Apollo struck me' " (*MC*, 5).

11   See *MC*, 121, note 1. The English *split* here translates the Italian *lacerazione*, which itself is a translation of Hegel's German *Zerrissenheit*—"the state of being torn."

12   Luc Ferry sets the time for the emergence of "aesthetic taste" in the seventeenth century: "It's around the middle of the seventeenth century that, first in Italy and Spain, then in France and England and, finally, Germany, where there was some difficulty finding in the word *Geschmack* an adequate translation—the term acquires pertinence in the designation of a new faculty, capable of distinguishing the beautiful from the ugly .... And it is beginning with the representation of such a faculty that we enter definitely into the universe of 'modern aesthetics' (the juxtaposition of these two terms being, besides, practically a pleonasm)" (Luc Ferry, *Homo Aestheticus: The Invention of Taste in the Democratic Age*, trans. Robert de Loaiza [Chicago, IL: University of Chicago Press, 1993], 14–15). R. G. Saisselin also writes, "Taste as the ultimate criterion for judging the fine arts first appeared in the midst of the scientific revolution of the *Grand Siècle*" (R. G. Saisselin, *Taste in Eighteenth Century France: Critical Reflections of the Origins of Aesthetics or an Apology for Amateurs* [Syracuse, NY: Syracuse University Press, 1965], 15). Regarding the transformation of the activity of taste into a *faculty* of taste, see Howard Caygill, *Art of Judgement* (Oxford: Basil Blackwell, 1989), 38–44.

13   For an analysis of the theme of the judgment of taste in Kant's work, see Paul Guyer, *Kant and the Claims of Taste*, 2nd ed. (Cambridge: Cambridge University Press, 1997); Brent Kalar, *The Demands of Taste in Kant's Aesthetics* (London: Continuum, 2006).

14   The romantic Subject is thus not the sincere creative Genius. Benjamin notes that F. Schlegel "is responsible for the decisive overcoming of aesthetic dogmatism" (*SW*, 154), the overcoming of the rationalist conventions of eighteenth-century rhetorical criticism. Moreover, the romantic work is not the manifestation of the psychologizing tendency of the *Sturm und Drang*, namely "the boundless cult of creative power understood as the mere expressive force of the creator" (*SW*, 154).

15   In Benjamin's analysis, it is possible to conceive the contours of what in *The Literary Absolute* will become the dialectical relation between the infinite progression of the work and the fragmentary ideal of connectedness (see *LA* 46, 106, and 135, note 26). In *The Literary Absolute,* the romantic

"infinitization" of the Subject compares to Benjamin's understanding of the romantic work's "limitless capacity of self-reflection," and the "fragmentary ideal" of connectedness correlates to "the continuum of forms" (cf. *SW*, 116–48; *LA*, 39–58).

16 Dieter Henrich notes that Hegel did not allow that art could itself be reflection *of* art, since philosophy is the reflection *on* art: "Hegel did not allow for the reflectedness *of the work of art itself.* ... Philosophy is the concept of its method and of its system. In Hegel's theory there is no reason for denying to art the same characteristics" (Dieter Henrich, "Art and Philosophy of Art Today: Reflections with Reference to Hegel," in *New Perspectives in German Literary Criticism: A Collection of Essays*, ed. Richard E. Amacher and Victor Lange [Princeton, NJ: Princeton University Press, 1979], 107–33 [128]).

Chapter 12

1 Edgar Wind, *Art and Anarchy*, 3rd ed. (Chicago, IL: Northwestern University Press, 1985), 39.

2 Ibid., 32.

3 Ibid., 36.

4 Ibid.

5 Ibid.

6 For studies on Barthes's lecture course on the preparation of the novel, see Lucy O'Meara, *Roland Barthes at the Collège de France* (Liverpool: Liverpool University Press, 2012), 163–99; Sam Ferguson, "Forgetting Gide: A Study of Barthes's 'Ursuppe,'" *Barthes Studies*, vol. 1 (2015), 17–34; Antoine Compagnon and Rosalind Krauss, "Roland Barthes's Novel," *October*, vol. 112 (2005), 23–34; Kris Pint, "How to Become What One Is: Roland Barthes's Final Fantasy," *Paragraph*, vol. 31, no. 1 (2008), 38–49; Jonathan Culler, "Preparing the Novel: Spiralling Back," *Paragraph*, vol. 31, no. 1 (2008), 109–20; Andy Stafford, "'*Préparation du romanesque*' in Roland Barthes's Reading of *Sarrasine*," *Paragraph*, vol. 31, no. 1 (2008), 95–108. A recurrent question is whether Barthes is actually writing a novel or rather preparing novel. Compagnon and Krauss presuppose that Barthes was writing a novel, and they focus on the fact that Barthes never did (Barthes did however produce eight sheets of paper contained in a red cardboard folder marked VITA NOVA in capital letters, see *PN*, 389–406). Pint also speaks of "Barthes's inability actually to write his novel" (Pint, "How to Become What One Is," 46) but also recognizes that the concern for Barthes is the "fantasy [of the novel] itself, rather than in the completion [of the actual novel]" (Pint, "How to Become What One Is," 48). Culler identifies that Barthes's proposed task is "not writing a novel but working *as if* he were writing a novel" (Culler, "Preparing the Novel," 110). Stafford notes that "there is no novel, but there is an acting of a novelist about to write" (Stafford, "'*Préparation du romanesque*,'" 102). O'Meara writes that "much of Barthes's work from

late 1978 is concerned with the planning and projection of a work that is not intended to be written" (O'Meara, *Roland Barthes at the Collège de France*, 164). Moreover, O'Meara notes the importance of *The Literary Absolute* for Barthes's late lecture course (see O'Meara, *Roland Barthes at the Collège de France*, 164). Barthes explicitly states from the beginning of the course that he is not writing a novel: "I've even heard it said (the path rumours usually take) that I'm writing one [i.e. a novel], which isn't true; if it were, I clearly wouldn't be in a position to propose a lecture course on its preparation: writing requires secrecy" (*PN*, 11). Barthes is in the position of the critic as a deferred writer, as a writer who cannot not-write intransitively but appropriates this intransitivity as the very possibility of a novel life, which is a literary life precisely because the writer is writing the absence of work. From this perspective, the question is not whether Barthes was writing a novel or not, but that the truth of literature as an intransitive "work" can never actualize itself in an actual work. From the perspective of this truth of literature, the *Vita Nova* (the eight sheets of "writing") is a trace of the impossibility of writing an actual *literary* work.

7   Rainer Maria Rilke, *Letters to a Young Poet & The Letter from the Young Worker*, trans. Charlie Louth (London: Penguin, 2011), 7–8.

8   For studies concerned with Barthes as a "writer-critic" and less with his place within the "movements" of literary criticism, see Andrew Brown, *Roland Barthes: The Figures of Writing* (New York: Clarendon Press, 1992); Réda Bensmaïa, *The Barthes Effect: The Essay as Reflective Text*, trans. Pat Fedkiew (Minneapolis: University of Minnesota Press, 1987). Brown notes that Barthes is neither simply a pure writer nor a pure literary theorist (see Brown, *Roland Barthes*, 3). Bensmaïa focuses on the fragmentary tendency of Barthes "reflective text" in which the producer and the user, the author and the critic are brought together "in one writing movement" (Bensmaïa, *The Barthes Effect*, xxvi). For a studies of Barthes's different positions within the field of literary criticism, see Annette Lavers, *Roland Barthes: Structuralism and After* (London: Methuen, 1982); Jonathan Culler, *Barthes* (London: Fontana Press, 1990); Rick Rylance, *Roland Barthes* (Hertfordshire: Harvester Wheatsheaf, 1994); Steven Ungar, *Roland Barthes: The Professor of Desire* (Lincoln: University of Nebraska Press, 1983).

9   Regarding this conference, see Chapter 8.

10 Barthes, "To Write: An Intransitive Verb?," in *The Structuralist Controversy: The Languages of Criticism and the Sciences of Man*, ed. Richard Macksey and Eugenio Donato (Baltimore, MD: Johns Hopkins University Press, 2007), 142.

11 See my Introduction.

12 Gérard Genette, "The Obverse of Signs," in Gérard Genette, *Figures of Literary Discourse*, trans. Alan Sheridan (New York: Columbia University Press, 1982), 27–44 (41).

13 Barthes, *Roland Barthes by Roland Barthes*, trans. Richard Howard (New York: Hill and Wang, 2010), 52.

14 Roland Barthes, "Inaugural Lecture, Collège de France," in Roland Barthes, *A Barthes Reader*, ed. Susan Sontag (London: Jonathan Cape, 1982), 457–78 (462).

15 Cf. Barthes, "Inaugural Lecture, Collège de France," 476.

16 Barthes, *Roland Barthes by Roland Barthes*, 49.

17 Ibid.; Roland Barthes, *Roland Barthes par Roland Barthes* (Paris: Seuil, 1975), 53.

18 Barthes, *Roland Barthes by Roland Barthes*, 52.

19 Ibid.; Barthes, *Roland Barthes par Roland Barthes*, 56.

20 Barthes, *Roland Barthes by Roland Barthes*, 85.

21 Ibid., 97.

22 Ibid., 140–1; Barthes, *Roland Barthes par Roland Barthes*, 144.

23 Barthes, *Roland Barthes by Roland Barthes*, 141.

24 Ibid.

25 Giorgio Agamben, *Remnants of Auschwitz: The Witness and the Archive*, trans. Daniel Heller-Roazen (New York: Zone, 2002), 146. Regarding the question of contingency, see also "Bartleby, or On Contingency," in Giorgio Agamben, *Potentialities: Collected Essays in Philosophy*, trans. Daniel Heller-Roazen (Stanford, CA: Stanford University Press, 1999), 243–71.

26 Giorgio Agamben, "On Potentiality," in *Potentialities*, 177–84 (183).

27 Alexandre Kojève, *Introduction to the Reading of Hegel: Lectures on the Phenomenology of Spirit*, ed. Allan Bloom, trans. James H. Nichols, Jr. (Ithaca, NY: Cornell University Press, 1980), 154.

28 Ibid., 153.

29 See Henrich, *Hegel im Kontext*, Vierte, veränderte Auflage (Frankfurt am Main: Suhrkamp, 1971), 159

30 Stephen Houlgate, "Necessity and Contingency in Hegel's *Science of Logic*," *Owl of Minerva*, vol. 27, no. 1 (1995), 37–49 (41).

31 Houlgate, "Necessity and Contingency in Hegel's *Science of Logic*," 41–2. Regarding Hegel's understanding of the necessity of contingency, see also George di Giovanni, "The Category of Contingency in the Hegelian Logic," in *Art and Logic in Hegel's Philosophy*, ed. Warren E. Steinkraus and Kenneth L. Schmitz (Sussex: Harvester Press, 1980), 179–200; John W. Burbidge, "The Necessity of Contingency," in *Art and Logic in Hegel's Philosophy*, ed. Warren E. Steinkraus and Kenneth L. Schmitz (Sussex: Harvester Press, 1980), 201–17.

Afterthought on Literary Inoperativity

1 Jacques Derrida, *Of Grammatology*, trans. Gayatri Chakravorty Spivak, Corrected Edition (Baltimore, MD: Johns Hopkins University Press, 1997), 314.

2 Ibid.

3 In "*Pardes*: The Writing of Potentiality," Agamben aims to think the potentiality of deconstruction (see Giorgio Agamben, *Potentialities: Collected Essays in Philosophy*, trans. Daniel Heller-Roazen [Stanford, CA: Stanford University Press, 1999], 205–19). However, in *Language and Death*, Agamben argues that Derrida's thought of the *grammata* is not the thinking of inoperativity. Agamben argues that metaphysics is not simply a metaphysics of presence, of the voice, of *phone*, but always already a metaphysics of writing, of the *gramma*, of the removal of voice: "*Metaphysics is always already grammatology and this is* fundamentology *in the sense that the* gramma *(or the Voice) functions as the negative ontological foundation*" (*LD*, 39). On the relation between Agamben's thinking of potentiality and Derrida's deconstructive thinking, see William Watkin, *Agamben and Indifference: A Critical Overview* (London: Rowman & Littlefield, 2014), 107–35.

4 Agamben, "*Pardes*: The Writing of Potentiality," in *Potentialities*, 217.

5 Ibid., 217–18.

BIBLIOGRAPHY

Abrams, M. H., *The Mirror and the Lamp: Romantic Theory and the Critical Tradition* (London: Oxford University Press, 1971).

Adorno, Theodor W., "Parataxis: On Hölderlin's Late Poetry," in *Notes to Literature, Volume Two*, edited by Rolf Tiedemann, translated by Shierry Weber Nicholsen (New York: Columbia University Press, 1992), 109–49.

Agamben, Giorgio, "The Author as Gesture," in *Profanations*, translated by Jeff Fort (New York: Zone, 2007), 61–72.

Agamben, Giorgio, *The End of the Poem: Studies in Poetics*, translated by Daniel Heller-Roazen (Stanford, CA: Stanford University Press, 1999).

Agamben, Giorgio, *Il linguaggio e la morte: un seminario sul luogo della negatività* (Torino: Giulio Einaudi, 1982).

Agamben, Giorgio, *The Kingdom and the Glory: For a Theological Genealogy of Economy and Government*, translated by Lorenzo Chiesa (Stanford, CA: Stanford University Press, 2011).

Agamben, Giorgio, *Language and Death: The Place of Negativity*, translated by Karen E. Pinkus and Michael Hardt (Minneapolis: University of Minnesota Press, 1991).

Agamben, Giorgio, *L'uomo senza contenuto* (Macerata: Quodlibet, 1994).

Agamben, Giorgio, *The Man without Content*, translated by Georgia Albert (Stanford, CA: Stanford University Press, 1999).

Agamben, Giorgio, *Means without End: Notes on Politics*, translated by Vincenzo Binetti and Cesare Casarino (Minneapolis: University of Minnesota Press, 2000).

Agamben, Giorgio, *Opus Dei: An Archaeology of Duty*, translated by Adam Kotsko (Stanford, CA: Stanford University Press, 2013).

Agamben, Giorgio, *Potentialities: Collected Essays in Philosophy*, translated by Daniel Heller-Roazen (Stanford, CA: Stanford University Press, 1999).

Agamben, Giorgio, *Remnants of Auschwitz: The Witness and the Archive*, translated by Daniel Heller-Roazen (New York: Zone, 2002).

Agamben, Giorgio, *The Signature of All Things: On Method*, translated by Luca D'Isanto and Kevin Attell (New York: Zone, 2009).

Aristotle, *Selections*, edited by Terence Irwin and Gail Fine (Indianapolis, IN: Hackett, 1995).

Arnim, Bettina von, *Die Günderode* (Frankfurt am Main: Insel Verlag, 1982).

Ball, Patricia M., "Sincerity: The Rise and Fall of a Critical Term," *Modern Language Review*, vol. 59, no. 1 (1964), 1–11.

Barthes, Roland, "Authors and Writers," in *A Barthes Reader*, edited by Susan Sontag (London: Jonathan Cape, 1982), 185–93.

Barthes, Roland, "The Death of the Author," *Aspen*, nos 5–6 (1967).

Barthes, Roland, "The Death of the Author," in Roland Barthes, *Image, Music, Text*, translated by Stephen Heath (London: Fontana Press, 1977), 142–8.

Barthes, Roland, "Écrivains et écrivants," in *Essais Critiques* (Paris: Éditions du Seuil, 1964), 147–54.

Barthes, Roland, "Inaugural Lecture, Collège de France," in Roland Barthes, *A Barthes Reader*, edited by Susan Sontag (London: Jonathan Cape, 1982), 457–78.

Barthes, Roland, "La Mort de l'auteur," *Manteia*, no. 5, 1968.

Barthes, Roland, *La Préparation du roman: cours au Collège de France 1978–1979 et 1979–1980*, edited by Nathalie Léger (Paris: Seuil, 2015).

Barthes, Roland, *The Preparation of the Novel: Lecture Courses and Seminars at the Collège de France, 1978–1979 and 1979–1980*, edited by Nathalie Léger, translated by Kate Briggs (New York: Columbia University Press, 2011).

Barthes, Roland, *Roland Barthes by Roland Barthes*, translated by Richard Howard (New York: Hill and Wang, 2010).

Barthes, Roland, *Roland Barthes par Roland Barthes* (Paris: Seuil, 1975).

Barthes, Roland, *S/Z* (Paris: Seuil, 1970).

Barthes, Roland, *S/Z*, translated by Richard Miller (Oxford: Basil Blackwell, 1990).

Barthes, Roland, "To Write: An Intransitive Verb?," in *The Structuralist Controversy: The Languages of Criticism and the Sciences of Man*, edited by Richard Macksey and Eugenio Donato (Baltimore, MD: Johns Hopkins University Press, 2007), 134–45.

Barthes, Roland, *Writing Degree Zero*, translated by Annette Lavers and Colin Smith (New York: Hill and Wang, 2012).

Baugh, Bruce, *French Hegel: From Surrealism to Postmodernism* (New York: Routledge, 2003).

Beaumarchais, Jean-Pierre de, Daniel Couty, and Alain Rey, eds., *Dictionnaire des littératures de langue française* (Paris: Bordas, 1998).

Beiser, Frederick C., *The Romantic Imperative: The Concept of Early German Romanticism* (Cambridge, MA: Harvard University Press, 2003).

Benjamin, Walter, *The Correspondence of Walter Benjamin, 1910–1940*, edited by Theodor W. Adorno and Gershom Gerhard Scholem, translated by Manfred R. Jacobson and Evelyn M. Jacobson (Chicago, IL: University of Chicago Press, 1994).

Benjamin, Walter, *Gesammelte Briefe*, edited by Christoph Gödde and Henri Lonitz (Frankfurt am Main: Suhrkamp, 1995), vol. I.

Benjamin, Walter, *Gesammelte Schriften*, edited by Rolf Tiedemann and Hermann Schweppenhäuser (Frankfurt am Main: Suhrkamp, 1991), vol. I–VII.

Benjamin, Walter, *Selected Writings: Volume 1, 1913–1926*, edited by Michael W. Jennings and Marcus Bullock (Cambridge, MA: Belknap Press of Harvard University Press, 2004).

Benjamin, Walter, *Selected Writings: Volume 4, 1938–1940*, edited by Michael W. Jennings (Cambridge, MA: Belknap Press of Harvard University Press, 2006).

Bensmaïa, Réda, *The Barthes Effect: The Essay as Reflective Text*, translated by Pat Fedkiew (Minneapolis: University of Minnesota Press, 1987).

Benveniste, Émile, *Problems in General Linguistics*, translated by Mary Elizabeth Meek (Coral Gables, FL: University of Miami Press, 1971).

Bernstein, Susan, "Re-Re-Re-Reading Jena," *MLN*, vol. 110, no. 4 (1995), 834–55.

Bertaux, Pierre, *Friedrich Hölderlin* (Frankfurt am Main: Suhrkamp, 1978).

Bident, Christopher, "The Movements of the Neuter," in *After Blanchot: Literature, Criticism, Philosophy*, edited by Leslie Hill, Brian Nelson, and Dimitris Vardoulakis (Newark: University of Delaware Press, 2005), 13–34.

Blanchot, Maurice, *The Book to Come*, translated by Charlotte Mandell (Stanford, CA: Stanford University Press, 2003).

Blanchot, Maurice, *The Infinite Conversation*, translated by Susan Hanson (Minneapolis: University of Minnesota Press, 1993).

Blanchot, Maurice, "L'Athenaeum," *La Nouvelle Revue Française*, no. 140 (1964), 301–13.

Blanchot, Maurice, "La Folie par excellence," *Critique*, no. 45 (1951), 99–118.

Blanchot, Maurice, "La Littérature et le droit à la mort," *Critique*, no. 20 (January 1948), 30–47.

Blanchot, Maurice, *La Part du feu* (Paris: Gallimard, 1949).

Blanchot, Maurice, *L'Entretien infini* (Paris: Gallimard, 1969).

Blanchot, Maurice, *L'Espace littéraire* (Paris: Gallimard, 1955).

Blanchot, Maurice, "L'Interruption," *La Nouvelle Revue Française*, no. 137 (1964), 869–81.

Blanchot, Maurice, "L'Oubli, la déraison," *La Nouvelle Revue Française*, no. 106 (1961), 676–86.

Blanchot, Maurice, "Madness *par excellence*," in *Maurice Blanchot, The Blanchot Reader*, edited by Michael Holland (Oxford: Blackwell, 1995), 110–28.

Blanchot, Maurice, *The Space of Literature*, translated by Ann Smock (Lincoln: University of Nebraska Press, 1982).

Blanchot, Maurice , *The Work of Fire*, translated by Charlotte Mandell (Stanford, CA: Stanford University Press, 1995).

Blanchot, Maurice, *The Writing of the Disaster*, translated by Ann Smock (Lincoln: University of Nebraska Press, 1995).

Bothe, Henning, *"Ein Zeichen sind wir, deutungslos": Die Rezeption Hölderlins von ihren Anfängen bis zu Stefan George* (Stuttgart: Metzler, 1992).

Bourdieu, Pierre, *The Rules of Art: Genesis and Structure of the Literary Field*, translated by Susan Emanuel (Stanford, CA: Stanford University Press, 1996).

Brooks, Cleanth, "The Formalist Critics," *Kenyon Review*, vol. 13, no. 1 (1951), 72–81.

Brooks, Cleanth, *Modern Poetry and the Tradition* (Chapel Hill: University of North Carolina Press, 1939).

Brooks, Cleanth, *The Well Wrought Urn: Studies in The Structure of Poetry*, Revised Edition (London: Dennis Dobson, 1968).

Brown, Andrew, *Roland Barthes: The Figures of Writing* (New York: Clarendon Press, 1992).

Bungay, Stephen, *Beauty and Truth: A Study of Hegel's Aesthetics* (Oxford: Oxford University Press, 1987).

Burbidge, John W., "The Necessity of Contingency," in *Art and Logic in Hegel's Philosophy*, edited by Warren E. Steinkraus and Kenneth L. Schmitz (Sussex: Harvester Press, 1980), 201–17.

Burke, Seán, *The Death and Return of the Author: Criticism and Subjectivity in Barthes, Foucault and Derrida*, 3rd ed. (Edinburgh: Edinburgh University Press, 2008).

Butler, Judith, *The Psychic Life of Power: Theories in Subjection* (Stanford, CA: Stanford University Press, 1997).

Butler, Judith, *Subjects of Desire: Hegelian Reflections in Twentieth-Century France* (New York: Columbia University Press, 1987).

Canguilhem, Georges, "The Death of Man, or Exhaustion of the Cogito?," in *The Cambridge Companion to Foucault*, edited by Gary Gutting, 2nd ed. (Cambridge: Cambridge University Press, 2005), 74–94.

Cassin, Barbara, ed., *Dictionary of Untranslatables: A Philosophical Lexicon* (Princeton, NJ: Princeton University Press, 2014).

Caygill, Howard, *Art of Judgement* (Oxford: Basil Blackwell, 1989).

Caygill, Howard, *A Kant Dictionary* (Oxford: Blackwell, 1995).

Caygill, Howard, *Walter Benjamin: The Colour of Experience* (London: Routledge, 1998).

Clark, Timothy, *Derrida, Heidegger, Blanchot: Sources of Derrida's Notion and Practice of Literature* (Cambridge: Cambridge University Press, 1992).

Clemens, Justin, "The Role of the Shifter and the Problem of Reference in Giorgio Agamben," in *The Work of Giorgio Agamben: Law, Literature, Life*, edited by Justin Clemens, Nicholas Heron, and Alex Murray (Edinburgh: Edinburgh University Press, 2008), 43–65.

Cohen, S. Marc, "Substances," in *A Companion to Aristotle*, edited by Georgios Anagnostopoulos (Chichester: Wiley-Blackwell, 2009), 197–212.

Colebrook, Claire, "Agamben: Aesthetics, Potentiality, and Life," *South Atlantic Quarterly*, vol. 107, no. 1 (2008), 107–20.

Comay, Rebecca, "Benjamin and the Ambiguities of Romanticism," in *The Cambridge Companion to Walter Benjamin*, edited by David S. Ferris (Cambridge: Cambridge University Press, 2004), 134–51.

Compagnon, Antoine, and Rosalind Krauss, "Roland Barthes's Novel," *October*, vol. 112 (2005), 23–34.

Cook, Daniel J., *Language in the Philosophy of Hegel* (The Hague: Mouton, 1973).

Critchley, Simon, *The Ethics of Deconstruction: Derrida and Levinas*, 3rd ed. (Edinburgh: Edinburgh University Press, 2014).

Critchley, Simon, "*Il y a*—Holding Levinas's Hand to Blanchot's Fire," in *Maurice Blanchot: The Demand of Writing*, edited by Carolyn Bailey Gill (London: Routledge, 1996), 108–22.

Critchley, Simon, *Very Little … Almost Nothing: Death, Philosophy, Literature*, 2nd ed. (London: Routledge, 2004).

Culler, Jonathan, *Barthes* (London: Fontana Press, 1990).

Culler, Jonathan, "Preparing the Novel: Spiralling Back," *Paragraph*, vol. 31, no. 1 (2008), 109–20.

Cusset, François, *French Theory: How Foucault, Derrida, Deleuze, & Co. Transformed the Intellectual Life of the United States*, translated by Jeff Fort (Minneapolis: University of Minnesota Press, 2008).

"Das älteste Systemprogramm des deutschen Idealismus," in Georg Wilhelm Friedrich Hegel, *Frühe Schriften*, Werke 1, edited by Eva Moldenhauer and Karl Markus Michel (Frankfurt am Main: Suhrkamp 1979), 234–6.

Davies, Paul, "The Work and the Absence of the Work," in *Maurice Blanchot: The Demand of Writing*, edited by Carolyn Bailey Gill (London: Routledge, 1996), 91–107.

Davis, Bret W., *Heidegger and the Will: On the Way to* Gelassenheit (Evanston, IL: Northwestern University Press, 2007).

de la Durantaye, Leland, *Giorgio Agamben: A Critical Introduction* (Stanford, CA: Stanford University Press, 2009).

Deleuze, Gilles, *Foucault*, translated by Seán Hand (London: Athlone Press, 1988).

de Man, Paul, *Allegories of Reading: Figural Language in Rousseau, Nietzsche, Rilke, and Proust* (New Haven, CT: Yale University Press, 1979).

de Man, Paul, "Sign and Symbol in Hegel's 'Aesthetics'," *Critical Inquiry*, vol. 8, no. 4 (1982), 761–75.

Derrida, Jacques, "Cogito and the History of Madness," in *Writing and Difference*, edited by Alan Bass (London: Routledge, 2001), 36–76.

Derrida, Jacques, *Dissemination*, translated by Barbara Johnson (Chicago, IL: University of Chicago Press, 1981).

Derrida, Jacques, "From Restricted to General Economy: A Hegelianism without reserve," in *Writing and Difference*, edited by Alan Bass (London: Routledge, 2001), 317–50.

Derrida, Jacques, "La Parole soufflée," in *Writing and Difference*, edited by Alan Bass (London: Routledge, 2001), 212–45.

Derrida, Jacques, *Of Grammatology*, translated by Gayatri Chakravorty Spivak, Corrected Edition (Baltimore, MD: Johns Hopkins University Press, 1997).

Derrida, Jacques, "The Pit and the Pyramid: Introduction to Hegel's Semiology," in *Margins of Philosophy*, translated by Alan Bass [Brighton: Harvester Press, 1982], 69–108.

Derrida, Jacques, "Structure, Sign, and Play in the Discourse of the Human Sciences," in *The Structuralist Controversy: The Languages of Criticism and the Sciences of Man*, edited by Richard Macksey and Eugenio Donato (Baltimore, MD: Johns Hopkins University Press, 2007), 247–72.

Derrida, Jacques, "This Strange Institution Called Literature: An Interview with Jacques Derrida," in *Acts of Literature*, edited by Derek Attridge (New York: Routledge, 1992), 33–75.

Descombes, Vincent, *Modern French Philosophy*, translated by L. Scott-Fox and J. M. Harding (Cambridge: Cambridge University Press, 1980).

Desmond, William, *Art and the Absolute: A Study of Hegel's Aesthetics* (Albany: State University of New York Press, 1986).

Desmond, William, "Art and the Absolute Revisited: The Neglect of Hegel's Aesthetics," in *Hegel and Aesthetics*, edited by William Maker (Albany: State University of New York Press, 2000), 1–12.

di Giovanni, George, "The Category of Contingency in the Hegelian Logic," in *Art and Logic in Hegel's Philosophy*, edited by Warren E. Steinkraus and Kenneth L. Schmitz (Sussex: Harvester Press, 1980), 179–200.

Djaballah, Marc, *Kant, Foucault, and Forms of Experience* (New York: Routledge, 2008).

Donnelly, Michael, "Foucault's Genealogy of the Human Sciences," in *Towards a Critique of Foucault*, edited by Mike Gane (London: Routledge & Kegan Paul, 1986), 15–32.

Doussan, Jenny, *Time, Language, and Visuality in Agamben's Philosophy* (Basingstoke: Palgrave Macmillan, 2013).

Dreyfus, Hubert L., and Paul Rabinow, *Michel Foucault: Beyond Structuralism and Hermeneutics*, 2nd ed. (New York: Harvester Wheatsheaf, 1982).

During, Simon, *Foucault and Literature: Towards a Genealogy of Writing* (London: Routledge, 1992).

Ehrmann, Jacques, ed., *Structuralism* (New York: Doubleday, Anchor Books). Reprint of special issue of *Yale French Studies*, nos 36–7 (1966).

Eliot, T. S., "Tradition and the Individual Talent," *Perspecta*, vol. 19 (1982), 36–42.

Empson, William, *Seven Types of Ambiguity*, 3rd ed. (London: Chatto and Windus, 1963).

Falzon, Christopher, "Making History," in *A Companion to Foucault*, edited by Christopher Falzon, Timothy O'Leary, and Jana Sawicki (Chichester: Wiley-Blackwell, 2013), 282–98.

Fenves, Peter, *The Messianic Reduction: Walter Benjamin and the Shape of Time* (Stanford, CA: Stanford University Press, 2011).

Ferguson, Sam, "Forgetting Gide: A Study of Barthes's 'Ursuppe,' " *Barthes Studies*, vol. 1 (2015), 17–34.

Ferry, Luc, *Homo Aestheticus: The Invention of Taste in the Democratic Age*, translated by Robert de Loaiza (Chicago, IL: University of Chicago Press, 1993).

ffrench, Patrick, *The Time of Theory: A History* of *Tel Quel (1960–1983)* (Oxford: Clarendon Press, 1995).

Fichte, Johann Gottlieb, "Foundations of the Entire Science of Knowledge," in *The Science of Knowledge*, edited by Peter Lauchlan Heath and John Lachs (Cambridge: Cambridge University Press, 1982).

Fichte, Johann Gottlieb, *Grundlage der gesammten Wissenschaftslehre*, in *Fichtes Werke*, edited by Immanuel Hermann Fichte (Berlin: Walter de Gruyter, 1971), vol. I, 83–328.

Fink, Bruce, *The Lacanian Subject: Between Language and Jouissance* (Princeton, NJ: Princeton University Press, 1995).

Fort, Jeff, *The Imperative to Write* (New York: Fordham University Press, 2014).

Foucault, Michel, *Aesthetics, Method, and Epistemology. Essential Works of Foucault, 1954–1984. Volume 2*, edited by James Faubion (London: Penguin, 2000).

Foucault, Michel, *The Archaeology of Knowledge and the Discourse on Language*, translated by A. M. Sheridan Smith (New York: Vintage, 2010).

Foucault, Michel, *Discipline and Punish: The Birth of the Prison*, translated by Alan Sheridan, 2nd ed. (New York: Vintage, 1995).

Foucault, Michel, *Dits et écrits I. 1954–1975*, edited by Daniel Defert, François Ewald, and Jacques Lagrange (Paris: Gallimard, 2001).

Foucault, Michel, *Dits et écrits II. 1976–1988*, edited by Daniel Defert, François Ewald, and Jacques Lagrange (Paris: Gallimard, 2001).

Foucault, Michel, *Folie et déraison. Histoire de la folie à l'âge classique* (Paris: Plon, 1961).

Foucault, Michel, *Histoire de la folie à l'âge classique* (Paris: Gallimard, 1972).

Foucault, Michel, *History of Madness*, edited by Jean Khalfa, translated by Jonathan Murphy and Jean Khalfa (London: Routledge, 2009).

Foucault, Michel, "La Pensée du dehors," *Critique*, no. 229 (1966), 523–46.

Foucault, Michel, "La Vie des hommes infâmes," *Les Cahiers du Chemin*, no. 29 (1977), 12–29.

Foucault, Michel, "Le 'Non' du père," *Critique*, no. 178 (1962), 195–209.

Foucault, Michel, *Les Mots et les choses: une archéologie des sciences humaines* (Paris: Gallimard, 1966).

Foucault, Michel, "Lives of Infamous Men," in *Power: Essential Works of Foucault, 1954–1984. Volume 3*, edited by James Faubion (London: Penguin, 2002), 157–75.

Foucault, Michel, *The Order of Things: An Archaeology of the Human Sciences* (London: Routledge, 2002).

Foucault, Michel, "Qu'est-ce qu'un auteur?," *Bulletin de la Société Française de Philosophie*, 63ᵉ année, no. 3 (1969), 73–104.

Foucault, Michel, "The Subject and Power," in *Power: Essential Works of Foucault, 1954–1984. Volume 3*, edited by James Faubion (London: Penguin, 2002), 326–48.

Frank, Manfred, *Einführung in die frühromantische Ästhetik: Vorlesungen* (Frankfurt am Main: Suhrkamp, 1989).

Freud, Sigmund, "Mourning and Melancholia," in *The Standard Edition of the Complete Psychological Works of Sigmund Freud. Volume 14 (1914–1916). On the History of the Psycho-Analytic Movement. Papers on Metapsychology and Other Works*, edited by James Strachey (London: Hogarth Press and the Institute of Psycho-Analysis, 1957), 243–58.

Frey, Hans-Jost, "The Last Man and the Reader," in *The Place of Maurice Blanchot*, edited by Thomas Pepper (New Haven, CT: Yale University Press, 1998), 252–79.

Fricke, Harald, ed., *Reallexikon der deutschen Literaturwissenschaft* (Berlin: Walter de Gruyter, 2000).

Fry, Paul H., "I. A. Richards," in *The Cambridge History of Literary Criticism. Volume 7. Modernism and the New Criticism*, edited by A. Walton Litz, Louis Menand, and Lawrence Rainey (Cambridge: Cambridge University Press, 2000), 181–99.

Fynsk, Christopher, "Crossing the Threshold: On 'Literature and the Right to Death,'" in *Maurice Blanchot: The Demand of Writing*, edited by Carolyn Bailey Gill (London: Routledge, 1996), 70–90.

Gabriel, Markus, *Transcendental Ontology: Essays in German Idealism* (New York: Continuum, 2011).

Gasché, Rodolphe, "The Felicities of Paradox: Blanchot on the Null-Space of Literature," in *Maurice Blanchot: The Demand of Writing*, edited by Carolyn Bailey Gill (London: Routledge, 1996), 34–69.

Gasché, Rodolphe, "The Sober Absolute: On Benjamin and the Early Romantics," in *Walter Benjamin and Romanticism*, edited by Beatrice Hanssen and Andrew Benjamin (London: Continuum, 2002), 51–68.

Genette, Gérard, "The Obverse of Signs," in *Figures of Literary Discourse*, translated by Alan Sheridan (New York: Columbia University Press, 1982), 27–44.

Gethmann-Siefert, Annemarie, *Einführung in Hegels Ästhetik* (München: Wilhelm Fink Verlag, 2005).

Gordon, Colin, "*History of Madness*," in *A Companion to Foucault*, edited by Christopher Falzon, Timothy O'Leary, and Jana Sawicki (Chichester: Wiley-Blackwell, 2013), 84–103.

Guilhamet, Leon, *The Sincere Ideal: Studies on Sincerity in Eighteenth-Century English Literature* (Montreal: McGill-Queen's University Press, 1974).

Gutting, Gary, *Michel Foucault's Archaeology of Scientific Reason* (Cambridge: Cambridge University Press, 1989).

Guyer, Paul, *Kant and the Claims of Taste*, 2nd ed. (Cambridge: Cambridge University Press, 1997).

Haase, Ullrich, and William Large, *Maurice Blanchot* (London: Routledge, 2001).

Hamacher, Werner, "Afformative, Strike: Benjamin's 'Critique of Violence,' " in *Walter Benjamin's Philosophy: Destruction and Experience*, edited by Andrew Benjamin and Peter Osborne (London: Routledge, 1994), 110–38.

Hamacher, Werner, "The End of Art with the Mask," in *Hegel after Derrida*, edited by Stuart Barnett (London: Routledge, 1998), 105–30.

Hamacher, Werner, " 'Now': Walter Benjamin on Historical Time," in *The Moment: Time and Rupture in Modern Thought*, edited by Heidrun Friese (Liverpool: Liverpool University Press, 2001), 161–96.

Hamacher, Werner, *Pleroma: Reading in Hegel*, translated by Nicholas Walker and Simon Jarvis (London: Athlone Press, 1998).

Hamacher, Werner, *Premises: Essays on Philosophy and Literature from Kant to Celan*, translated by Peter Fenves (Stanford, CA: Stanford University Press, 1999).

Han, Béatrice, "The Analytic of Finitude and the History of Subjectivity," in *The Cambridge Companion to Foucault*, edited by Gary Gutting, 2nd ed. (Cambridge: Cambridge University Press, 2005), 176–209.

Han, Béatrice, *Foucault's Critical Project: Between the Transcendental and the Historical*, translated by Edward Pile (Stanford, CA: Stanford University Press, 2002).

Hansen, Frank-Peter, *"Das älteste Systemprogramm des deutschen Idealismus": Rezeptionsgeschichte und Interpretation* (Berlin: Walter de Gruyter, 1989).

Hanssen, Beatrice, " 'Dichtermut' and 'Blödigkeit': Two Poems by Friedrich Hölderlin, Interpreted by Walter Benjamin," in *Walter Benjamin and Romanticism*, edited by Beatrice Hanssen and Andrew Benjamin (London: Continuum, 2002), 139–62.

Hart, Kevin, *The Dark Gaze: Maurice Blanchot and the Sacred* (Chicago, IL: University of Chicago Press, 2004).

Hegel, Georg Wilhelm Friedrich, *Aesthetics: Lectures on Fine Art. Volume 1*, translated by T. M. Knox (Oxford: Clarendon Press, 1975).

Hegel, Georg Wilhelm Friedrich, *Hegel's Science of Logic*, translated by Arnold V. Miller (New York: Humanities Press, 1976).

Hegel, Georg Wilhelm Friedrich, *Phänomenologie des Geistes*, Werke 3, edited by Eva Moldenhauer and Karl Markus Michel (Frankfurt am Main: Suhrkamp, 1986).

Hegel, Georg Wilhelm Friedrich, *Phenomenology of Spirit*, edited by J. N. Findlay, translated by A. V. Miller (Oxford: Oxford University Press, 1977).

Hegel, Georg Wilhelm Friedrich, *Vorlesungen über die Ästhetik I–II*, Werke 13–14, edited by Eva Moldenhauer and Karl Markus Michel (Frankfurt am Main: Suhrkamp, 1986).

Hegel, Georg Wilhelm Friedrich, *Wissenschaft der Logik*, I–II, Werke 5–6, edited by Eva Moldenhauer and Karl Markus Michel (Frankfurt am Main: Suhrkamp, 1969).

Heidegger, Martin, *The Basic Problems of Phenomenology*, Revised Edition, translated by Albert Hofstadter (Bloomington: Indiana University Press, 1988).

Heidegger, Martin, *Being and Time*, translated by Joan Stambaugh (Albany: State University of New York Press, 1996).

Heidegger, Martin, "Der Ursprung des Kunstwerkes," in *Holzwege*, edited by F.-W. von Herrmann (Frankfurt am Main: Vittoria Klostermann, 1980), 1–72.

Heidegger, Martin, *Elucidations of Hölderlin's Poetry*, translated by Keith Hoeller (Amherst, NY: Humanity, 2000).

Heidegger, Martin, *The End of Philosophy*, translated by Joan Stambaugh (Chicago, IL: University of Chicago Press, 2003).

Heidegger, Martin , *Erläuterungen zu Hölderlins Dichtung* (Frankfurt am Main: Vittorio Klostermann, 2012).

Heidegger, Martin, *The Essence of Human Freedom: An Introduction to Philosophy*, translated by Ted Sadler (London: Continuum, 2005).

Heidegger, Martin, "Hegels Begriff der Erfahrung," in *Holzwege* (Frankfurt am Main: Vittorio Klostermann, 1980), 111–204.

Heidegger, Martin, "Hegel's Concept of Experience," in *Off the Beaten Track*, translated by Julian Young and Kenneth Haynes (Cambridge: Cambridge University Press, 2002), 86–156.

Heidegger, Martin, *Hegels Phänomenologie des Geistes*, Gesamtausgabe, Band 32 (Frankfurt am Main: Vittorio Klostermann, 1980).

Heidegger, Martin, *Hegel's Phenomenology of Spirit*, translated by Parvis Emad and Kenneth Maly (Bloomington: Indiana University Press, 1994).

Heidegger, Martin, *Identity and Difference*, translated by Joan Stambaugh (Chicago, IL: University of Chicago Press, 2002).

Heidegger, Martin, *Introduction to Metaphysics*, translated by Gregory Fried and Richard Polt (New Haven, CT: Yale University Press, 2000).

Heidegger, Martin, *Kant and the Problem of Metaphysics*, translated by Richard Taft, 5th ed., Enlarged (Bloomington: Indiana University Press, 1997).

Heidegger, Martin, "Kants These über das Sein," in *Wegmarken* (Frankfurt am Main: Vittorio Klostermann, 1967), 273–307.

Heidegger, Martin, "Kant's Thesis about Being," in *Pathmarks*, edited by William McNeill (Cambridge: Cambridge University Press, 1998), 337–63.

Heidegger, Martin , *Kant und das Problem der Metaphysik*, Fünfte, vermehrte Ausgabe (Frankfurt am Main: Vitorrio Klostermann, 1991).

Heidegger, Martin, *Nietzsche II* (Pfullingen: Neske, 1961).

Heidegger, Martin, *On Time and Being*, translated by Joan Stambaugh (Chicago, IL: University of Chicago Press, 2002).

Heidegger, Martin, "The Origin of the Work of Art," in *Basic Writings*, edited by David Farrell Krell, Revised and Expanded Edition (New York: Harper Perennial, 2008), 139–212.

Heidegger, Martin, *Phenomenological Interpretation of Kant's Critique of Pure Reason*, translated by Parvis Emad and Kenneth Maly (Bloomington: Indiana University Press, 1997).

Heidegger, Martin, *Schellings Abhandlung über das Wesen der menschlichen Freiheit (1809)*, edited by Hildegard Feick (Tübingen: Max Niemeyer Verlag, 1995).

Heidegger, Martin, *Schelling's Treatise on the Essence of Human Freedom*, translated by Joan Stambaugh (Athens: Ohio University Press, 1985).

Heidegger, Martin, *Zur Sache des Denkens* (Tübingen: Max Niemeyer Verlag, 1969).

Helfer, Martha B., *The Retreat of Representation: The Concept of* Darstellung *in German Critical Discourse* (Albany: State University of New York Press, 1996).

Henrich, Dieter, "Art and Philosophy of Art Today: Reflections with Reference to Hegel," in *New Perspectives in German Literary Criticism: A Collection of Essays*, edited by Richard E. Amacher and Victor Lange (Princeton, NJ: Princeton University Press, 1979), 107–33.

Henrich, Dieter, *The Course of Remembrance and Other Essays on Hölderlin*, edited by Eckart Förster (Stanford, CA: Stanford University Press, 1997).

Henrich, Dieter, *Der Grund im Bewußtsein: Untersuchungen zu Hölderlins Denken (1794–1795)* (Stuttgart: Klett-Cotta, 1992).

Henrich, Dieter, *Hegel im Kontext*, Vierte, veränderte Auflage (Frankfurt am Main: Suhrkamp, 1971).

Hill, Leslie, *Blanchot: Extreme Contemporary* (London: Routledge, 1997).

Hill, Leslie, *Maurice Blanchot and Fragmentary Writing: A Change of Epoch* (London: Continuum, 2012).

Hiller, Marion, *Harmonisch Entgegengesetzt: Zur Darstellung und Darstellbarkeit in Hölderlins Poetik um 1800* (Tübingen: Max Niemeyer Verlag, 2008).

Hölderlin, Friedrich, *Essays and Letters*, edited by Jeremy Adler and Charlie Louth (London: Penguin, 2009).

Hölderlin, Friedrich, *Essays and Letters on Theory*, edited by Thomas Pfau (Albany: State University of New York Press, 1988).

Hölderlin, Friedrich, *Hyperion and Selected Poems*, edited by Eric L. Santner (New York: Continuum, 1990).

Hölderlin, Friedrich, *Sämtliche Werke (Grosse Stuttgarter Ausgabe)*, edited by Friedrich Beissner, Grosse Stuttgarter Ausgabe (Stuttgart: W. Kohlhammer Verlag, 1943).

Hölderlin, Friedrich, *Sämtliche Werke: Historisch-Kritische Ausgabe (Frankfurter Ausgabe)*, edited by. D. E. Sattler (Frankfurt am Main: Stroemfeld/Roter Stern, 1975).

Holt, Jason, "The Marginal Life of the Author," in *The Death and Resurrection of the Author?*, edited by William Irwin (Westport, CT: Greenwood Press, 2002), 65–78.

Hoolsema, Daniel J., "The Echo of an Impossible Future in 'The Literary Absolute,'" *MLN*, vol. 119, no. 4 (2004), 845–68.

Houlgate, Stephen, *An Introduction to Hegel's Philosophy: Freedom, Truth and History*, 2nd ed. (Oxford: Blackwell, 2005).

Houlgate, Stephen, "Necessity and Contingency in Hegel's *Science of Logic*," *Owl of Minerva*, vol. 27, no. 1 (1995), 37–49.

Hutchens, B. C., *Jean-Luc Nancy and the Future of Philosophy* (Chesham: Acumen, 2005).

Iyer, Lars, *Blanchot's Vigilance: Literature, Phenomenology, and the Ethical* (New York: Palgrave Macmillan, 2005).

Jakobson, Roman, "Linguistics and Poetics," in *Language in Literature*, edited by Krystyna Pomorska and Stephen Rudy (Cambridge, MA: Belknap Press of Harvard University Press, 1987), 62–94.

Jakobson, Roman, "Shifters, Verbal Categories, and the Russian Verb," in *Russian and Slavic Grammar: Studies 1931–1981*, edited by Linda R. Waugh and Morris Halle (Berlin: Mouton, 1984), 41–58.

Jakobson, Roman , "What Is Poetry?," in *Language in Literature*, edited by Krystyna Pomorska and Stephen Rudy (Cambridge, MA: Belknap Press of Harvard University Press, 1987), 368–78.

James, David, *Art, Myth and Society in Hegel's Aesthetics* (London: Continuum, 2009).

James, Ian, *The Fragmentary Demand: An Introduction to the Philosophy of Jean-Luc Nancy* (Stanford, CA: Stanford University Press, 2006).

Jaspers, Karl, *Karl Jaspers' Strindberg and Van Gogh: An Attempt at a Pathographic Analysis with Reference to Parallel Cases of Swedenborg and Hölderlin*, translated by Oskar Grunow and David Woloshin (Tucson: University of Arizona Press, 1977).

Jennings, Michael W., "Benjamin as a Reader of Hölderlin: The Origins of Benjamin's Theory of Literary Criticism," *German Quarterly*, vol. 56, no. 4 (1983), 544–62.

Kalar, Brent, *The Demands of Taste in Kant's Aesthetics* (London: Continuum, 2006).

Kant, Immanuel, *Critique of Pure Reason*, translated by Paul Guyer and Allen W. Wood (Cambridge: Cambridge University Press, 1998).

Kant, Immanuel, *Critique of the Power of Judgment*, translated by Paul Guyer and Eric Matthews (Cambridge: Cambridge University Press, 2000).

Kant, Immanuel, *Kritik der reinen Vernunft*, 1–2, edited by Wilhelm Weischedel (Frankfurt am Main: Suhrkamp, 1974).

Kant, Immanuel, *Kritik der Urteilskraft*, edited by Wilhelm Weischedel (Frankfurt am Main: Suhrkamp, 1974).

Kant, Immanuel, "The Only Possible Argument in Support of a Demonstration of the Existence of God," in *Theoretical Philosophy, 1755–1770*, translated by David Walford and Ralf Meerbote (Cambridge: Cambridge University Press, 1992), 107–201.

Keats, John, *The Letters of John Keats, Volume I, 1814–1821*, edited by Hyder Edward Rollins (Cambridge: Cambridge University Press, 1958).

Kojève, Alexandre, *Introduction to the Reading of Hegel: Lectures on the Phenomenology of Spirit*, edited by Allan Bloom, translated by James H. Nichols, Jr. (Ithaca, NY: Cornell University Press, 1980).

Kreuzer, Johann, *Erinnerung: Zum Zusammenhang von Hölderlins Theoretischen Fragmenten "Das untergehende Vaterland…" und "Wenn der Dichter einmal des Geistes mächtig ist…"* (Königstein: Verlag Anton Hain, 1985).

Kristeller, Paul Oskar, "The Modern System of the Arts: A Study in the History of Aesthetics (II)," *Journal of the History of Ideas*, vol. 13, no. 1 (1952), 17–46.

Kristeller, Paul Oskar, "The Modern System of the Arts: A Study in the History of Aesthetics Part I," *Journal of the History of Ideas*, vol. 12, no. 4 (1951), 496–527.

Kusch, Martin, *Foucault's Strata and Fields: An Investigation into Archaeological and Genealogical Science Studies* (Dordrecht: Kluwer, 1991).

Lacan, Jacques, *Écrits*, 1–2 (Paris: Seuil, 1999).

Lacan, Jacques, *Écrits: The First Complete Edition in English*, translated by Bruce Fink (London: W. W. Norton, 2006).

Lacan, Jacques, *The Ethics of Psychoanalysis 1959–1960. The Seminar of Jacques Lacan. Book VII*, edited by Jacques-Alain Miller, translated by Dennis Porter (London: Routledge, 1992).

Lacan, Jacques, *The Four Fundamental Concepts of Psychoanalysis. The Seminar of Jacques Lacan. Book XI*, edited by Jacques-Alain Miller, translated by Alan Sheridan (London: W. W. Norton, 1981).

Lacan, Jacques, *Freud's Papers on Technique 1953–1954. The Seminar of Jacques Lacan. Book I*, edited by Jacques-Alain Miller, translated by John Forrester (New York: W. W. Norton, 1991).

Lacoue-Labarthe, Philippe, "The Caesura of the Speculative," in *Typography: Mimesis, Philosophy, Politics*, edited by Christopher Fynsk (Stanford, CA: Stanford University Press, 1989), 208–35.

Lacoue-Labarthe, Philippe, *Ending and Unending Agony: On Maurice Blanchot*, translated by Hannes Opelz (New York: Fordham University Press, 2015).

Lacoue-Labarthe, Philippe, *Heidegger, Art and Politics: The Fiction of the Political*, translated by Chris Turner (Oxford: Basil Blackwell, 1990).

Lacoue-Labarthe, Philippe, "Introduction to Walter Benjamin's 'The Concept of Art Criticism in German Romanticism,'" *Studies in Romanticism*, vol. 31, no. 4 (1992), 421–32.

Lacoue-Labarthe, Philippe, "La Césure du spéculatif," in *L'Imitation des modernes (Typographies 2)* (Paris: Galilée, 1986), 39–69.

Lacoue-Labarthe, Philippe, *Le Sujet de la philosophie: typographies I* (Paris: Aubier-Flammarion, 1979).

Lacoue-Labarthe, Philippe, "L'Imprésentable," *Poetique*, no. 21 (1975), 53–95.

Lacoue-Labarthe, Philippe, *The Subject of Philosophy*, edited by Thomas Trezise (Minneapolis: University of Minnesota Press, 1993).

Lacoue-Labarthe, Philippe, and Jean-Luc Nancy, *L'Absolu littéraire: théorie de la littérature du romantisme allemand* (Paris: Seuil, 1978).

Lacoue-Labarthe, Philippe, and Jean-Luc Nancy, *Le Titre de la lettre: une lecture de Lacan* (Paris: Galilée, 1973).

Lacoue-Labarthe, Philippe, and Jean-Luc Nancy, *The Literary Absolute: The Theory of Literature in German Romanticism*, translated by Philip Barnard and Cheryl Lester (Albany: State University of New York Press, 1988).

Lacoue-Labarthe, Philippe, and Jean-Luc Nancy, *Retreating the Political*, edited by Simon Sparks (London: Routledge, 1997).

Lacoue-Labarthe, Philippe, and Jean-Luc Nancy, *The Title of the Letter: A Reading of Lacan*, translated by François Raffoul and David Pettigrew (Albany: State University of New York Press, 1992).

Lamarque, Peter, "The Death of the Author: An Analytical Autopsy," in *The Death and Resurrection of the Author?*, edited by William Irwin (Westport, CT: Greenwood Press, 2002), 79–91.

Lange, Wilhelm, *Hölderlin: Eine Pathographie* (Stuttgart: Ferdinand Enke, 1909).

Laplanche, Jean, *Hölderlin and the Question of the Father*, translated by Luke Carson (Victoria: ELS Editions, 2007).

Lavers, Annette, *Roland Barthes: Structuralism and After* (London: Methuen, 1982).

Lévi-Strauss, Claude, *The Savage Mind* (London: Weidenfeld and Nicolson, 1966).

Lönker, Fred, *Welt in der Welt: Eine Untersuchung zu Hölderlins "Verfahrungsweise des poetischen Geistes"* (Göttingen: Vandenhoeck & Ruprecht, 1989).

Makaryk, Irena R., ed., *Encyclopedia of Contemporary Literary Theory: Approaches, Scholars, Terms* (Toronto: University of Toronto Press, 1993).

Malabou, Catherine, *The Future of Hegel: Plasticity, Temporality and Dialectic*, translated by Lisabeth During (London: Routledge, 2005).

Mallarmé, Stéphane, *Divagations*, translated by Barbara Johnson (Cambridge, MA: Belknap Press of Harvard University Press, 2007).

Maniglier, Patrice, "*The Order of Things*," in *A Companion to Foucault*, edited by Christopher Falzon, Timothy O'Leary, and Jana Sawicki (Chichester: Wiley-Blackwell, 2013), 104–21.

Martis, John, *Philippe Lacoue-Labarthe: Representation and the Law of the Subject* (New York: Fordham University Press, 2005).

McCall, Tom, "Plastic Time and Poetic Middles: Benjamin's Hölderlin," *Studies in Romanticism*, vol. 31, no. 4 (1992), 481–99.

McLaughlin, Kevin, "Benjamin Now: Afterthoughts on the Arcades Project," *Boundary 2*, vol. 30, no. 1 (2003), 191–7.

Meillassoux, Quentin, *After Finitude: An Essay on the Necessity of Contingency*, translated by Ray Brassier (London: Bloomsbury, 2012).

Menninghaus, Winfried, "Walter Benjamin's Exposition of the Romantic Theory of Reflection," in *Walter Benjamin and Romanticism*, edited by Beatrice Hanssen and Andrew Benjamin (London: Continuum, 2002), 19–50.

Mill, John Stuart, "The Two Kinds of Poetry," in *Essays on Poetry*, edited by F. Parvin Sharpless (Columbia: University of South Carolina Press, 1976), 28–43.

Mill, John Stuart, "What Is Poetry?," in *Essays on Poetry*, edited by F. Parvin Sharpless (Columbia: University of South Carolina Press, 1976), 3–22.

Mills, Catherine, *The Philosophy of Agamben* (Stocksfield: Acumen, 2008).

Murray, Alex, *Giorgio Agamben* (London: Routledge, 2010).

Nancy, Jean-Luc, *The Birth to Presence*, translated by Brian Holmes and others (Stanford, CA: Stanford University Press, 1993).

Nancy, Jean-Luc, "The Calculation of the Poet," in *The Solid Letter: Readings of Friedrich Hölderlin*, edited by Aris Fioretos (Stanford, CA: Stanford University Press, 1999), 44–73.

Nancy, Jean-Luc, *The Discourse of the Syncope: Logodaedalus*, translated by Saul Anton (Stanford, CA: Stanford University Press, 2008).

Nancy, Jean-Luc, *The Inoperative Community*, edited by Peter Connor (Minneapolis: University of Minnesota Press, 1991).

Nancy, Jean-Luc, *La Remarque spéculative (un bon mot de Hegel)* (Auvers-sur-Oise: Éditions Galilée, 1973),

Nancy, Jean-Luc, *Le Discours de la syncope: I. Logodaedalus* (Paris: Aubier-Flammarion, 1976),

Nancy, Jean-Luc, *The Muses*, translated by Peggy Kamuf (Stanford, CA: Stanford University Press, 1996).

Nancy, Jean-Luc, *The Sense of the World*, translated by Jeffrey S. Librett (Minneapolis: University of Minnesota Press, 1997).

Nancy, Jean-Luc, *The Speculative Remark (One of Hegel's Bons Mots)*, translated by Céline Surprenant (Stanford, CA: Stanford University Press, 2001).

Nehamas, Alexander, "Writer, Text, Work, Author," in *The Death and Resurrection of the Author?*, edited by William Irwin (Westport, CT: Greenwood Press, 2002), 95–115.

Newman, Michael, "The Trace of Trauma: Blindness, Testimony and the Gaze in Blanchot and Derrida," in *Maurice Blanchot: The Demand of Writing*, edited by Carolyn Bailey Gill (London: Routledge, 1996), 153–73.

Newmark, Kevin, "L'Absolu littéraire: Friedrich Schlegel and the Myth of Irony," *MLN*, vol. 107, no. 5 (1992), 905–30.

Nietzsche, Friedrich, *The Will to Power*, edited by Walter Kaufmann, translated by Walter Kaufmann and R. J. Hollingdale (New York: Vintage, 1968).

Novalis, *Monolog*, in *Novalis Schriften: Die Werke Friedrich von Hardenbergs II*, edited by Paul Kluckhohn and Richard Herbert Samuel (Stuttgart: W. Kohlhammer Verlag, 1960), 672–3.

Novalis, *Monologue*, in *Philosophical Writings*, translated by Margaret Mahony Stoljar (Albany: State University of New York Press, 1997), 83–4.

O'Meara, Lucy, *Roland Barthes at the Collège de France* (Liverpool: Liverpool University Press, 2012).

Opelz, Hannes, and John Mckeane, eds., *Blanchot Romantique: A Collection of Essays* (Bern: Peter Lang, 2011).

Perkins, David, *Wordsworth and the Poetry of Sincerity* (Cambridge, MA: Belknap Press of Harvard University Press, 1964).

Peyre, Henri, *Literature and Sincerity* (New Haven, CT: Yale University Press, 1963).

Pfau, Thomas, "Thinking before Totality: Kritik, Übersetzung, and the Language of Interpretation in the Early Walter Benjamin," *MLN*, vol. 103, no. 5 (1988), 1072–97.

Pint, Kris, "How to Become What One Is: Roland Barthes's Final Fantasy," *Paragraph*, vol. 31, no. 1 (2008), 38–49.

Pippin, Robert, "The Absence of Aesthetics in Hegel's Aesthetics," in *The Cambridge Companion to Hegel and Nineteenth-Century Philosophy*, edited by Frederick C. Beiser (Cambridge: Cambridge University Press, 2008), 394–418.

Pippin, Robert, *Hegel's Idealism: The Satisfactions of Self-Consciousness* (Cambridge: Cambridge University Press, 1989).

Pöggeler, Otto, *Hegels Kritik der Romantik* (München: Wilhelm Fink Verlag, 1998).

Prozorov, Sergei, *Agamben and Politics: A Critical Introduction* (Edinburgh: Edinburgh University Press, 2014).

Rajchman, John, *Michel Foucault: The Freedom of Philosophy* (New York: Columbia University Press, 1985).

Rancière, Jacques, *Mute Speech: Literature, Critical Theory, and Politics*, translated by James Swenson (New York: Columbia University Press, 2011).

Rancière, Jacques, *The Politics of Aesthetics: The Distribution of the Sensible*, translated by Gabriel Rockhill (London: Bloomsbury, 2013).

Ransom, John Crowe, *The New Criticism* (Norfolk, CT: New Directions, 1941).

Rapp, Carl, "Hegel's Concept of the Dissolution of Art," in *Hegel and Aesthetics*, edited by William Maker (Albany: State University of New York Press, 2000), 13–30.

Redfield, Marc, "Romanticism, *Bildung*, and the Literary Absolute," in *Lessons of Romanticism: A Critical Companion*, edited by Thomas Pfau and Robert F. Gleckner (Durham: Duke University Press, 1998), 41–54.

Richards, I. A., *Practical Criticism: A Study of Literary Judgment* (London: Routledge & Kegan Paul, 1929).

Rilke, Rainer Maria, *Briefe an einen jungen Dichter* (Leipzig: Insel Verlag, 1929).

Rilke, Rainer Maria, *Letters to a Young Poet & The Letter from the Young Worker*, translated by Charlie Louth (London: Penguin, 2011).

Robinson, Keith A., *Michel Foucault and the Freedom of Thought* (Lewiston: Edwin Mellen Press, 2001).

Roth, Michael S., *Knowing and History: Appropriations of Hegel in Twentieth-Century France* (Ithaca, NY: Cornell University Press, 1988).

Rugo, Daniele, *Jean-Luc Nancy and the Thinking of Otherness: Philosophy and Powers of Existence* (London: Bloomsbury, 2013).

Russo, John Paul, "Belief and Sincerity in I. A. Richards," *Modern Language Quarterly*, vol. 47, no. 2 (1986), 154–91.

Rutter, Benjamin, *Hegel on the Modern Arts* (Cambridge: Cambridge University Press, 2010).

Ryan, Lawrence J., *Hölderlins Lehre vom Wechsel der Töne* (Stuttgart: W. Kohlhammer, 1960).

Rylance, Rick, *Roland Barthes* (Hertfordshire: Harvester Wheatsheaf, 1994).

Saghafi, Kas, "The 'Passion for the Outside': Foucault, Blanchot, and Exteriority," *International Studies in Philosophy*, vol. 28, no. 4 (1996), 79–92.

Saisselin, R. G., *Taste in Eighteenth Century France: Critical Reflections of the Origins of Aesthetics or an Apology for Amateurs* (Syracuse, NY: Syracuse University Press, 1965).

Sartre, Jean-Paul, *"What Is Literature?" and Other Essays*, translated by Steven Ungar (Cambridge, MA: Harvard University Press, 1988).

Schlegel, Friedrich, *Dialogue on Poetry and Literary Aphorisms*, translated by Ernst Behler and Roman Struc (London: Pennsylvania State University Press, 1968).

Schlegel, Friedrich, *Friedrich Schlegel's Lucinde and the Fragments*, translated by Peter Firchow (Minneapolis: University of Minnesota Press, 1971).

Schlegel, Friedrich, *Kritische Friedrich-Schlegel-Ausgabe. Bd. 2. Charakteristiken und Kritiken 1 (1796–1801)*, edited by Hans Eichner (Paderborn: Verlag Ferdinand Schöningh, 1967).

Schlegel, Friedrich, *Kritische Friedrich-Schlegel-Ausgabe. Bd. 18. Philosophische Lehrjahre (1796–1806)*, edited by Ernst Behler (Paderborn: Verlag Ferdinand Schöningh, 1963).

Schlegel, Friedrich, "On Goethe's Meister," in *Classic and Romantic German Aesthetics*, edited by J. M. Bernstein (Cambridge: Cambridge University Press, 2003), 269–86.

Sheppard, Darren, Simon Sparks, and Colin Thomas, eds., *On Jean-Luc Nancy: The Sense of Philosophy* (London: Routledge, 1997).

Speight, Allen, "Hegel and the 'Historical Deduction' of the Concept of Art," in *A Companion to Hegel*, edited by Stephen Houlgate and Michael Baur (Oxford: Wiley-Blackwell, 2011), 353–68.

Stafford, Andy, "'*Préparation du romanesque*' in Roland Barthes's Reading of *Sarrasine*," *Paragraph*, vol. 31, no. 1 (2008), 95–108.

Strathman, Christopher A., *Romantic Poetry and the Fragmentary Imperative: Schlegel, Byron, Joyce, Blanchot* (Albany: State University of New York Press, 2006).

Szondi, Peter, *Poetik und Geschichtsphilosophie I: Antike und Moderne in der Ästhetik der Goethezeit. Hegels Lehre von der Dichtung*, edited by Senta Metz and Hans-Hagen Hildebrandt (Frankfurt am Main: Suhrkamp, 1974).

"The Oldest Programme for a System of German Idealism," in Friedrich Hölderlin, *Essays and Letters*, edited by Jeremy D. Adler and Charlie Louth (London: Penguin, 2009), 341–2.

Toumayan, Alain, "Blanchot, Reader of Baudelaire: 'Baudelaire's failure,'" in *After Blanchot: Literature, Criticism, Philosophy*, edited by Leslie Hill, Brian Nelson, and Dimitris Vardoulakis (Newark: University of Delaware Press, 2005), 137–48.

Träger, Claus, ed., *Wörterbuch der Literaturwissenschaft* (Leipzig: Veb Bibliographisches Institut, 1986).

Ungar, Steven, *Roland Barthes: The Professor of Desire* (Lincoln: University of Nebraska Press, 1983).

Wall, Thomas Carl, *Radical Passivity: Levinas, Blanchot, and Agamben* (Albany: State University of New York Press, 1999).

Warminski, Andrzej, "Dreadful Reading: Blanchot on Hegel," *Yale French Studies*, no. 69 (1985), 267–75.

Wasserman, George R., *Roland Barthes* (Boston, MA: Twayne, 1981).

Watkin, William, *Agamben and Indifference: A Critical Overview* (London: Rowman & Littlefield, 2014).

Watkin, William, *The Literary Agamben: Adventures in Logopoiesis* (London: Continuum, 2010).

Weber, Samuel, *Benjamin's -Abilities* (Cambridge, MA: Harvard University Press, 2008).

Weber, Samuel, "Criticism Underway: Walter Benjamin's *Romantic Concept of Criticism*," in *Romantic Revolutions: Criticism and Theory*, edited by Kenneth R. Johnston et al. (Bloomington: Indiana University Press, 1990), 302–19.

Wellek, René, *Discriminations: Further Concepts of Criticism* (New Haven, CT: Yale University Press, 1970).

Wellek, René, and Austin Warren, *Theory of Literature*, 3rd ed. (London: Jonathan Cape, 1966).

Wicks, Robert, "Hegel's Aesthetics: An Overview," in *The Cambridge Companion to Hegel*, edited by Frederick C. Beiser (Cambridge: Cambridge University Press, 1993), 348–77.

Wilson, Adrian, "Foucault on the 'Question of the Author': A Critical Exegesis," *Modern Language Review*, vol. 99, no. 2 (2004), 339–63.

Wimsatt, W. K., *The Verbal Icon: Studies in the Meaning of Poetry* (Kentucky: University of Kentucky Press, 1954).

Wimsatt, W. K., and M. C.Beardsley, "The Affective Fallacy," *Sewanee Review*, vol. 57, no. 1 (1949), 31–55.

Wimsatt, W. K., and M. C.Beardsley, "The Intentional Fallacy," *Sewanee Review*, vol. 54, no. 3 (1946), 468–88.

Wind, Edgar, *Art and Anarchy*, 3rd ed. (Evanston, IL: Northwestern University Press, 1985).

Wiseman, Mary Bittner, *The Ecstasies of Roland Barthes* (London: Routledge, 1989).

Wohlfart, Günter, *Der Spekulative Satz: Bemerkungen zum Begriff der Spekulation bei Hegel* (Berlin: Walter de Gruyter, 1981).

Wordsworth William, *The Poetical Works of William Wordsworth*, edited by E. de Selincourt and Helen Darbishire (Oxford: Clarendon Press, 1947), vol. IV.

Wordsworth William, *Wordsworth's Literary Criticism*, edited by W. J. B. Owen (London: Routledge & Kegan Paul, 1974).

Žižek, Slavoj, "Burned by the Sun," in *Lacan: The Silent Partners*, edited by Slavoj Žižek (London: Verso, 2006), 217–30.

Žižek, Slavoj, *How to Read Lacan* (New York: W. W. Norton, 2007).

Žižek, Slavoj, *Less Than Nothing: Hegel and the Shadow of Dialectical Materialism* (London: Verso, 2012).

Žižek, Slavoj, *The Sublime Object of Ideology* (London: Verso, 1989).

INDEX

Abrams, M. H. 105–6, 192n. 21
absence of work (*see also* intransitivity)
  and the author 113, 117
  and criticism 134, 141, 148–9, 153–
    4, 185n. 11
  and desire 87–9, 97–101
  lack and affirmation 26, 30,
    53–4, 60, 62
  and madness 74–6, 68, 73
  possibility and impossibility
    156–7, 159
actuality
  and atopia 149–50
  in Blanchot 82
  and criticism 140–1
  and desire 82, 91
  in Hegel 25–6, 57–8,
  in Hölderlin and the romantics 35–7,
    42–3, 47, 53–4, 60–2, 132
  and potentiality 152–3, 170n. 18
Adorno, Theodor W. 199n. 11
Aesthetics (*see also* art; taste) 14
  destruction 135–6
  Hegel 10–11, 81, 129–33, 143–4,
    184n. 8
  and inoperativity 136–9
  Kant and the Romantics 120,
    133–4, 138
Agamben, Giorgio 3, 14,
  "Author as Gesture" 114–18
  End of the Poem 198n. 2
  Language and Death 114–18,
    209n. 3
  Man without Content 135–43,
    203n. 7, 205n. 10
  Means without End 115
  Opus Dei 36, 170n. 18
  Potentialities 152, 157
  Signature of All Things 5, 12, 178n. 5

alienation 8–10, 138, 188n. 25
amateur 14, 149–54, 157
aporia 6–7, 152, 154, 156–7, 163n. 26,
  177n. 19
archaeology 2–8, 10–14, 124,
  156–7, 159–60
  and contingency 177n. 19, 181n. 14
  in Foucault 67–74, 79–80
  historical a priori 5–6
  paradigm 5–12
  truth and acceptability 4
art (*see also* literature) 1, 31, 33–5, 108
  experience 2, 76, 83, 118, 143–4,
    203n. 7
  and life 52, 80, 88–9, 115, 117, 120–
    3, 135–41, 148, 150
  and literature 10–11, 106, 201n. 4
  and philosophy 27, 40–1, 55, 60,
    121, 206n. 16
  as a thing of the past 14,
    81–2, 129–41
Artaud, Antonin 67, 75
Athenaeum (*see* Early German
  Romantics)
Aufhebung (sublation) 24–5, 30, 37–9,
  47, 153, 169n. 6, 189n. 31
authenticity (*see* sincerity)
author 8, 13, 38, 40, 48, 105–9, 119,
  125, 138, 144
  death 14, 111–18, 135
  gesture 114–18

Barthes, Roland 3, 14, 141, 154, 162n.
  20, 206n. 6
  "Authors and Writers" 112–13
  "Death of the Author" 111–13
  Preparation of the Novel 144–52
  Roland Barthes by Roland Barthes
    10, 150

"To Write: Intransitive Verb?" 7
Writing Degree Zero 9–10, 147
Beardsley, Monroe C. 108–9
Being, *Sein* (*see also* language; positing; will) 100–1, 125
  in Aristotle 175n. 10
  atopic 150–1
  and the author 109, 112–14, 116–18
  in Blanchot 80, 82–4, 148
  and desire 88–9, 92–3, 98
  in Foucault 69, 71, 76, 179n. 6
  in Hamacher 177n. 19
  in Heidegger 47, 136–7, 170n. 18, 172n. 30, 203n. 7
  in Kant 20–2, 25
  literature 56–9, 61–2, 141, 156
  in romanticism 35–6, 41–3
  uppercase and lowercase 165n. 59
Belles Lettres 9
Benjamin, Walter
  Concept of Criticism 40–1, 121, 140–1, 168n. 3, 171n. 27, 205n. 14, 205n. 15
  letter to Martin Buber 121
  "Theses on history" 123–4
  "Two Poems by Friedrich Hölderlin" 14, 119–24
biographism (*see* author)
Blanchot, Maurice (*see also* unworking) 100, 125
  and Agamben 138
  "Athenaeum" 43–6
  and Barthes 148
  experience of literature 3, 10–13, 58–9, 61–3
  in Foucault 71, 73
  "Literature and the Right to Death" 7, 56
  "Madness par excellence" 75, 98
  and psychoanalysis 90–1, 94
  Space of Literature 2, 79–85, 118
Bourdieu, Pierre 8, 10–11, 161n. 5
bourgeoisie 8–10
Brooks, Cleanth 108–9, 192n. 33, 194n. 46

caesura 15, 48, 55, 60, 152, 174n. 56, 196n. 30

classicism 10–11, 130–1
connoisseur 143
content (*see* form and content)
contingency
  and dialectical necessity 38, 117–18, 137, 153, 188n. 31
  and history 6–7, 70–6, 187n. 10
  literary absolute 14, 88–90, 141
  and writing 80, 83–5, 96–101, 151–7, 159–60, 162n. 19
criterion of literature (*see under* literature)
the critic (*see under* literary criticism)
criticism (*see* literary criticism)

Darstellung, presentation 19, 22–3, 35, 53–4, 133
death of the author (*see under* author)
deconstruction 3, 30, 32, 111, 172n. 30, 209n. 3
de Man, Paul 111, 177n. 20, 180n. 12
  Allegories of Reading 2, 195n. 17, 197n. 1
demand, exigency 80, 82, 98, 148
  demand of the system 25
  fragmentary exigency 29, 33, 43, 185n. 11
Derrida, Jacques 3
  and Agamben 155–7, 209n. 3
  and Foucault 178n. 2, 178n. 5
  Of Grammatology 31–2, 34, 37, 155, 162n. 16, 169n. 5
  and Hegel 45, 166n. 12
  on literature 11, 56, 58, 175n. 11
  "Structure, Sign, and Play" 111
de Sade, Marquis 67
dialectic (*see also* unworking) 2, 125
  aesthetics 129–30, 136
  connotation of word 40
  contingency 116–18, 120, 136, 188n. 31
  desire to write 87–96, 152–5, 157
  exigency 43
  in *Literary Absolute* 29–34
  literature 7, 8, 10–13, 15, 57–61, 71, 73, 141, 148, 159
  non-dialectic (*see* unworking)
  and *Witz* 36–40
  writerly necessity 79–84

dissemination 45, 72, 111, 175n. 11

Early German Romantics (*see also*
  Schlegel) 3, 10, 22, 147
  Athenaeum 11, 13, 19, 23–4, 27–49,
    54, 57–60, 121, 144, 153
  "Fragment 116" 33, 35
  and Hölderlin 34–5, 46–61
  Witz 36–41, 45, 170n. 23
eighteenth century
  and aesthetics 143, 201n. 4
  and literature 8, 182n. 30, 190n. 3
  and madness 74
  and writerly necessity 4, 12, 80, 105
Eliot, T. S. 109
Empson, William 107
epochē 136, 166n. 12, 167n. 1, 203n. 7
exigency (*see* demand)
expression (*see* sincerity)

Fichte, J. G. 25, 39–41, 60
fiction (*see under* literature)
finitude 20, 22–3, 60, 68, 95, 179n. 6,
  180n. 13
Flaubert, Gustave 145
form and content
  art and literature 8–1, 71, 130–8,
    141, 154
  and the writer 47, 54–5, 59, 82,
    148–9
formalism (*see* New Criticism)
Foucault, Michel
  archaeology of literature 10, 12–14,
    67–77, 182n. 30
  "Father's 'No'" 68, 74, 76, 178n. 5
  History of Madness 67–8, 74–7,
    182n. 30
  method 3–5, 70, 79
  Order of Things 68–74, 100
  "Thought of the Outside" 71, 75
  "What Is an Author?" 113–14
Fragment, fragmentation
  and Foucault 69, 72
  and the Romantics 2, 27–49, 54, 59,
    133–4, 143
French Revolution 8–9
Freud, Sigmund 87, 92–3

Genette, Gérard 149

genius 37, 81, 132–4, 143, 205n. 14
German idealism 24–5, 35–42, 45–8,
  54, 115
gesture (*see under* author)
Goethe, Johann Wolfgang von 2,
  198n. 4

Hamacher, Werner 124, 166n. 7, 177n.
  19, 196n. 30, 199n. 11, 202n. 11
Hegel, G. W. F. 3, 13–15, 115
  Aesthetics 81, 129–33, 143
  and Blanchot 7, 80, 134, 148
  in French thought 8–10, 39–40, 70
  and Hölderlin 46–7, 54
  judgement on art 135–7, 139–40
  necessity and contingency 152–3
  and reading 23–32, 36–8
  and the Romantics 41–2, 57–8, 60–1,
    129, 137–8
  speculative proposition 26
Heidegger, Martin 3, 12–13, 36, 80,
  115, 148
  Hegel's Phenomenology of Sprit
    24–6, 30
  history of being 36, 42, 56–8, 136,
    170n. 18, 172n. 30, 175n. 11,
    203n. 1, 203n. 7
  *Kant and the Problem of
    Metaphysics* 20–2
  Origin of the Work of Art 136–7, 139
  reading of Hölderlin 46–7
  Schelling's Treatise 24–5, 37
  subjectivity and subjectity 42,
    173n. 43
Henrich, Dieter 46, 153, 206n. 16
historical a priori (*see under*
  archaeology)
Hölderlin, Friedrich (*see also* Early
  German Romantics) 13–15,
  62, 84–5
  in Agamben's thought 115, 137
  in Benjamin's thought 119–24,
    171n. 29
  in Blanchot's thought 80
  in Foucault's thought 67–8,
    74–5, 100
  letters 51–4, 88–99
  in *Literary Absolute* 19, 34–5, 46–9,
    57, 59–60

Operations of the Poetic Spirit 54–6
"Remarks on 'Oedipus' " 53, 131,
   174n. 56
in Žižek's thought 188n. 31

idealism (*see* German idealism)
idleness (*see* unworking)
imagination 21–2, 91, 132, 201n. 4
inoperativity (*see* unworking)
interruption (*see* unworking)
intransitivity
  in Agamben 138, 141
  in Barthes 147, 149
  as criterion 4, 14, 105, 111–26,
    195n. 17
  in Foucault 68–9, 72–3
  as interruption or self-reference 44–5
  as question of literature 7–11, 13, 26,
    58–63, 152, 156–7, 159
  and writerly necessity 83–4, 90, 92,
    98, 100, 134
in-transitivity 14, 149, 154
intuitus originarius 20, 22, 25
irony 29, 60, 133, 138, 168n. 3, 202n. 11

Jakobson, Roman 112, 186n. 4, 195n. 16
Johns Hopkins University 7, 111, 146

Kafka, Franz 145, 183n. 4, 196n. 30
Kant, Immanuel 3, 13, 61, 159
  and archaeology 5, 10, 180n. 13
  and Benjamin 120, 198n. 3
  first *Critique* 5, 19–27, 31, 57
  and German idealism 35, 37–40,
    42, 57–8
  third *Critique* 133, 138–9
Keats, John 186n. 9

Lacan, Jacques 87–99, 111
Lacoue-Labarthe, Philippe (see also
  Literary Absolute) 10, 73, 199n. 11
  "Caesura of the Speculative"
    48, 55, 60
  "The Fable" 155
  "The Unpresentable" 24
language 13, 119, 156
  in Agamben 115–17, 125, 157
  in Barthes 9, 112–3, 146, 150–1

in Blanchot 82–4
in Derrida 32, 37
and desire 88–101
in Foucault 67–77, 114
in Kant 133
in New Criticism 108
in Novalis 43–4, 59
and philosophical presentation 23
in Ranciere 11
Laplanche, Jean 68, 97–8
law (*see also* pleasure principle) 3, 97,
  99, 120, 123, 132
letter (*see* spirit and letter)
Literary Absolute 2, 7, 27–60
  and Barthes 144, 146
  and criticism 140–1
  and Kant 22, 24
  secondary literature 167n. 1, 169n. 4,
    171n. 28
  as starting point 3, 12–13, 79
literary criticism 3, 13–14, 103–26
  age of criticism 4, 31, 129–54
  as concept of literature 29–32, 49
  the critic 14, 108, 126, 134–41,
    143–54, 206n. 6
literary theory (*see also* literary
  criticism; literature) 14, 24,
    124–6, 139–40
  definition 3
  as science 11–12, 27–8, 39, 61, 133,
    173n. 43, 177n. 20
literature (*see also* art; philosophy;
  question of literature; writing)
    61, 100
  as absolute 27–49
  as condition of the writer 51–6,
    79–85, 87–99
  as contingency 70–1
  as counter-discourse 71–3
  criterion 2–3, 105–9, 111–24
  and democracy 8
  etymology 162n. 16
  as fiction 23, 27, 61–2, 159
  as ideology 9, 180n. 12
  and life in criticism 105–9, 111–25,
    135, 138–40, 159
  and life of the writer 1, 51–6, 62,
    79–85, 87–99, 145–6, 150, 186n. 9

and madness 13, 49, 67–8, 73–7, 90,
94, 96–8, 100–1
as theory 29, 129–53
as tragic 9

madness (*see under* literature)
Mallarmé, Stéphane 67, 72–3, 176n. 13,
182n. 30
mathematics 22
melancholy 9 (*see also* madness)
metaphysics of will (*see also* will)
aesthetics 136–7
history of Being 36–8, 41–3, 73, 81,
155–7, 172n. 30, 173n. 43
as link between fields 3, 12, 162n. 17
the writer 107, 144–9
Mill, John Stuart 106–7, 192n. 21
modernity 7, 9, 49, 69, 72–5, 100, 135–6

Nancy, Jean-Luc (*see also Literary
Absolute*) 10, 13, 32, 58–9
Discourse on the Syncope 19–23
"Menstruum Universale" 38
Speculative Remark 24–6, 30, 37
necessity to write (*see* writerly
necessity)
negativity
abstract 8–9
double negativity 84, 88, 90,
94, 99–101
place of negativity 115–18
question of literature 79, 141, 149,
154, 156–7
speculative 15, 26, 30, 45, 57, 63
New Criticism 3, 14, 107–9
nineteenth century
connoisseur 143
form and content 8
in Foucault 69, 73, 182n. 30
literary criticism 2, 4, 13, 97, 105–7,
112, 125, 162n. 16
Novalis (Friedrich von Hardenberg) 11,
29, 41, 43–4, 49, 58–60, 121

operation (*see* work)
outside 69–72, 75–7

paradigm (*see under* archaeology)

philosophy (*see also* literature) 61
and art 81, 129–30
and Hölderlin 51–2
and literature 11–13, 19–28, 30, 32,
35, 47, 58, 155
question of whatness 56
and the Romantics 3, 11, 41–2
and will 38
plasticity 26, 198n. 3
pleasure principle 92–3, 96
politics 3, 119–24, 168n. 3, 199n. 11
positing, *Setzung*
in Agamben 116
aporia 6–7, 177n. 19
in Barthes and Foucault 113–14
in Benjamin 124
in Kant and Hegel 57–8
and literature 2, 4, 10–12, 33, 73,
101, 153–4, 156
and madness 76, 99
in New Criticism 108
in the Romantics 40–1, 45
poststructuralism 3
potentiality 35–6, 117, 122, 137, 140,
152–3, 157, 209n. 3
psychoanalysis 87–99

question of literature (*see also*
literature)
in Foucault 73
and Hegel 26, 129
in *Literary Absolute* 3, 28–9
meaning of the question 22–4, 45–7,
56–62, 153, 155, 159
as object of knowledge 7–12
and writerly necessity 81, 149–50

Ranciére, Jacques 8, 10–11
Ransom, John Crowe 107, 192n. 33
reader, reading 8, 24, 26–7, 29–30, 45,
56, 108–9, 115, 135
reason, rationality 11, 20, 22–3, 41, 68,
74–6, 98, 129
reflection
and art 129, 131, 138–41
and the Romantics 29–30, 40–2, 133,
168n. 3
and writing 155

Richards, I. A. 2, 105, 107–9
Rilke, Rainer Maria 1–3, 118, 145, 148, 195n. 17, 197n. 1
romanticism (see Early German Romantics)

Sartre, Jean-Paul 8–10, 175n. 6
Schelling, F.W.J. 24, 37, 39, 46, 115
Schlegel, Friedrich 3, 11, 23, 28–9, 37, 41, 43
    Critical Fragments 2, 133–4
    Dialogue on Poetry 121
    "On Goethe's Meister" 2
Schlegel, August W. 28–9
self-reference (see intransitivity)
seventeenth century 69, 205n. 12
shifter 112, 116, 186n. 4
sincerity 2, 4, 105–9, 111–12, 119, 124–5, 143–4
spectator 135, 138–9
spirit and letter 54–5, 60, 130–4, 141
structuralism 3, 111
Sturm und Drang 205n. 14
subject
    era of the Subject 39–46
    subjectivity and subjectity 42
    subject position 3–6
    subject–predicate relation 26, 57–8
    uppercase and lowercase 6
suicide 93, 95
supplement (see under writing)
symbolic
    art form 14, 130–3
    symbolic of literature 87–99, 186n. 9
synthesis 21–2, 38, 57, 79, 199n. 11, 202n. 11
"System-Programme" 46, 115, 173n. 46
Szondi, Peter 130

taste 133, 139, 143, 205n. 12
teleology 70, 72
theology 3
theory (see literary theory)
thesis (see positing)
tragic (see under literature)
truth (see under archaeology)

unworking, inoperativity
    as criterion of literature 4, 118, 125

as interruption 43–6, 48–9, 59–61, 63, 76, 136–7, 139, 141
and writerly necessity 80–2, 90, 96, 148, 154–7
unthought, unsaid
    in Foucault 70, 75
    in Heidegger 28
    in Kant 21
    in literary criticism 59, 107–8, 114, 119, 141, 154
    in the Romantics 43–9, 58–60

vocation 43, 98–9, 129, 145, 149

Wellek, René and Austin Warren 193n. 45
will to system (see also metaphysics of will) 25–6, 38, 42–3, 47, 144, 172n. 35
Wimsatt, Wlliam K. 2, 108–9
Wirklichkeit (see actuality)
Witz (see under Early German Romantics)
Wordsworth, William 107, 190n. 3, 192n. 21
work (see unworking, absence of work)
writerly necessity
    as condition of literary truth 105–26
    as paradigm 1–12
    as subject position 19, 51–6, 79–85
writing (see also literature) 1, 3–4, 7–10, 13–14, 75–6, 155–7
    act 79–85, 112–14, 117, 144–9
    a priori 19–26, 119–24
    desire 87–99
    essence 56–63
    fragments 27–39
    love 149–53
    as supplement 31–2, 140–1, 155–6, 166n. 12
writer (see also writerly necessity; amateur)
    as essence of romanticism 43–5
    as neurotic 90–4
    as perverse 94–6
    as psychotic 96–9
    social function 8–9, 28

Žižek, Slavoj 89, 91, 186n. 9, 188n. 31

Lightning Source UK Ltd.
Milton Keynes UK
UKHW051451110320
359884UK00025B/295